Social Policies, Labour Markets and Motherhood

The relationship between fertility and the participation rate of women in the workforce is an increasingly important area of study for economists, demographers and policy-makers. Recent data show important differences in the relationship between employment rates of women and fertility across Europe. For example, in Southern Europe, low fertility rates are combined with low rates of female participation. In contrast, Nordic countries are experiencing relatively high fertility rates combined with high female labour market participation. *Social Policies, Labour Markets and Motherhood* analyses the effects of policies aimed to reconcile motherhood and labour market participation. Making extensive use of European Community Household Panel data, it compares the outcomes of policies in several European countries analysing why they succeed in some environments but not in others. It will be of interest to researchers, policy-makers and graduate students working on labour markets, population economics, demography and the methodology of applied microeconomics.

DANIELA DEL BOCA is Professor of Economics at the University of Turin and Fellow of Collegio Carlo Alberto.

CÉCILE WETZELS is Senior Researcher in the Department of Economics at the University of Amsterdam.

Social Policies, Labour Markets and Motherhood

A Comparative Analysis of European Countries

Edited by

Daniela Del Boca and Cécile Wetzels

CAMBRIDGE
UNIVERSITY PRESS

CAMBRIDGE UNIVERSITY PRESS
Cambridge, New York, Melbourne, Madrid, Cape Town, Singapore,
São Paulo, Delhi

Cambridge University Press
The Edinburgh Building, Cambridge CB2 8RU, UK

Published in the United States of America by Cambridge University Press, New York

www.cambridge.org
Information on this title: www.cambridge.org/9780521877411

First published 2007

Printed in the United Kingdom at the University Press, Cambridge

A catalogue record for this publication is available from the British Library

ISBN 978-0-521-87741-1 hardback

Contents

Contents   vii

Figures

Tables

Contributors

DANIELA DEL BOCA is Professor of Economics at the University of Turin and Fellow of Collegio Carlo Alberto. She received a Ph.D. from the University of Wisconsin-Madison in 1988 and has been a visiting professor at New York University, Johns Hopkins University and The Italian Academy at Columbia University. She has published several books and articles in the area of labour economics and the economics of the family. Her articles have appeared in international journals, including *American Economic Review*, *Journal of Human Resources*, *Journal of Population Economics*, *Labour Economics*, *Review of Income and Wealth*, *Structural Change and Economic Dynamics*. She is a co-editor of *Labour* and member of the advisory board of *Review of Economics of the Household*. Since 2000 she has been Director of the Centre for Household, Income, Labour and Demographic Economics (CHILD). In 2000 she was President of the European Society of Population Economists (ESPE).

JÉRÔME DE HENAU is a researcher at the Department of Applied Economics of the Université Libre de Bruxelles (DULBEA) and Research Fellow at the Open University, UK. He has a Ph.D. in Management Science from the Solvay Business School (ULB). His main research interests are gender, female employment, family policies (especially relating to young children) and long-term home care. He is also a member of the International Association for Feminist Economics (IAFFE).

SIV GUSTAFSSON is Professor of Economics at the University of Amsterdam. She defended her dissertation 'Determination and Structure of Wages in the Government Sector of Sweden' at the Stockholm School of Economics in 1976. She has published in journals and books on female labour supply, family taxation, childcare subsidies and country comparative policy analyses on the compatibilities of parenting and work. She is co-editor with Adriaan

Kalwij of *Education and Postponement of Maternity: Economic Analyses of Industrial Countries* (2006).

EIKO KENJOH is an Associate Professor in Economics at Asia University in Tokyo, Japan. After completing her study at the Graduate School of Keio University in Tokyo, she obtained teaching and research experience in Japan, England and the Netherlands. She received her Ph.D. at the Department of Economics of the University of Amsterdam. Her main research fields are population and labour economics. She is currently pursuing research projects in women's employment, fertility and non-standard work arrangements, both from a national point of view and in international comparison. She is author of *Balancing Work and Family Life in Japan and Four European Countries: Econometric Analyses on Mothers' Employment and Timing of Maternity* (Amsterdam).

MARILENA LOCATELLI is Adjunct Professor at AVSC (Graduate program in Complex System) and Research Fellow in the Department of Economics 'C. De Martiis' at the University of Turin. She received her Ph.D. from the Polytechnic University of Milan. Her research interest are in applied microeconometrics, economics of the family and public economics. Her articles have appeared in national and international journals such as *Labour, Journal of Cultural Economics and Review of Economics of the Household*. She is a member of the European Society of Population Economists and Fellow of the Centre for Household, Income, Labour and Demographic Economics (CHILD).

DANIÈLE MEULDERS is Professor of Economics at the University of Brussels, Belgium and Invited Professor at the University of Strasbourg, France. She is supervisor of the research team on labour economics at the Department of Applied Economics of the University of Brussels and a past president of the Labour Institute. She was a founder member of the European Association of Labour Economists; member of the executive committee of the Applied Econometrics Association (organiser of different conferences on gender issues); and member of the EU expert group on Gender, Social Inclusion and Employment (EGGSIE). Her research interests are in labour economics, gendered evaluation of employment policies, wage and income distribution, segregation and atypical employment, motherhood gaps, comparative public finance, social protection (individualisation), income taxation, microsimulation models (Euromod) and the impact of social policies on women's choices.

SÍLE O'DORCHAI has been a researcher and assistant at the Department of Applied Economics (DULBEA) at the Universitè Libre de Bruxelles (ULB) in Belgium since 2001. In 1997, she graduated in Slavic Studies at the Catholic University of Leuven, in 2001 in Economics at the Universite Libre de Bruxelles and in 2007 she finished her doctoral thesis. Her main research interests are in the field of labour economics, household fertility choices and the influence of public policies. Her scientific activities have focused on the 2001–04 European research project 'The Rationale of Motherhood Choices: Influence of Employment Conditions and of Public Policies (MOCHO)' of the Fifth Framework Programme of the European Commission. Besides many research reports and newsletter contributions, she has published articles in the *Journal of Comparative Policy Analysis*, *Transfer*, *International Journal of Manpower* and *Brussels Economic Review*.

SILVIA PASQUA is Assistant Professor of Economics at the University of Turin. She has an M.Phil. and a Ph.D. in the Economics of Developing Countries from the University of Cambridge and a Ph.D. in Economics from the University of Pavia. She is a member of ESPE (European Association of Population Economists) and of the Executive Committee of CHILD (Centre for Household, Income, Labour and Demographic Economics). She has published in *Labour*, *Review of Income and Wealth*, *Review of Economics of the Household* and several collected publications and books.

CHIARA PRONZATO is a Ph.D. student in Economics at the Institute for Social and Economic Research, University of Essex. She is a member of CHILD (Centre for Household, Income, Labour and Demographic Economics) and collaborates with Statistics Norway. Her research interests are in the fields of labour economics and family economics. Results from her research appeared in *Labour*, and in several working papers. She is Graduate Teaching Assistant at the University of Essex.

CÉCILE WETZELS is Senior Researcher in the Department of Economics and Econometrics at the University of Amsterdam and affiliated with the Tinbergen Institute, the Amsterdam Institute for Labour Studies and IZA in Bonn. She graduated in economics from Tilburg University and received a Ph.D. in Population Economics from the University of Amsterdam in 1998. She obtained teaching, research and management experience in the Netherlands, the UK, Germany and Sweden. Her core interest is to analyse implications from human capital theory across welfare states and futhermore to understand the potential impacts of social policies, migrant background and culture. Her empirical work is based on national and European Household Panel data, public health data and web-based national and European survey data. The evaluation of the impact of social policy on the labour market outcomes of individuals and on (the timing) of events such as family formation, has led to a number of projects linked to various government agencies both in the Netherlands and in Europe, including the European Commission. She has published in the *European Journal of Population Economics, Journal of Public Finance and Management, Information and Management, Labour* and the *Journal of Cultural Economics*, and contributed to several books. She is also trained as a visual artist.

Preface

This book aims to explore two crucial questions concerning the different patterns of fertility rates and women's participation rates in Europe: Why are fertility and participation so different across countries? Why have fertility rates continued to decline in Southern Europe (where women's participation rates are very low) but have grown in Nordic Europe (where participation rates are relatively high)? The decline of fertility has important implications: low fertility reduces the potential sustainability of the pension system, and implies lower growth as well as lower savings. An understanding of the relationship between participation and fertility is therefore relevant in ways which go beyond theoretical speculations.

In fact, the recent pattern of fertility and its relationship with women's participation rates are increasingly becoming an object of interest for economists, demographers and policy-makers. Data from the last decade indicate important differences in the relationship between employment rates of women and fertility in different countries. Although the rising long-term trend in the female participation rate is similar for most countries, persistent differences in women's levels as well as in career perspectives suggest that different countries are constrained by country-specific institutional and social factors.

The comparison of relevant institutional characteristics can help to interpret these differences. In Nordic European countries and in some Continental European countries, governments have developed policies with the objective of simultaneously encouraging both fertility and the participation of women in the labour force. These programmes have supported dual-earner families, while shifting some of the economic burden of child rearing to the state. Public childcare availability, generous optional maternity leave as well as part-time opportunities have allowed women to choose either to remain in the labour market during their childbearing years and maintain a continuous relationship with the labour market or to take care of their children themselves by using long, optional maternity leave. In the Anglo-Saxon countries and some continental countries with strong breadwinner regimes, governments have implemented programmes only for the poor. In this context, where long optional paid parental leave is not available, mothers have to choose between working part-time combined with the use of private childcare and leaving the labour market in their childbearing years.

Finally, in Southern European countries, on the contrary, governments have developed high-quality public childcare, but it is very limited in supply and in hours of service. This has made the service compatible with part-time work but not with full-time activities. However, given that part-time work is very limited, married women are forced to choose between no paid work and full-time work, neither of which is necessarily their preferred option. In Southern Europe where both part-time work and childcare are limited, and optional parental leave is of short duration, women need to rely on family support in order to continue working when their children are young.

Other important institutional differences concern the labour markets. In the Southern European countries unlike in the Anglo-Saxon countries, strict rules still exist regarding the hiring and firing of workers and (flexible) employment arrangements are very limited. These labour market regulations have been largely responsible for the high unemployment rates, particularly among women and young adults. Thus, the labour market indirectly imposes high fertility costs on families even when the mother does not work, and therefore it discourages fertility both directly and indirectly. Because of the high unemployment rates, women have a hard time taking breaks in their working life during their childbearing years, and then find it difficult to re-enter the labour market.

In this book, we analyse and interpret the different patterns across countries reviewing the relevant literature, discussing the appropriate methodological frameworks. In Part I the differences between welfare states across Europe are analysed in Chapter 1 (Danièle Meulders and Síle O'Dorchai). These authors use different classification methods and assess to what degree they account for differences across welfare states regarding childcare provision, parental leave, family cash assistance and working mothers' time constraints. With this analysis, we aim to contribute to the debate on the explanatory power of welfare state, typologies while assessing the issue not just from the point of view of women in general but also from that of mothers in particular. Over the course of Chapters 2, 3 and 4, we focus especially on those childcare systems and parental leave and child benefits which have been more relevant in explaining differences in mothers' participation to the labour market across Europe (Jérôme de Henau, Danièle Meulders, Síle O'Dorchai and Helene Périvier). In this part a detailed ranking of countries according to their generosity in supporting women's work and fertility is presented.

In Part II we provide a review and interpretations of several empirical analyses of European fertility patterns and their relationship with women's labour market participation as well as with earnings. First, Chapter 5 focuses closely on the link between motherhood and women's work and the impact of social policies (Daniela Del Boca and Marilena Locatelli). In Chapter 6 the temporal changes in levels and timing of fertility are described and analysed (Siv Gustafsson and Eiko Kenjoh), while in Chapter 7 several aspects of the relationship between wages and motherhood are considered, as well as the impact of social policies on wage differentials (Cécile Wetzels).

In Part III we use ECHP panel data to provide empirical estimates of various social policies on fertility, labour market participation and earnings (Daniela Del Boca, Chiara Pronzato, Silvia Pasqua and Cécile Wetzels). The results show that, while age, education and women's non-labour income (both from other household sources and from public transfers) have the expected sign in all countries, the impact of social policies on the decision to work and have children is quite consistent with the hypotheses developed in the chapters. The empirical analysis of Part III on the wage differentials between childless women and mothers shows that in Nordic countries the correlation between being a participant in the labour market and having children is less strong than in Central and Southern European countries.

Each chapter contains extensive references and appendices with up-to-date data on each aspect of the issues discussed. This book can serve as an important tool for graduate and senior graduate students for work in classes, seminars and theses. It can also be an important reference work for all researchers in the field of population economics, demography, labour economics and applied microeconomics.

DANIELA DEL BOCA AND CÉCILE WETZELS

Part I

1 The position of mothers in a comparative welfare state perspective

Danièle Meulders and Sile O'Dorchai

1.1 Introduction

In most European countries welfare states developed after World War II. Until 1960 most countries developing a welfare state were led by the idea that families would be provided for by their male heads, and therefore the design of social security schemes was based on a household-with-bread-winner perspective. Since the 1970s, however, labour force participation rates for women have risen in some European countries, especially in the 1980s and 1990s. In addition, mothers increasingly have combined paid work and motherhood, even when children were still very young. Today, women's greater investment in education has resulted in their having equal levels of initial training. Although there are differences in men's participation rates across countries, the differences in women's partici-pation rates are more significant, especially after children are born into the family. Women with a similar level of education behave differently in terms of both the age at which they choose to give birth to children and their labour force participation after childbirth. Moreover, the types of jobs women have vary considerably across welfare states.

In order to understand welfare states and the difference between welfare states across Europe, social scientists began to classify countries according to various welfare criteria. Typologies can be used for different purposes and can focus on variables related to causes, institutions and/or outcomes. The most influential attempt to create a welfare state typology has been that of Esping-Andersen (1990). He uses the concept of welfare state regimes to characterise and to describe the complex relationships between the state, the labour market and the family. By underlining the multi-dimensional nature of welfare state variation, Esping-Andersen's typology is innovative and useful, and it has stimulated much research. His three-fold clustering of welfare state regimes labels them according to their main ideological currents, which are Conservative-Corporatist, 'Liberal' and Social Democratic. Since Esping-Andersen's primary interest was to

3

describe the contours of the relationships between states, labour markets and families, his typology is based on a broad set of indicators that refer to outcomes as well as to institutions. The basic concepts used to motivate his typology are decommodification, social stratification and the state–market nexus (Esping-Andersen 1990).

Although critics have questioned the theoretical and empirical value of a welfare state typology based on ideal-types, Arts and Gelissen (2001, 2002) have clearly pointed out that ideal-types such as those created by Esping-Andersen are not goals in themselves. However, these ideal-types serve to represent a reality that cannot yet be described using laws, given the fact that the comparative macro-sociology of welfare states is still *in statu nascendi*. In welfare state research there is still a lack of theory, which ideal-types *à la* Esping-Andersen help to overcome. Therefore, typologies do play an important role as instruments in developing more general conclusions on the ways in which welfare states across Europe accommodate the specific needs of women with children.

Welfare state classifications have developed over time. Typology-builders have gradually needed to incorporate an ever-increasing number of variables in their analyses of welfare states in order to stay in line with social attitudes and ideas, as well as with political and economic reality. Indeed, the feminist literature has pointed to the numerous inadequacies of many typologies with respect to the new work/life balance of modern women who refuse to be confined to homemaking and thus challenge the traditional male breadwinner model.

In this chapter, we aim to contribute to the debate on the explanatory power of welfare state typologies, assessing the issue not just from the point of view of women but also indeed from that of mothers. While women's increased presence in the labour market results mainly from their emancipatory battle, which launched the move from the traditional male-breadwinner to a dual-earner model of the family, the labour participation of mothers combines both emancipation effects and time-sharing challenges.

In this chapter, we present different classification methods and assess to what degree they account for differences across welfare states regarding childcare provision, parental leave, family cash assistance, working mothers' time constraints, etc.

1.2   Welfare state typologies built around the concept of redistribution

A first cluster of typologies contains fewer complex typologies. Just one variable is studied in order to draw up a classification, be it the proportion of tax receipts to GDP, the degree of corporatism, the proportion of GDP represented by transfers, the state's level of social expenditure, or still other relevant measures of social protection. In other words, the touchstone of the first cluster is the concept of social amelioration, focusing on measures of public expenditure and redistribution.

Examples of this first cluster are the welfare state classifications by MacFarlan and Oxley (1996) and Adema *et al.* (1996). MacFarlan and Oxley (1996) examined the level of transfers to the active population as a percentage of GDP. As a result, the Nordic countries scored best, while the Southern European countries were the least generous. Adema *et al.* (1996) constructed a typology based on net social expenditure and observed a great difference compared with a typology based on gross social expenditure as it figures in state budgets. Gross social expenditure overestimates the social effort of countries, and their ranking changes when net expenditure is considered instead. The Netherlands, for example, is ranked as one of the poorest performers on this measure.

Another example of this cluster is the 1988 categorisation of welfare state regimes by Calmfors and Driffill based on the degree of corporatism. The 'hump shape hypothesis', first introduced by Calmfors and Driffill (1988), states that countries with highly decentralised (USA, Italy) and highly centralised (Sweden, Austria) wage-bargaining processes have a superior performance in terms of unemployment compared to countries with an intermediate degree of centralisation (Germany, France and the Netherlands). In the latter, unions are strong enough to cause major disruption but not sufficiently encompassing to bear their share of the cost of their actions.

1.3 Welfare state typologies based on the interplay between the state, the market and the family

1.3.1 Esping-Andersen as a catalyst for new comparative welfare state research

Until the seminal contribution of Esping-Andersen (1990), most empirical work relied on comparing the amount of social security expenditures with distributive outcomes. In the second cluster of welfare state typologies, the central object of analysis is broadened to the state–market nexus or the relationship between paid work and welfare. To study this relationship and, accordingly, construct welfare state typologies, a whole range of measures and policies is considered. The most important example of the second cluster of comparative analysis is Esping-Andersen's three-fold typology of Conservative-Corporatist, 'Liberal' and Social-Democratic welfare state regimes (Esping-Andersen 1990). Four concepts are at the core of Esping-Andersen's three-fold typology: decommodification, defamilialisation, social stratification and the state–market nexus. Esping-Andersen understands 'decommodification' as the degree to which welfare states weaken the cash nexus by granting entitlements independent of market participation. A familialistic welfare regime is seen as one that assigns a maximum of welfare obligations to the household. As a consequence, the concept of 'defamilialisation' is to capture policies that lessen individuals' reliance on the family, and maximise individuals' command of economic resources independently of familial or conjugal reciprocities. 'Stratification' is defined as the unequal rights and perquisites of different positions in a society. Finally, the state–market nexus refers to the mix of state and market provisions within welfare state programmes. In terms of these four phenomena, first, at the lower end of the welfare spending spectrum or at the market end of the state–market nexus, Ireland and the UK are classified as liberal welfare state regimes characterised by a low degree of decommodification (given the important welfare role of the market compared with the residual responsibilities of the state), a narrow definition of social risks (predominance of means-tested social assistance versus a poorly developed social insurance scheme with limited eligibility and low benefits compensated by private insurance by the richest layers of the population), a high level of social stratification, and no labour market management (it is feared that disincentive effects would be introduced if the free play of the market were disrupted). Second, with an intermediate level of welfare spending or with a balanced state–market nexus, Austria, Belgium, France, Germany, Greece, Italy, Luxembourg and Spain are the representative countries of Esping-Andersen's Conservative-Corporatist welfare cluster. They simultaneously implement a system of social assistance and insurance. Their tradition of etatism narrows down the welfare role played by the market. Moreover, led by the principle of subsidiarity, extended family ties are heavily relied upon in the provision of social protection (a low degree of defamilialisation). Finally, social protection differs according to work status and therefore Conservative-Corporatist welfare state regimes are characterised by a high level of social stratification. Thirdly, with the highest level of welfare spending or at the state end of the state–market nexus, the Social-Democratic welfare cluster includes the Nordic countries (Denmark, Finland and Sweden) and the Netherlands. Here, the market intervenes little, given that a universal system of social insurance is organised by the state with a broad definition of social risks, generous benefits and individualised social rights. The principle of universalism guarantees access to social protection based on citizenship and not on work status so that social stratification is low. In terms of labour market management, the major goal is to achieve full employment.

Esping-Andersen's typology has received different kinds of criticism that have paved the way for a whole set of alternative welfare state typologies.

1.3.1.1 The value of typologies First, critics have questioned the theoretical and empirical value of a welfare state typology based on ideal-types. However, it has been pointed out by Arts and Gelissen (2001, 2002) that ideal-types, such as those created by Esping-Andersen, are not goals in themselves but serve to represent a reality that cannot yet be described using laws, given the fact that the comparative macrosociology of welfare states is still in its infancy. In welfare state research there is still a lack of theory; ideal-types *à la* Esping-Andersen help to overcome this.

1.3.1.2 The contestable character of Esping-Andersen's three regime clusters Second, critics have contested Esping-Andersen's assumption that countries have crystallised into three distinct regime clusters with different underlying welfare state logics. As a result, a fourth cluster has at times been suggested or at least the reclassification of certain countries in another cluster than the one in which they were classified by Esping-Andersen.

The low level of public welfare spending and the strong reliance on (tough) means testing in Australia and New Zealand has led Esping-Andersen to classify these countries as liberal welfare state regimes. However, in the case of Australia, its long-standing commitment to wages-as-welfare, with centralised wage-bargaining machinery that is reminiscent of post-war Sweden, cannot be ignored. Income guarantees through market regulation play a large role. Moreover, as Castles and Mitchell (1993) have pointed out, high thresholds result in a large part of the population receiving means-tested benefits. In the Antipodean countries, leftist political activity has pursued equality in pre-tax, pre-transfer income rather than equalisation through social policy. Korpi and Palme constructed a typology of welfare states based on the institutional characteristics of old-age pensions and sickness cash benefits (Korpi and Palme 1998; see also Korpi 1983, 1989; and for a similar analysis, see Lumen *et al.* 2000). They consider three aspects of these benefits: targeting versus universalism, the extent of protection and the type of governance of the social insurance programme. While Australia was identified as a targeted model,[1] the liberal countries of Ireland and the United Kingdom were believed to belong to a basic security model with non-universal coverage.[2] In terms of women's choice it does seem to make sense to group Australia and New Zealand with the United Kingdom and Ireland: their fertility rates are very similar (below replacement level) and mothers of young children have very low workforce involvement (for more details, see Gornick *et al.* 1997). Moreover, weak financial incentives to work in the tax/benefit systems of Australia, Ireland, New Zealand and the UK contribute to only around 50% of single parents working (Adema 2005).

Esping-Andersen (1990) classifies the Netherlands as a social-democratic welfare state regime and gives the country a place within the same category as the Nordic countries. However, historically, the process of 'democratic pacification' (via pillarisation) in the Netherlands has led, on the one hand, to tolerance and accommodation, mainly in the public sphere, and to basic income policies, and, on the other, to a strengthened idea of family privacy and women homemakers. According to Knijn (1991), the Netherlands, like Germany, has a low level of individualisation, no equal access to the labour market, the polity or state institutions, and a very low state and market household service profile. Knijn, therefore, groups the Dutch welfare regime with Germany.

We could say there is some truth in both arguments: Wetzels and Zorlu (2003) confirm that Knijn (1991) is correct in classifying the Dutch system, as it existed before 1990, as being of the conservative, Christian-democratic kind. Welfare state policies were designed to induce mothers to take care of young children on a full-time basis. Nevertheless, they also support Esping-Andersen's interpretation of the Dutch welfare state as a social-democratic one by pointing out the profound changes that have marked the Dutch regime during the 1990s. Social policies have increasingly focused on facilitating the work/life balance for Dutch mothers, thus fitting in with the social-democratic welfare model. Moreover, Gustafsson (1994) has supported Esping-Andersen (1990) in noting the Netherlands as a social-democratic welfare regime as far as its outcome in terms of poverty alleviation is

[1] Targeted models are characterised by low levels of means-tested benefits.
[2] The basic security model of the liberal countries is non-universal because eligibility relies on the payment of social contributions (as opposed to Denmark, where citizenship bestows the right to various allowances and benefits). Moreover, allowances are either lump-sum or tied to very low income ceilings which exclude a large proportion of the population.

concerned. Finally, note that the particular expansion of part-time work in the Netherlands has also encouraged women with young children to participate at least on a part-time basis in employment, whereas in Germany social values are such as to put pressure on mothers to completely withdraw from the labour market in order to devote themselves to caregiving duties during their children's early years of life. In addition, in Germany the fertility rate has been adjusted downwards much more markedly than in the Netherlands.

Leira (1989) has shown that Esping-Andersen's idea of a Nordic welfare regime breaks down as soon as gender is given serious consideration. She found that the Norwegian model, which treated women primarily as wives and mothers, was closer in many respects to that of the UK than it was to the Swedish model. However, with its recent introduction of family-friendly policies, Norway seems to have secured its position in the Nordic cluster. Today, Norway no longer seems very different from Sweden in terms of its welfare state model. However, after considerable debate, Norway enacted a law which introduced a child-rearing grant in 1998 that provides a cash benefit to parents of children aged 12–36 months. It is provided on condition that the child does not attend publicly funded childcare. Norway's policy has been controversial. Although it was intended to give families more time to care for children and more choices in care arrangements, and to equalise the benefits offered to families who do, and do not, use publicly funded care for children under 3 years of age, the law has in fact led to an expansion in the use of private care and has eased the pressure to expand publicly funded care and, more importantly, it risks inducing women to stay out of the labour force longer. The difference with Finland, which was the first to introduce an early childhood benefit in 1985, is that Finland guarantees a publicly funded childcare place for all children aged 1 year or older whose parents desire one, so that the early childhood benefit gives parents a real choice between parental care, private childcare or public childcare. As for Sweden, a law introducing a childrearing grant was enacted in 1994 but was repealed the following year before it actually came into effect owing to concerns about the law's impact on the country's commitment to publicly funded childcare. This example shows that Norwegian policy-makers may still be driven by slightly different standards and ideas than their colleagues in the other Nordic countries.

Finally, critics have pointed to Esping-Andersen's misspecification of the Mediterranean welfare states as immature versions of the conservative continental model. Not only Esping-Andersen but also Katrougalos (1996) see the Mediterranean countries as an underdeveloped species of the continental welfare state model. These countries have in common the immaturity of their social protection systems and a shared set of social and family structures. However, Ebbinghaus (1998) has derived a 'Latin' residual welfare state cluster by differentiating some countries from the conservative cluster. What distinguishes those countries is the fact that they are welfare laggards. The principle of subsidiarity prevails in these societies, and therefore, there is a more heavy reliance on traditional intermediary institutions such as the church and the family. The social security system of these Latin countries seems to be more fragmented and corporatist than the Bismarckian model common to the conservative cluster of welfare state regimes. Other proponents of a unique Southern European regime include Leibfried (1992), who distinguishes between a rudimentary policy model for the countries of the South of Europe, the modern model of the Nordic countries, the institutional model of the Bismarckian countries and the residual policy model of the Anglo-Saxon countries. He has justified the separate classification of the Mediterranean countries on the basis of the absence in those countries of an articulated social minimum and a right to welfare. Ferrera (1997) also identified a separate Southern European cluster characterised by a high level of fragmentation of the social protection systems (see Ebbinghaus 1998), the generosity of some benefits (old-age pensions, health care as a right derived from citizenship) despite the absence of an articulated social minimum, the low degree of state intervention in the welfare sphere, and the high level of particularism with regard to cash benefits and financing, expressed in strong clientelism. Bonoli (1997) used the low level of social expenditure as a proportion of GDP and the small percentage of social expenditure financed through contributions to support his preference for a separate Mediterranean cluster. Finally, Trifiletti (1998), in her comparison of family policies in Europe, argued that in Mediterranean countries family and employment continue to be in competition rather than in balance. The traditional division of care work relies both on the fact that time for caregiving remains a private matter and on the compulsive rather than the supportive nature of subsidiarity. These arguments are supported by the situation that today fertility rates observed in the South of Europe are amongst the lowest in the world. Women face the dichotomous choice either to have children or to pursue a career. Motherhood gives rise to severe employment penalties, which further dampen women's low employment rates.

Esping-Andersen (1999) has taken this claim for a fourth welfare state cluster very seriously. 'The case for a unique Southern Europe regime depends ultimately on the centrality of families. This was the weak link in the original "three worlds" model ... [However,] as far as my choice of attributes and measurements is concerned, a simple "three worlds" typology may suffice' (Esping-Andersen 1999: 92, 94).

Esping-Andersen has a very reasonable point here. The question of how to identify and classify welfare regimes will remain open because researchers will always differ in terms of which attributes they consider vital and how they should be measured. If we allow too many cross-country differences to each give rise to new regime clusters or 'worlds', then we must be aware that the desired explanatory value of our typologies will, at least partially, be sacrificed. We must ensure that the additional value of typologies, as compared with individual comparisons, is safeguarded.

1.3.1.3 The omitted gender dimension   In addition to receiving criticism on the looseness of his groupings' boundaries, Esping-Andersen was attacked by feminists accusing him of neglecting gender. Esping-Andersen has replied as follows: '[Feminists often argue] that models of welfare regimes that have been specified via a political economy perspective fail to hold up when subject to a gendered analysis. Alternative "gendered" typologies do, in fact, often contradict "political economy" typologies. But the contradiction may be spurious because different phenomena are being explained and compared' (Esping-Andersen 1999: 49–50).

Indeed, feminists have pointed out that in comparative welfare state research, women only enter the analysis as they become more visible as paid workers. Unfortunately, they are simply granted a place within the same paid work/welfare schedule that was primarily designed with male breadwinners in mind.

As mentioned above, the concept of decommodification plays an important role in Esping-Andersen's typology (Esping-Andersen 1990). 'De-commodification' is understood as the 'degree to which welfare states weaken the cash nexus by granting entitlements independent of market participation' (Esping-Andersen 1999: 43), or, in other words, grant benefit entitlements regardless of whether one participates in the labour market or not. The concept presupposes that individuals are already commodified. It may adequately describe the relationship between welfare states and the standard, full-career male worker, but it is not easily applicable to women, considering that their economic role is often non-commodified (Esping-Andersen 1999: 44). Much of the welfare work undertaken by women within the household has never been part of the market and continues to be performed outside the purview of the welfare state (Sainsbury 1994; Orloff 2001). The concept of decommodification is inoperable for women unless welfare states help them become commodified (Esping-Andersen 1999: 44).

Furthermore, the concept of familialisation has received special attention, particularly in Esping-Andersen's later work (1999). According to Esping-Andersen (1999: 45), a familialistic welfare regime is one that assigns a maximum of welfare obligations to the household. Therefore, the concept of 'defamilialisation' serves to capture policies that lessen individuals' reliance on the family and maximise individuals' command over economic resources despite familial or conjugal reciprocities.

Given that women's, or at least mothers', family responsibilities restrict their ability to gain full economic independence solely via work, their defamilialisation can be achieved only by the welfare state (Esping-Andersen 1999: 45). Women carefully weigh the gains and losses of work given their time-consuming childcare responsibilities. Part-time employment, although enabling women to deal with their double burden, is hardly ever enough to guarantee full economic independence. In other words, it was the feminist critique that led Esping-Andersen (1999) to realise that female independence necessitates 'defamilialising' welfare obligations rather than 'decommodifying' them.

Feminist critique of 'mainstream' male-centred welfare state theory has led Esping-Andersen (1999) to reconsider the family.[3] To quote Esping-Andersen:

The stable one-earner family is no longer standard but atypical. Cohabitation and single-person households are growing. Childhood today more likely means growing up with parents who both work, or with a single parent. Being a child today also means having few, if any, siblings and a fair risk of seeing one's parents separate or divorce ... Such turmoil signals an emerging welfare deficit: the family that was the model for post-war welfare state reformers is still the linchpin of policy even if it is becoming extinct. (Esping-Andersen 1999:49)

Esping-Andersen has accepted that family welfare services have still not generally been replaced by welfare-state-provided services and that women provide these services on a decommodified basis (Esping-Andersen 1999). Any national comparative analysis of the contrasting composition of welfare services in terms of the mix of decommodified public service provision and commodified market provision therefore fails

---

[3] Gender under the form of 'family' is present in two of his three categories of welfare state regimes. The corporatist welfare states strongly hold on to the family in its traditional form, while a major goal of the social-democratic welfare state regime is individual independence.

to take into account the significant amount of unpaid, decommodified welfare work undertaken by women (Wheelock *et al.* 2003).

The key issue is thus the way women's unpaid work as providers of welfare (mainly within the family) is valued and accepted as a legitimate ground for social entitlements. Esping-Andersen's criterion of the state–market nexus has not yet been convincingly and successfully replaced by that of the state–market–family nexus or the relationship between paid work, unpaid work and welfare. Despite progress towards a more equal division of paid work, the latter nexus necessarily remains gendered, given that the division of unpaid work is still very much gendered (see Chapter 8, this volume). Alternatively, as Esping-Andersen himself states (1999): 'Most welfare states are still income transfer biased, and only a handful pursues a *de facto* reduction of the family's welfare burden' (Esping-Andersen 1999: 55). The unequal division of unpaid work thus adds a gender dimension to the meaning of concepts such as 'de commodification' or 'dependency'.

Feminist discussion has not been blind to this issue of social entitlements and citizenship. Feminists have pointed out that in a great many approaches to social citizenship, women's full integration into waged work or, in other words, full provision of childcare, is the avenue to full citizenship of women and to gender equality.

Recapturing Pateman's arguments (1989), we could state that, in modern welfare states, social rights attach to those who are 'independent', and such independence is achieved through labour market integration. Because the division of paid and unpaid work is unequal between men and women, women's social rights become problematic. The comparative literature on welfare regimes has, thus far, failed to integrate the analysis of unpaid work. However, in modern societies, continuous paid work, independence and economic rights are inevitably built on their opposites: unpaid work, discontinuity, dependence and immobility. Paid, continuously working, mobile men face unpaid or low-paid, immobile, caring women, mothers, daughters and wives.

Unlike Pateman, many of her feminist colleagues have rejected a notion of gender equality as resting on women's employment, arguing that this represents an unacceptable androcentrism, and preferring what is often thought of as a strategy of 'equality in difference', by which women's 'traditional' domestic and caregiving activities are valued and serve as a basis for citizenship rights and political standing. Knijn and Kremer (1997) use the term 'including' citizenship to stress the fact that social citizenship should include the right to care, as well as the right to be cared for, as guaranteed and promoted by the welfare state.

1.3.2   The aftermath of Esping-Andersen: from welfare regime clusters to gender regime clusters

Studies reflecting on gender equality have led Lewis and Ostner (1994) to suggest an alternative categorisation of welfare regimes based on the gender division of work and using the strength of the male-breadwinner/ family wage model as a proxy measure. They observed that, when gender is treated as a full variable in the structuring of welfare regimes, it cuts across established typologies because of the division of paid and unpaid work. In most welfare systems, women's rights to welfare have been indirect, a function of their presumed dependence on a male breadwinner. While potential or actual motherhood has often provided the continued justification for making the grounds of women's social entitlements different from those of men, it has been as wives rather than as mothers that women have qualified for benefits in most state social security systems. Furthermore, Lewis and Ostner (1994) observed substantial variation in the degree to which parliaments also grant entitlements to women as paid workers. However, they believe, and hope to demonstrate in their welfare regime classification, that the tendency has been to make a dichotomous choice between treating women as wives and mothers, or as workers, with the former approach being chosen far more often than the latter.

According to Lewis and Ostner (1994), this has meant, first, that women's substantial contributions to welfare, particularly their unpaid contributions, have been ignored and with them the direct entitlements that should have been their due; and second, that women's needs have been defined in terms of motherhood as a social function rather than on the basis of individual need.

Because of the prevalence of the bourgeois family form, Lewis and Ostner (1994) have suggested that a majority of modern welfare states may be categorised as exemplars of a 'strong' male-breadwinner model. In its ideal form, this model prescribes breadwinning for men and homemaking/caring for women. However, they found that, while the vast majority of European countries recognise the male breadwinner role, there are significant differences in the extent to which women are confined to homemaking and motherhood, or – as married women and mothers – also recognised as workers. As a result, different national welfare settings produce different outcomes in terms of women's entitlement to benefits, the level of the social wage, public expenditure for social services and women's labour force participation. In response, Lewis and Ostner (1994) have distinguished between 'strong', 'moderate' and 'weak' male-breadwinner states.

Strong male-breadwinner countries such as the UK, Germany and the Netherlands have all tended towards treating adult women as dependent wives for the purposes of social entitlements. To quote Wheelock *et al.*: 'The UK policy-makers' family-wage model of the post-war years assumed a single utility function for the household. This model hid gender imbalances inside the household. The welfare state remained largely outside the front door, leaving the individuals within to manage the financial dependence of wives and the domestic dependence of husbands in whatever way they saw fit' (Wheelock *et al.* 2003: 21). Similarly, Gustafsson has pointed out the conservative nature of the Dutch welfare regime as far as women's roles are concerned (Gustafsson 1994). As a result, these strong male-breadwinner states are characterised by very high motherhood-induced employment penalties, which in Germany take the form of a complete withdrawal from the labour market in the presence of young children, whereas, in the Netherlands and the UK, mothers more frequently adjust their working hours to part-time. That is also why the fertility rate has remained higher in the latter two countries than in Germany where it dropped nearly as low as in the South of Europe.

By contrast, France has continued to recognise and promote women as both wives and mothers and as workers and may therefore be categorised as a moderate male-breadwinner model.

Finally, Sweden (or Denmark) is considered a weak male breadwinner state: since the 1970s, women have been defined as workers rather than as wives and mothers.

Both in the moderate and strong male breadwinner states, public childcare provision is the most efficient and encompassing of the whole of Europe and therefore motherhood does not force women to rein in their professional ambitions.

Despite its pioneer value, Lewis and Ostner's gendering of welfare states has turned out to be preliminary and incomplete.

Gornick *et al.* (1997) examined childcare arrangements and maternity and parental leave provisions in fourteen different countries in the mid 1980s. They then classified countries according to their score on two indices: the index of policies that support employment for mothers with children aged 3 and under, and the index of policies that support employment for mothers with pre-school-age children. Both indices reflect the availability of publicly funded childcare, different forms of tax relief, the length of maternity leave and parental leave, and the wage replacement rate during each of these types of leave, as well as whether legislation provides for job protection during the period of leave.

The study presents a relatively strong correspondence between the degree of support provided by child-related policies of maternal employment and women's employment profiles. Those countries where the age of the youngest child matters (Germany, Ireland, Luxembourg and the Netherlands: see below) are less supportive of employed mothers than those that use the number of children as the factor for precipitating a change in mothers' labour force participation. A striking exception to the correlation between policies and participation rates is presented by the liberal countries, especially the USA (low support but high participation). An individual exception is also presented by Portugal (low support but high participation). For Italy, it is important to know that, although the provision for children over 3 years is very generous, all other aspects of policies to support female employment tend to lag behind those of other countries.

A direct comparison can be made between these findings and the results of Letablier's analysis of the family-employment relationship. Letablier (1998)[4] has devoted a great deal of attention to the different conceptualisations of women's work and the varying degrees of acceptance of children's early socialisation. When the state intervenes in this area, it is not always for the same reasons: in France, it is to protect mothers at work, whereas in the Nordic countries, it is mainly to improve equality between men and women. However, in both cases (and in Belgium), it is due to significant public policy support that employment is made compatible with family life.

In line with the findings of Gornick *et al.* (1997), Letablier found that in strong male breadwinner states such as Austria, Germany, Luxembourg and the Netherlands, an important determinant for the family employment relationship is the age of the youngest child. Indeed, in those countries, policies designed to help parents combine paid work outside the home with childrearing duties presume that one parent, most often the mother, ceases or reduces her economic activity in order to return home to raise young children. Care work is more or less recognised by the state in the form of paid parental leave and/or access to social rights.

In the liberal countries, the rule for governments is not to interfere in private lives except when families fail. Thus, care is seen as a family obligation. In this sense, the UK and Ireland have long opposed the European regulation projects concerning maternity and parental leave because they are considered as limitations to employers' liberty. As a result, state support is low and associated with movements in and out of employment. Wheelock *et al.* (2003), in their study of the UK, have pointed out that the shift from the family wage model to a model of family employment has generally involved part-time employment for women, enabling mothers to retain their traditional caring roles. The gendering of working time is thus

---

[4] See also Hantrais and Letablier (1996).

one example of the different forms a regime of insecurity can take, depending on historical and institutional factors. In the new model, wives appear to have achieved only a very constrained level of financial independence, as households still tend to consider any childcare costs as a deduction from women's wages, rather than from household income. Men continue, as before, to be domestically dependent. In its concern to 'make work pay', the British government has identified childcare as a macro-economic issue which, if made affordable, could move both two-parent and one-parent households into family employment. In this strategy, the reference unit for public policy is the coresident model of the household (whether one- or two-parent) with impermeable boundaries (which are in fact widening so as to include the non-resident grandparental generation[5]). As a result, the 'make work pay' campaign merely modifies traditional gendered caring roles by implicitly delivering to mothers state additions to childcare in particular (Wheelock et al. 2003).

Finally, Letablier found the rejection of state intrusion into family affairs to be equally characteristic of Spain. However, in Southern Europe, the weakness of state support tends to be motivated by financial constraints rather than by liberal convictions. In the Mediterranean countries, family and employment are difficult to combine. A major role is played by family networks and intergenerational solidarity to substitute for little state support and an underdeveloped system of social protection. For Italy, Del Boca et al. (2003) explain: 'Assistance provided by grand-mothers and husbands appears to be of crucial significance to Italian mothers who are seeking to reconcile the difficulties stemming from the rigidity of the labour market and the limitations of childcare. Rationing, both of public and private childcare, also proves to be an important factor affecting households' choices.'[6] In addition, in the South and especially in Italy, decision-making mainly takes place at the local level giving rise to large disparities. The generous provision for children over 3 years old that was observed by Gornick et al. (1997) nevertheless signals some tradition of state policy (legislation) intended to protect working mothers even though women's activity rates are quite low.

---

[5] Wheelock et al. 2003 found that grandparents were giving up their own paid work to look after grandchildren in order to allow their daughters and daughters-in-law to earn a wage. They thereby illustrate the complexity of the shifts between paid and unpaid work between generations and the way in which they reproduce the gendered provision, organisation and management of childcare.

[6] For a detailed analysis of the interactions and mutual effects of employment and fertility in Italy, as well as for a comprehensive overview of public policies that facilitate the reconciliation of work and family life for Italian mothers, we would like to refer the reader to Del Boca (2000), Del Boca, Locatelli and Pasqua (2000), Del Boca and Pasqua (2002), Del Boca et al. (2003), and Del Boca and Repetto-Alaia (2003).

Another interesting study of family policy systems and of their similarities and differences was carried out by Forssén and Hakovirta (2000). They have compared the levels of family policies in thirteen countries, acknowledging that mothers' labour supply is influenced by both their preferences and labour market conditions, and also by family policies. Therefore, the study focused on direct cash transfers and taxation, as well as on social services that enable mothers to be active in the labour market. A family policy index was constructed. It includes both cash transfers for families with children and taxation and childcare arrangements so as to reflect two dimensions: first, the *work incentive* dimension, which refers to those measures, such as separate taxation and childcare policies, that encourage women to participate in the labour force, and second, the *home care incentive* dimension, which includes those measures that encourage mothers to stay at home, such as paid maternity leave, extended leave and economic support during the extended leave. The Nordic countries, France, Belgium, as well as Italy and Spain, all have a wide range of family policy legislation. However, the outcome of this legislation in terms of women's, and particularly mothers', employment is quite different. In the Nordic countries, France and Belgium, family policies in combination with other tax and child-related policies facilitate a balance between professional and family responsibilities, whereas, in the Southern European countries, the wide range of family policies does not translate into high female participation rates, with the exception of Portugal.

Northern European states tend to reject special protection for women as mothers in the labour market on the grounds of equality objectives. Therefore, generous state provision of childcare, paid parental leave for both men and women, and favourable working-time arrangements have to be understood as measures supporting women's access to the labour market. In France and Belgium, the focus has been on improving the quality of life of working people, on protecting the standard of living of families, and on achieving greater equality between men and women in the labour market.

An underdeveloped system of social protection characterises those countries where governments have deliberately abstained from interfering in the private lives of individuals (the UK, the USA, and Australia). Public childcare is designed primarily to protect children in need, while the issue of mothers' paid employment receives only secondary attention. Paid parental leave is not a universal right, it is merely an area of negotiation between employees and employers. In this sense, the USA's reliance on its substantial private market in (low-cost) childcare stands at the opposite pole from the Nordic welfare regime (strong state support for welfare services for household caring, both direct services and tax and family allowances). In the UK, the limited availability of both market- and state-provided childcare suggests a concomitant welfare state and market failure (Wheelock *et al.* 2003).

When parental leave, leave to care for sick children and childcare are considered together, it is clear that the Nordic countries have gone much further than other countries in assisting parents in reconciling employment with family life. The liberal welfare states lack this kind of support almost entirely.

Finally, it appears that not only the coverage of daycare matters but also its cost. The daycare fees of single parents in relation to their incomes are highest in the UK (28%) and the USA (22%). In Australia, high daycare fees have forced women to return to or stay at home. In the Nordic countries, daycare coverage and state subsidies for daycare costs are both very high.

Recently, Korpi (2000) categorised 'gender policy models' according to the level of public care services and the level of family support through transfers. While services tend to increase female employment, transfers usually have the opposite effect. Korpi (2000) found that the dual-earner model was the most compatible with the gender-egalitarian politics of the social-democratic parties of the Nordic countries.[7] The dual-earner model is characterised by a great number of public services and only a few transfers. The centralised state structure and encompassing system of social partnership which are typical of the Nordic countries have encouraged a well-developed welfare state.

While unionisation and social partnership have a relatively strong tradition on the European continent as well, the political context is much more conservative (see also Stryker and Eliason 2002). This is the result of status concerns and the strong role played by the church. The presence and activity of unions has contributed to a labour market which is highly regulated, entailing extensive protection for workers, as opposed to citizens, as is the case in the Nordic countries. Confessional parties trying to protect 'traditional' family relations in the face of capitalist market pressures have contributed to the strengthening of a general family model. Since the general family model involves many transfers and a

---

[7] In Sweden, the issue goes back as far as the 1930s, when Alva and Gunnar Myrdal first used the term 'women-friendly' policy with reference to pro-natalist policies concerned with assuring that working women can also have the option to have children, work being an obligation rather than a choice. By the 1960s, the male breadwinner model had become dominant and women's increased educational attainment required different policies than before in order to assure that mothers could also have access to the labour market. Today, most Swedish women want to work and a growing minority are even willing to postpone or totally refrain from maternity for the sake of a satisfying professional career.

concomitantly reduced provision of services, it corresponds to the traditional breadwinner model.

Finally, Korpi's market-oriented model refers to the logic of secular conservative parties which put market forces above gender or family considerations. Compared with the Nordic countries, industrial relations tend to be more decentralised in liberal regimes resulting in more market-friendly but less egalitarian welfare systems. The market-oriented model is characterised by low levels of both transfers and services resulting in a level of female employment that is situated somewhere between the levels of the dual-earner and the general family models.

Building on a wide spectrum of earlier research, Walby (2001) further developed the concept of gender regimes encompassing additional, relevant aspects other than just the welfare state (Walby 2001). Beginning with Lewis's and Ostner's simplistic distinction between strong, moderate and weak male breadwinner models (1994), she uses previous works by a wide range of authors to add to her analysis new and interesting sources of variation between different countries' welfare and gender regimes. Gender regimes are compared according to: whether women's family role is considered in terms of their being wives, mothers or workers; whether care is provided in the form of services, money to purchase services or money to allow for more time at home; and, finally, the actual outcome in terms of women's incomes and well-being.

In line with her predecessors, Walby (2001) acknowledged that the concept of 'welfare state', as opposed to 'gender regime', does not capture certain areas of state activity that nevertheless have a significant impact on the balance of women's paid and unpaid work and therefore also on gender relations. In this respect, she refers to the regulation of the labour market, marriage and divorce, abortion and contraception, male violence against women and education. Furthermore, the concept of gender regime also takes into account the second and often neglected component of women's unpaid labour, that is, housework (besides caregiving).[8]

The central thesis of Walby's theory on gender regimes is that there is a continuum along which gender regimes move from domestic to public (Walby 2001). Different countries are at different points along this

---

[8] Too often the analysis of unpaid work is limited to caregiving. Nevertheless, it is true that the extent to which household members' wages are used to purchase care constitutes an important factor of variance in the patterns of gender relations over time and between countries. Countries where domestic labour is socialised through the state suffer less social inequality since there is a more egalitarian provision of childcare. On the other hand, socialisation through the market favours the rich and excludes the poor who resort to career breaks since they cannot afford to purchase care on the market. These career breaks, in turn, have a negative impact on their lifetime earnings.

continuum and move at different times and rates under the impulse of modernisation and restructuring. The transition from domestic to public takes place through both state and marketised mechanisms although different countries use both routes to a different extent.

In theory, there are three possibilities as to the nature of changes taking place in gender regimes.

First, *gender regimes may change over time but all changes are rooted in national particularities and are therefore confined to a fixed range because of the continued importance of original national differences.* Walby (2001) refers to this scenario as the thesis of 'entrenched national differences'.

Second, *changes in gender regimes may result from modernisation. In the strong version of this thesis, the processes converge. In the weak version, modernisation causes similar and parallel changes in different countries but initial differences may remain.* Walby (2001) calls this the 'modernisation' thesis.

A third possible option is that of *an interaction between a process of major structural change (economic modernisation) and pre-existing differences (political institutions). This interaction is believed to lead to common outcomes in new social patterns which may reverse the rankings of the differences between the countries or create new ones.* Walby (2001) names this the 'restructuring' thesis.

While gender regimes move from domestic to public along a continuum, their position on the continuum at any given moment is determined by their performance in all of four fields which Walby (2001) considers to be constitutive of what she calls a gender regime: employment, family,[9] fertility,[10] and political representation.[11] She tested each of her three preliminary hypotheses in these four fields.

[9] Besides divorce rates, Walby analysed the birthrate outside marriage as an indicator of the extent to which marriage fully encapsulates women's lives. It measures the strength of marriage in domesticating women. The higher the birthrate outside marriage, the more public is the gender regime and the weaker the male breadwinner model. This rate has increased considerably over time.

[10] The lowest fertility rates and the greatest falls in these rates appear in those European countries with the strongest traditions in restricting the availability of abortion and contraception. Strikingly, Walby showed that fertility and female employment do not, in any way, preclude each other. All depends on the available package of financial incentives and childcare provisions to facilitate women's combination of work and childrearing. In other words, the gendered patterns of welfare provision seem to be decisive.

[11] The period 1970–95 witnessed a general transition to higher female political representation. Different factors seem to affect women's level of representation: female employment, electoral system, extent of legislature and of party competition, party organisation, and the process of recruitment of candidates within parties. All of these factors can potentially increase or decrease women's representation. However, they do not explain the observed increase in the number of women in parliament over time. For a more elaborate analysis of the importance of political factors in shaping women's employment policies and larger welfare politics, we refer to Korpi's work which we discussed briefly earlier in this chapter (Korpi 1983; Korpi 2000).

Her analysis proves the latter two theses to be dominant. The commodification of women's labour has thus proved to be a common stage of development for all welfare state regimes and in no way unique to the social-democratic regime. Differences between countries are due primarily to their stage in the transition process. At any moment, it is possible to identify clusters of countries with similar patterns of gender relations. The main source of variation is their stage in the transition process from domestic to public. A secondary source of variation is the interaction between deeply embedded social institutions and the restructuring process. Modernisation means that the same changes are replicated everywhere but not in an identical fashion, since the interaction with social institutions can lead to the emergence of new patterns.

1.3.3   The role of culture in shaping gender regimes

Although feminists have actively participated in the debate on social citizenship, they have often neglected the role of cultural values and ideals which are crucial to explain why social citizenship is defined in different ways in different welfare states, and why social practices of citizenship vary. However, exceptions exist. On the basis of a Jamaican case study, Wyss has argued for the culturally specific nature of childcare and examined how these cultural determinants have been accounted for by economic models of child support behaviour (Wyss 1999). In his more recent work, Esping-Andersen has also focused on the cultural side of childcare by analysing cross-country differences in the mix of state, market and household-based childcare. Furthermore, Pfau-Effinger (2000) has incorporated different cultural beliefs into her comparative analysis and classification of Western European gender cultural models.

These models differ with respect to two features: first, with respect to cultural ideas regarding the gender division of labour, the main spheres of work for women and men, the social valuation of these spheres, and the way dependencies between men and women are generated; and, second, with respect to the cultural construction of the relationship between generations, or, in other words, the construction of motherhood, fatherhood and childhood. Based on these underlying features, Pfau-Effinger (2000) has distinguished six gender cultural models: the family economic gender model; the male breadwinner/female home carer model; the male breadwinner/female part-time carer model; the dual breadwinner/state carer model, the dual breadwinner/dual carer model, and the dual earner/marketised female carer model. These models are not mutually exclusive. In Sweden, the dual breadwinner/

Table 1.1 *An overview of welfare state typologies (in chronological order)*

Author	Date	Main subject of analysis
Calmfors and Driffill	1988	degree of corporatism
Esping-Andersen	1990, 1999	de-commodification, social stratification, de-familialisation and the state/family/market nexus to classify welfare states in three clusters: social-democratic, liberal and conservative
Leibfried	1992	rudimentary/modern/institutional/residual policy models
Lewis and Ostner	1994	strong/moderate/weak male breadwinner typology
MacFarlan and Oxley	1996	transfers as a % of tendential GDP
Adema	1996	net public social expenditures as a % of GDP
Bonoli	1997	social expenditure as a % of GDP and the part of social expenditures financed through contributions
Gornick *et al.*	1997	policies that support the employment of mothers of young children
Korpi and Palme	1998	institutional characteristics of old-age pensions and sickness cash benefits
Letablier	1998	family policy models: explicitly family-oriented, less explicitly family-oriented and implicit state support
Letablier	1998	family–employment relationship
Ebbinghaus	1998	subsidiarity principle and intergenerational welfare provision
Trifiletti	1998	family policies, gender division of paid/unpaid work, subsidiarity principle
Korpi	2000	gender policy models (balance in cash/in kind support) and political tendencies
Forssén and Hakovirta	2000	family policy index
Pfau-Effinger	2000	gender cultural models
Walby	2001	gender regimes instead of welfare states

dual carer model is combined with elements of private care for children. Mothers tend to work part-time for a long period of time during the phase of active motherhood. The male breadwinner/female part-time carer model is dominant in former West Germany while the dual-breadwinner/dual-carer model prevails in former East Germany. Finally, the Netherlands seems to be in a transitory phase, the dual breadwinner/ dual carer model prevailing at the cultural level, while in practice the male breadwinner/female part-time carer model is still dominant.

1.4   Conclusion

At the beginning of the 1990s, Esping-Andersen's three-fold typology of welfare state regimes launched a very lively debate on the usefulness of research that tries to group together into clusters similar welfare state regimes. Throughout the 1990s, new welfare state typologies have relied on an ever-increasing number of welfare state characteristics in order to reflect adequately new political and economic patterns emerging in European societies. The proliferation of variables underlying comparative welfare state research has substantially complicated the task of identifying distinct welfare clusters. This chapter has shown that, although most typologies were easily applicable to welfare states organised according to the dominant male-breadwinner logic, problems arise when they are applied to today's welfare state reality that relies heavily on women in terms of both their participation in the labour market and their willingness to bear children.

When the specific situation of mothers is considered, the main finding of this chapter is that welfare states are usually not pure types but are instead hybrid cases that foster mothers' welfare in different forms and to different extents. However, this has not led us to conclude that welfare state classifications have no use. In fact, typologies help in modelling reality and unravelling the latent organising principles and laws of modern welfare states, especially from the point of view of mothers. In this sense, typologies have a significant explanatory value even though welfare states have proven to be rather unique specimens which do not easily lend themselves to crystallisation into distinct 'worlds of welfare'.

References

Adema, W. 2005. 'Babies and bosses', *OECD Observer*, no. 248, March.

Adema, W., M. Einerhand, B. Eklind, J. Lotz and M. Pearson 1996. *Net Public Social Expenditure*, Labour Market and Social Policy Occasional Papers no 39, Paris: OECD.

Arts, Wil and John Gelissen 2001. 'Welfare states, solidarity and justice principles: does the type really matter?', *Acta Sociologica* 44, 283–99.

2002. 'Three worlds of welfare capitalism or more? A state-of-the-art report', *Journal of European Social Policy* 12; 2: 137–58.

Bonoli, G. 1997. 'Classifying welfare states: a two-dimension approach', *Journal of Social Policy* 26 (3), 351–72.

Calmfors, L. and J. Driffill 1988. 'Bargaining structure, corporatism and macroeconomic performance', *Economic Policy* 6, 16–61.

Castles, F. G. and D. Mitchell 1993. 'Worlds of welfare and families of nations', in F. G. Castles (ed.), *Families of Nations: Patterns of Public Policy in Western Democracies*, Aldershot: Dartmouth Publishing Company.

Del Boca, D. 2000. 'Participation and fertility behaviour of Italian women: the role of market rigidities', *CHILD Working Paper 10*.

Del Boca, D. and S. Pasqua 2002. 'Labour market participation of mothers in Italy: facts, studies and public policies', *CHILD Working Paper 04*.

Del Boca, D. and M. Repetto-Alaia 2003. *Women's Work, the Family and Social Policy: Focus on Italy in a European Perspective*, New York: Peter Langs Publishing, 216pp.

Del Boca, D., M. Locatelli and S. Pasqua 2000. 'Employment decisions of married women: evidence and explanations', *CHILD Working Paper 8*.

Del Boca, D., M. Locatelli and D. Vuri 2003. 'Childcare choices by Italian households', *CHILD Working Paper 30*.

Ebbinghaus, B. 1998. 'European labour relations and welfare state regimes: a comparative analysis of their "elective affinities"', Background Paper for Cluster 3: 'The Welfare State and Industrial Relations Systems, Conference on 'Varieties of Welfare Capitalism in Europe, North America and Japan', Max Planck Institute for the Study of Societies, Cologne, 11–13 June.

Esping-Andersen, G. 1990. *The Three Worlds of Welfare Capitalism*, Cambridge: Polity Press.

1999. *Social Foundations of Postindustrial Economies*, Oxford: Oxford University Press.

Ferrera, M. 1997. 'General introduction', in Mire Florence Conference, *Comparing Social Welfare Systems in Southern Europe*, vol. III, Paris: Mire, 13–24.

Forssén, Katja and Mia Hakovirta 2000. 'Family policy, work incentives and employment of mothers: findings from the Luxembourg Income Study', Paper presented at The Year 2000 International Research Conference on Social Security ('Social Security in the Global Village'), organised by the Finnish member organisations of the International Social Security Association (ISSA) and held in Helsinki, Finland, 25–27 September.

Gornick, J. C., M. K. Meyers and K. E. Ross 1997. 'Supporting the employment of mothers: policy variation across fourteen welfare states', *Journal of European Social Policy* 7 (1), 45–70.

Gustafsson, S. 1994. 'Childcare and types of welfare states', in D. Sainsbury (ed.), *Gendering Welfare States*, London: Thousand Oaks, 45–61.

Hantrais, L. and M.-T. Letablier 1996. *Families and Family Policies in Europe*, London and New York: Longman.

Katrougalos, G. S. 1996. 'The South European welfare model: the Greek welfare state in search of an identity', *Journal of European Social Policy* 6 (1), 39–60.

Knijn, T. 1991. 'Citizenship, care and gender in the Dutch welfare state', Paper presented at the European Feminist Research Conference 'Women in a Changing Europe', University of Aalborg, 18–22 August.

Knijn, T. and M. Kremer 1997. 'Gender and the caring dimension of welfare states: toward inclusive citizenship', *Social Politics* 5 (3), 328–61.

Korpi, W. 1983. *The Democratic Class Struggle*, London: Routledge.

1989. 'Power, politics, and state autonomy in the development of social citizenship: social rights during sickness in eighteen OECD countries since 1930', *American Sociological Review* 54 (3), 309–28.

2000. 'Faces of inequality: gender, class, and patterns of inequalities in different types of welfare states', *Social Politics* 7, 127–91.

Korpi, W. and J. Palme 1998. *The Paradox of Redistribution and Strategies of Equality: Welfare State Institutions, Inequality and Poverty in the Western Countries*, February.

Leibfried, S. 1992. 'Towards a European welfare state: on integrating poverty regimes into the European Community', in Z. Ferge and J. Kolberg (eds.), *Social Policy in a Changing Europe*, Frankfurt am Main and Boulder, CO: Campus Verlag/Westview Press, 245–79.

Leira, A. 1989. *Models of Motherhood: Welfare State Policies and Everyday Practices: The Scandinavian Experience*. Oslo: Institute for Social Research.

Letablier, M.-T. 1998. *Comparing Family Policies in Europe*. Periodic Progress Report No 1 of the Thematic Network: 'Working and Mothering: Social Practices and Social Policies', TSER Programme of the European Commission, Area III: Research into Social Integration and Social Exclusion in Europe, 1st TSER Seminar held in Lund, 26–28 November.

Lewis, J. and I. Ostner 1994. 'Gender and the evolution of European social policies', Universität Bremen, Zentrum für Sozialpolitik (Centre for Social Policy Research), ZeS-Arbeitspapier nr. 4/94.

Lumen, J., J. Le Cacheux and D. Meulders 2000. *Policy Digest*.

MacFarlan, M. and H. Oxley 1996. 'Social transfers: spending patterns, institutional arrangements and policy responses', *OECD Economic Studies*, no. 27.

Myrdal, A. and G. Myrdal 1934. *Kris I befolkningsfrågan*, Stockholm.

Orloff, Ann Shola 2001. 'Gender equality, women's employment: cross-national patterns of policy and politics', Paper prepared for the meeting of the International Sociological Association Research Committee 19, Poverty, Social Welfare and Social Policy 'Old and New Social Inequalities: What challenges for Welfare States?', University of Oviedo, Spain, 6–9 September.

Pateman, C. 1989. 'Feminist critiques of the public/private dichotomy', in C. Pateman (ed.), *The Disorder of Women*, Stanford: Stanford University Press, 118–40.

Pfau-Effinger, B. 2000. 'Changing welfare states and labour markets in the context of European gender arrangements', Centre for Comparative Welfare State Studies, Aalborg University, Denmark, COST A13 Action 'Changing

Labour Markets, Welfare Policies and Citizenship', Gender Group Working Paper.(www.socsci.auc.dk/cost/gender/workingpapers.html)

Sainsbury, Diane (ed.) 1994. *Gendering Welfare States*, London: Sage Modern Politics Series, vol. XXXV.

Stryker, R. and S. R. Eliason 2002. 'The welfare state, gendered labor markets and political orientations in France, Belgium, Germany, Italy, Denmark and Britain 1977–1994', Paper presented at the Gender Studies Program, October.

Trifiletti, R. 1998. Comments on *Comparing Family Policies in Europe*. Periodic Progress Report No 1 of the Thematic Network: 'Working and Mothering: Social Practices and Social Policies', TSER Programme of the European Commission, Area III: Research into Social Integration and Social Exclusion in Europe, 1st TSER Seminar held in Lund, 26–28 November.

Walby, S. 2001. 'From gendered welfare state to gender regimes: national differences, convergence, or re-structuring?', Paper presented to Gender and Society Group, Stockholm University, January.

Wetzels, Cecile and Aslan Zorlu 2003. 'Wage effects of motherhood: a double selection approach', Paper presented to the conference 'Family, Employment and Welfare Issues in Europe: The Quantitative Approach', 18–20 February, Brussels. Presented to the 17th meeting of the European Society of Population Economics (13–15 June, New York State University, New York).

Wheelock, Jane, Elizabeth Oughton and Susan Baines 2003. 'Getting by with a little help from your family: toward a policy-relevant model of the household', *Feminist Economics* 9 (1), 19–45.

Wyss, Brenda 1999. 'Culture and gender in household economics: the case of Jamaican child support payments', *Feminist Economics* 5 (2), 1–24.

2 Making time for working parents: comparing public childcare provision

Jérôme De Henau, Danièle Meulders and Síle O'Dorchai

2.1 Introduction

Early childhood education and care differ substantially across countries. First, opinions diverge as to the optimal age at which children's socialisation should begin, that is, the age at which children should be cared for outside the family circle, and these differences are reflected in the way a country's childcare system is organised (Letablier 1998). Some countries emphasise the importance of outside childcare options being available for children from as early as the end of maternity leave onwards. Others are in favour of children being cared for in the close family circle when they are very young and do not focus on developing outside care until children are 3 years of age (and up to the age at which they enter primary school). Second, countries also differ as to the sharing of childcare responsibilities between the domestic, the public and the private sphere. In some countries, 'having children' is considered to be a private choice, so that parents have to pay for the cost of children. In others, it is considered to be a public matter, in which case the state helps parents maintain their standard of living when they decide to have children. As a result, the former countries rely heavily on market intervention, while the latter focus on making the public system as all-encompassing as possible.

Governments can act on three levels to provide care for children and to avoid deterring dual-earner families from having children. These levels are related to the different conceptions of children's socialisation and public intervention in this process, mentioned above (Martin 2003). They are also related to budget constraints and financial priorities. The three main forms that state interventions can take are:

– direct supply and organisation (and/or supervision) of public (publicly funded) childcare (collective places or registered childminders);

- replacement income and/or job protection for parents who temporarily quit their job to take care of their children (maternity and paternity leave around birth, and parental leave later on);
- direct financial support to families to help them purchase care on the market (cash and tax benefits that can sometimes be used beyond mere care purposes).

This three-fold institutional setting relies on different assumptions as to how care for young children should be provided, by public services, by relatives at home or by private services.

If preference is given to children being looked after by their own parents, the focus will be on the parental leave system; if the private sphere is seen as the preferred locus for the organisation of care, the government will assist parents financially to buy services in the market (private nurseries, childminders, nannies) with a series of child benefits, tax credits or care allowances. A third way of dealing with the issue is to provide public formal childcare by means of subsidised services.

As far as outside childcare options are concerned, countries have generally implemented a two-fold system:

- collective childcare systems (crèches, kindergartens, play-schools): these are public or private reception facilities with skilled staff providing care for young children during the day;
- subsidised professional childminders who receive children in their own home (family daycare).

Moreover, most countries distinguish between two periods of pre-primary care and education, an earlier period being more related to care (from birth to the child's third birthday) and a later one to education (from 3 years until the age of compulsory education). The locus of authority usually shifts from one period to the other: infants fall under the auspices of the Ministry of Social Affairs, while pre-school children are the responsibility of the Ministry of Education.

The Barcelona European Council of March 2002 put forward the improvement of childcare provision as an important instrument within the set of active policies aimed at full employment. The Council acknowledged the need to improve public and private childcare provision in order to increase female participation rates. Moreover, accessible and high-quality childcare is considered of prime importance to enhance social inclusion of all vulnerable groups in society. Two very precise targets were adopted: by 2010, Member States should provide care facilities to cover, first, at least 90% of children aged between

3 years and the age at which compulsory schooling begins and, second, at least 33% of children below 3 years of age. These objectives have appealed to governments to substantially improve their childcare systems.

This chapter provides a critical overview of a comprehensive set of relevant childcare characteristics as well as a consistent comparison of all EU-15 Member States. Our goal goes far beyond describing each country's childcare system since we aim to assess and compare countries with respect to a large number of criteria which we have grouped into two main categories that adequately and exhaustively describe a public childcare system. These categories are: (i) the coverage rate of the childcare system measured by three indicators (proportion of children covered, public share in the costs and opening hours of care facilities); (ii) the child/staff ratio (number of children per full-time equivalent qualified carer). To complete the latter category, public spending on education for children aged 3–5 is also considered. Many studies show that each of these criteria plays an important role in facilitating the dual-earner model without jeopardising families' fertility choices (e.g. Gornick *et al.* 1997; Rostgaard and Fridberg 1998; Del Boca *et al.* 2000; Gornick and Meyers 2000; Adema 2001; Kamerman 2001; Bradshaw and Finch 2002; Eurostat 2002 and Del Boca and Repetto-Alaia 2003). Therefore, the point is to evaluate a country's performance on each of these criteria and compare it with other countries. The assumptions underlying each of the childcare components are the following: (i) the higher the coverage rate, the longer the opening hours of care facilities and the larger the public share of the cost, the greater the proportion of children in public (and publicly funded) full-time free care and therefore the easier it is for parents to engage in paid work, even at atypical hours; (ii) the smaller the number of children per trained carer, the higher the level of professionalism of a country's public childcare system and the better its quality; and (iii) the higher the level of public spending per child in education, the better the system's infrastructure, the more attractive employment in this branch, and the higher the quality of child development.

The analysis is carried out *ex ante*, without investigating the actual impact of policies on women's labour participation or fertility decisions. We build on the literature to assess the potential effects of policies, and thus to decide on the direction each element should take if dual-earner families are to be privileged. Budget constraints also need to be considered, in order to understand trade-offs made by countries between different elements. As a matter of fact, we have assumed a perfect substitution framework of costs: guaranteeing a place for all children of a certain age on a half-day basis is equivalent to guaranteeing to half of the children of the same age a place on a full-day basis.[1]

The different aspects of childcare have been described and commented upon by a wide range of authors, providing substantial information for our work. In addition to the overarching research activity in the field of childcare by organisations such as the OECD (2001a, 2002, 2003) and Eurostat (2002), individual authors have covered the question of childcare. Math (2003) provides a description of public policies for families over the period 1990–2000 in Europe. An overview of benefits that foster the reconciliation of work and family life in OECD countries was presented by Adema (2001). His analysis is based on a large set of indicators including public expenditure on family benefits, the coverage rates of childcare systems, maternity and parental leave arrangements, employment-related tax credits and benefit programmes, incidence of part-time employment, etc. Thus, Adema's study extends far beyond the childcare system itself. Furthermore, his data refer to the late 1990s (1997–99). An extensive analysis of early childhood education and care was carried out by Kamerman (2001) and also by Gornick and Meyers (2000) who used a rich set of interesting data concerning institutional arrangements for the provision of childcare with details on the opening hours of facilities and the age category of the children served in each of these arrangements. Government subsidies for childcare, tax relief, employer contributions and parent fees are also discussed. Moreover, coverage rates of childcare systems and quality indicators such as the staff/child ratio are given ample attention.

However, Kamerman's study has two main drawbacks. First, not all of the EU-15 countries are analysed (only ten). Secondly, data refer to the situation in the mid-1990s and as such are becoming out of date. Several European research networks have focused on the issue of childcare. A rich set of data was gathered by TSFEPS[2] (2002) and Care Work in Europe at the beginning of this decade. Finally, Bradshaw and Finch (2002) compared child benefit packages in twenty-two countries in 2002 in the framework of research commissioned by the Department for Work and Pensions in the UK. Besides these more or less comprehensive

---

[1] Note that our data allow us to disentangle both types of models. This is helpful to compare the actual effect of either model on employment outcomes (see Part III).

[2] 'Transformations des Structures Familiales et Evolution des Politiques Sociales' or TSFEPS (2001–04) is a European research project financed by the 5th Framework Programme of the EC. Its aim is to analyse childcare services in eight European countries (Belgium, France, Italy, Spain, Great Britain, Sweden, Bulgaria and Germany) as well as the social cohesion issues that are at stake in the development of the care sector.

childcare studies, many analyses or reports exist at the national level. Unfortunately, these are difficult to compare across countries (lack of comparable and harmonised data).

Collecting comparable data on childcare systems across Europe raises difficulties because complete harmonised data sources are not available, in particular not for the youngest children. We have dealt with this problem by gathering a large set of different data sources, subjecting them to critical comparison, and retaining the most reliable data which we have then harmonised in order to allow for sound cross-country comparisons. However, a problem of accounting for regional hetero-geneity persists since data are not sufficiently disaggregated. Indeed, in most countries local communities play an important role in the provi-sion of childcare, which often leads to a high degree of diversity within countries: this is especially true for Italy, France, Germany and the UK.[3] For example, disparities are commonly observed between rural and urban areas with regard to the number of childcare places locally available (Del Boca *et al.* 2003). Moreover, care for 0–3 year olds is often provided through private services or informal intra-family agree-ments that are not easy to measure formally. Nevertheless, our aim is to evaluate the degree to which a state takes care of its children, since public childcare structures should have more universal access. As a result, our analysis is not hindered by the lack of data on private or informal childcare availability.

The added value of this work is (i) to cover all countries of the EU-15; (ii) to update information on childcare policy elements; (iii) to consider a wider range of policy elements and discuss their interrelationships; (iv) to process this information into comparable harmonised indicators that can be used for assessing employment outcomes (see Part III).

First, we will briefly describe childcare and early education systems across countries and then review our set of indicators one by one, positioning countries with respect to each indicator before establishing a final overall classification of countries.

2.2   Great institutional heterogeneity of early education and care

According to the Eurydice Network (2002), three main categories of formal care or education structures can be distinguished based on age and educational content (see Appendix Figure 2.A.1). The first category

---

[3] Partial information on regional coverage is available upon request to the authors for France, Denmark, Sweden, Finland, Belgium, Italy and to some extent, Germany.

comprises a wide range of arrangements targeted at children of the youngest age group (aged 0–2 generally) such as daycare centres, playgroups and nurseries, all of which put the emphasis on care (as opposed to education) and allow parents to work. These structures can be private and independent (Ireland, the UK), private but publicly funded (Portugal, the Netherlands, most structures in Germany), or public (France, Italy, Belgium, Greece, Austria, Denmark, Sweden, Finland).

In the Nordic countries, all of these facilities are operated by staff with tertiary educational skills. Moreover, these countries propose age-integrated structures until the age at which compulsory schooling begins (7 years, with a one-year period of pre-school classes), alongside crèches (0–2) and kindergartens (3–6).

In the other countries, the move from infant care to care for children of the next age group – generally from 3 years old – corresponds to a change in formal arrangements, mostly shifting responsibility to the education system (all but Austria and Germany). For some of these countries, such education-based care is the only form provided for pre-school-age children (France, Belgium and Italy) from the age of 3 years onwards. In Greece, Ireland and the Netherlands, educational enrolment starts at 4 years of age.

For the purpose of harmonisation, we have divided children into two age groups: infants, 0–2 years of age (third birthday), and pre-school children, 3–5 (sixth birthday).[4]

Such a procedure does not accommodate children between 6 and 7 years of age in the Nordic countries. However, since coverage is almost 100% in free public classes with a substantial educational component, the Nordic arrangements are almost identical to the usual primary classes in other countries. In the Netherlands, Greece and Ireland, a change in care structure takes place at the age of 4 years. In order to take into account this latter arrangement, we have weighted the figures for care structures for 4–6 year olds in order to filter out what is available for 3–4 year olds).

Finally, we need to say a few words on the articulation between the age of compulsory school enrolment and children's entry into the first level of primary education (ISCED 1). In Appendix Figure 2.A.1, we see that Luxembourg is the country with the lowest age to start statutory education: at 4 years of age children start a pre-primary curriculum. The UK and the Netherlands follow with compulsory enrolment at 5 years of

---

[4] In the following sections and chapters, children of the first category (zero to third birthday) are referred as infants or 0–2 year olds or under-threes, while children of the second category are called pre-school-age children, preschoolers, or 3–5 year olds.

age, also in the pre-primary system (primary school starting at the age of 6 in those three countries).

Most European countries have let the age of compulsory schooling coincide with entry into primary education, that is 6 years of age in most countries. The same is true for the Nordic countries but at 7 years of age. In Ireland, primary school starts at the age of 4, while compulsory schooling begins only at 6 years of age.

Here, we do not go into the more subtle rules regarding the way to measure a child's age to assess whether or not enrolment is compulsory (according to date of birth in some countries, while in others the child's age at the end of the calendar year counts). The Eurydice (2002) report offers additional interesting information on this topic.

2.3   Method used for the construction of indicators

The first step of our research consists in gathering quantitative information on different childcare policy elements. In a second step these data are harmonised through different sub-stages: (i) first, we make the values of each of our original variables comparable[5] between countries; (ii) then, we sometimes combine them (creating so-called grouped variables) when it makes sense to do so in order to clarify the understanding of certain policy elements across countries;[6] (iii) once all useful direct variable combinations are made,[7] we transform each individual or grouped variable into an index using a method called Linear Scaling Technique and, finally (iv) we combine our scaled indices to obtain summary indicators of policies for each of the major policy fields (axes), by taking either simple or weighted averages according to the number of underlying original variables.

The Linear Scaling Technique (hereafter LST) has been extensively applied by the United Nations Development Programme (UNDP) to construct the Human Development Index (HDI), an index also used to compare countries according to their overall level of welfare.[8] LST standardises the range of a variable across countries. For each variable, the highest and lowest values identified among countries are denoted

---

[5] For example, monetary amounts, expressed either in PPP or in percentage of the relevant level of average national earnings.

[6] For example, number of available places per one hundred children combined with percentage of public share in the total costs.

[7] For example, public spending for preschoolers and average coverage rates of childcare are not directly 'combinable' (amounts in PPP versus percentages).

[8] For more details on the Linear Scaling Technique, its strengths and weaknesses and different applications, see Salzman (2003).

Max and Min, respectively. The value of a particular country i is then scaled relative to these bounds to obtain its score, according to the formula:

$$scaled[Criterion_i] = \frac{Value_i - Min}{Max - Min} \cdot 100$$

The obtained score is always in the range 0–100. The procedure is reiterated for each criterion considered relevant for the computation of the final indicator. Once all countries have a score (ranging from 0 to 100) for each criterion, these are combined to obtain a final indicator by simply taking their arithmetic average.

Note that if one criterion is expressed in the reversed order (the higher score is associated with the lowest value[9]), the formula to transform the criterion is as follows:

$$scaled^{-1}[Criterion_i] = \frac{Max - Value_i}{Max - Min} \cdot 100$$

Weighting criteria in the process of taking arithmetic averages is a critical question, varying with the underlying information we aim to synthesise. We have been careful to discuss it for each specification though, in some cases, an arbitrary weight is given to the scores, reflecting the number of primary criteria they are built on.

Note that this method results in a relative classification: it obscures a country's actual performance for criteria that have a definite maximum (childcare coverage, replacement rates, etc.).[10] However, it is a very relevant method to use when criteria do not have a consensual maximum (spending, child/staff ratios, flexibility of leave, etc.), and consequently for indicators that combine these two types of criteria, such as those presented in this analysis.

Finally, the last step consists in comparing our indicators across the three dimensions (axes) of child policy. Since our goal is to group countries into more or less homogeneous clusters, we have opted for a Euclidian-distance cluster analysis rather than a principal components analysis. The latter works better to identify cross-country correlation

---

[9] It means, for example, a criterion that goes in the opposite direction to the effect we try to measure – in our case parental work supportiveness (amount of parental fee for a childcare slot, for example, but also length of transferable parental leave, qualification for child benefits, as discussed in Chapters 3 and 4).

[10] For example, Denmark scores 100 on childcare coverage while it is far from offering a place to each infant (Table 2.1).

between variables than to position countries within a particular group according to the similarity of their scores on different indices.[11]

2.4   Degree of coverage of the childcare system

Three indicators are combined to evaluate the coverage rate of a childcare system, each broken down by age group (Table 2.1).[12]

First, there is what is commonly denoted as the 'coverage rate': it measures the proportion of children of a given age group received in some form of public or publicly funded childcare. In order to make sure that we account for availability and not statistical coverage, we have decided to retain the proportion of places available (during the whole range of daily opening hours) rather than the number of children enrolled, because some enrolled children can also attend facilities on a part-time basis.

A second element determining overall coverage of the childcare system is 'daily coverage': it refers to the spread of opening hours of formal childcare arrangements. If a system intends to adapt to parents' working hours, childcare centres and other care provisions are expected to offer a continuous service covering the entire working day or, in other words, without interruption at noon and continuing beyond the usual working hours in order to grant parents enough time to commute.

Finally, a third element that measures public commitment to offer affordable childcare is the way in which the cost of childcare is shared between public funds and parent or employer fees.

After a separate analysis of each of these three components of the degree of coverage of childcare systems, we have engaged in a summarising exercise by computing the combined generosity of a country on all of these indicators. All three components are considered to be equivalent and perfect substitutes in measuring the actual degree of coverage of a country's childcare system.

This indicator measures the proportion of children, within each age category, respectively, who have a full-time and free place in public or publicly funded childcare facilities. Of note is the large difference in coverage rates in both age groups. Coverage of the youngest children reaches 58% at most, and only in Denmark, whereas coverage of preschool-age children is hardly ever below this level, except for Greece, Ireland and Finland.

---

[11] Clusters are processed through the software Intercooled Stata 8.0.
[12] See Appendix Table 2.A.2 and 2.A.3 for more detailed figures and sources.

Table 2.1 *Ranking of the EU-15 Member States according to their score on six indicators of formal public and publicly funded care and education facilities*

Coverage for ages 0–2 (%)		Coverage for ages 3–5 (%)		Daily opening hours for ages 0–2		Daily opening hours for ages 3–5		Public share in the cost for ages 0–2 (%)		Public share in the cost for ages 3–5 (%)	
DK	58	BE	99	SE	11.5	SE	11.5	IE	100	BE	100
FR	39	DK	94	DK	10.5	DK	10.5	UK	94	EL	100
SE	37	FR	87	NL	10.5	FI	10.0	SE	92	ES	100
BE	30	IT	87	FR	10.2	FR	8.0	FI	85	FR	100
FI	23	SE	79	GE	10.0	IT	8.0	BE	83	IE	100
PT	12	ES	77	IT	10.0	BE	7.0	LU	83	LU	100
AT	10	LU	76	FI	10.0	NL	7.0	GE	82	NL	100
GE	9	GE	73	BE	9.0	GE	7.0	AT	82	PT	100
IT	7	PT	72	EL	9.0	AT	6.7	EL	80	UK	100
ES	5	AT	70	IE	9.0	UK	6.3	ES	80	SE	92
EL	3	NL	66	LU	9.0	ES	5.2	IT	80	IT	91
LU	3	FI	63	UK	8.0	LU	5.0	PT	80	FI	85
NL	2	UK	60	PT	7.5	PT	5.0	FR	78	GE	82
IE	2	IE	50	AT	7.5	EL	4.0	DK	75	AT	82
UK	2	EL	48	ES	5.0	IE	4.0	NL	65	DK	75

Note: BE stand for Belgium, DK for Denmark, DE for Germany, EL for Greece, ES for Spain, FR for France, IE for Ireland, IT for Italy, LU for Luxembourg, NL for the Netherlands, AT for Austria, PT for Portugal, FI for Finland, SE for Sweden, UK for the United Kingdom. These country codes are used in the whole document.

How to read the table: For example, concerning coverage for under 3s, Denmark is at the top of the ranking offering a place in public or publicly funded childcare to 58% of children in this age group, with average opening hours of care facilities equal to 10.5 hours each day and with a public share of 75% in the average cost of childcare.

Coverage rate of infants and pre-school-age children.

Source: See Appendix Tables 2.A.1 and 2.A.2. Data for 0–2s are mainly for 2003, those for 3–5s for 2002.

2.4.1   Availability of childcare slots

2.4.1.1 Lack of childcare slots for infants   Low public childcare coverage (between 0% and 10%) is observed in three groups of countries:

Anglo-Saxon countries where the provision of childcare relies almost entirely on private, marketised care options and firms' efforts at the local level;
Mediterranean countries where family support is high;
Luxembourg, Austria, the Netherlands and Germany where the traditional division of roles is institutionalised, and mothers are responsible for the socialisation of children, a task that requires their full-time commitment to childrearing (Letablier and Rieucau 2001).[13]

The most generous countries include Finland, Belgium, France, Sweden and Denmark. The latter country by far outperforms the former countries with 58% of under-threes covered by some form of public childcare (versus less than 40% for Sweden and France). France and Belgium have privileged early socialisation of children for two reasons: it facilitates mothers' employment and safeguards the principle of equality of all children (Letablier and Rieucau 2001). Moreover, a considerable percentage of children under 3 years of age are enrolled in pre-primary education (33% of 2 year olds in France and around 60% of $2\frac{1}{2}$ year olds in Belgium, both contributing to about 9% of total public coverage).

In the Nordic countries, given that the individual is at the core of the system, children have the right to a place in collective childcare from their first year of age onwards. Public policy evolves from the principle of equality between men and women. Therefore, it aims at maximising the degree to which both parents are involved in care for their children. Formal childcare is a legal right of every child. If almost no child under one year of age is cared for outside the family (12% in Denmark, 0% in Sweden and 1.3% in Finland), 82% of Danish children aged 1–2 attend public childcare facilities compared with, respectively, 55% of Swedish and 33% of Finnish children of the same age (Statistics Denmark 2005; Skolverket 2005a; Ministry of Social Affairs and Health 2004). These countries clearly favour parental leave schemes in the early stages of a child's life, lasting for one year in almost all cases (see Chapter 3).

---

[13] The Netherlands are positioned somewhere between the Anglo-Saxon and German-speaking countries, with a high degree of private or firm-organised care, even though total coverage does not exceed 12% (Berg-Le Clercq *et al.* 2002).

Box 1: Early socialisation in France

Since the 1980s, public investment in collective facilities in France has been gradually replaced by efforts to develop individual solutions such as care by childminders or by nannies within the home (Périvier 2003). As a result, in 2000, 11% of the under-2s were cared for within the framework of schools, 9% had a place in a crèche, 19% were cared for by childminders, 1.5% were cared for by a nanny at home, and around 40% were cared for by one of the two parents. Half of them made use of the parental leave system (*allocation parentale d'éducation*) (Fenet *et al.* 2001). Despite this diversity of childcare solutions, inequalities persist: availability and feasibility of most of the options depend on where the family lives as well as on its total income. In rural areas, the lack of collective facilities has led to a major role being played by childminders, a solution which is not financially affordable for low-income families. In urban areas, although more places are available in crèches, a problem of excess demand remains. Nannies are available for those families failing to get their children into crèches, but this solution is financially affordable only for high-income families and thus excludes part of the population. Recently, the French government enacted some reforms, implemented as of January 2004, which lower the price of childminders for low-income families (Périvier 2003). Concerning the cost of hiring a nanny at home, support is usually given through income tax reduction so that the lowest-income families are again excluded from the benefit of this childcare measure since their income is usually not taxed.

The trend towards the individualisation of the childcare system that characterised the 1980s and 1990s in France has reinforced women's and men's traditional social roles: women continue to be considered the only legitimate carers (Boyer 1999). Skilled women hire unskilled women to take care of their child(ren) (childminders and nannies are generally women with few or no skills). Be that as it may, domestic work remains a 'women's sphere of activity'. Despite recent reforms in France, institutions in charge of family matters, public decision-makers, employers and a large proportion of families themselves all share the same idea that caring for children remains a woman's business (Fagnani 2001).

2.4.1.2 Wide coverage of pre-school-age children   The picture is different when we focus on the age category composed of pre-school-age children, between 3 and 5 years old (Table 2.1). For this age group, public care and education facilities achieve more than 75% coverage in a series of countries, and even higher if private educational arrangements are taken into consideration (see Eurydice 2002). On the whole, three groups of countries can be distinguished. A first group of countries includes Belgium, Denmark, France, Italy and, to a lesser extent, Spain, with almost 100% of children covered, but with varying degrees of public coverage (lower in France, Italy and Spain). So, almost all children in those countries are enrolled in some form of early education – whether private or publicly funded – but mostly supervised by the Ministry of Education.

The coverage rate of pre-school-age children (public but also private) is somewhat lower in a second group of countries which include Luxembourg, Germany, Portugal, Sweden and Austria. It ranges between 70% and 79% of children of this age group.

The third group includes countries with more heterogeneous facilities and systems. The low coverage rate in the Netherlands, Greece and Ireland is mostly explained by the absence of public care arrangements for children aged 3 years while older children are indeed well covered by the public system (100% in the Netherlands and approximately 75% in Greece and Ireland for 4–5 year olds). Finland remains a country with a high proportion of pre-school children not covered by any formal facility: more than a quarter of children aged 5 were not covered by private or by public facilities at the end of 2003 (Ministry of Social Affairs and Health 2004). Finally, the UK is characterised by a large share of private institutions (25%). A French study of child performance in the first years of primary education has shown that early educational enrolment (around 4 years of age) is of crucial importance (Goldstein 2003). In other countries, efforts are made also to improve the enrolment rate of 4-year-old children (e.g., Portugal, Austria, the UK, Finland, Sweden and Denmark), especially in the more vulnerable categories of the population (Eurydice 2002).

2.4.2   *Opening hours of childcare provisions for infants and pre-school-age children*

The practical use of public childcare arrangements may be hindered by limited opening hours, forcing parents to work short hours or work out informal solutions to complement formal ones. Again, we distinguish between the opening hours of facilities for infants and those for pre-school-age children. For each age bracket, the indicator measures the number of hours during which children are cared for in the framework of public or publicly funded childcare facilities. The figures presented in Table 2.1 take into account the opening hours of the different arrangements that exist for each age group, computed on a weighted-average basis for each type of care arrangement (school, crèche, family daycare, etc.).

2.4.2.1 Infants   In most countries childcare facilities for this age group have long opening hours, especially in Sweden (more than 11 hours per day), Denmark, the Netherlands and France.[14] Such a degree of availability helps parents with very young children to combine their family and professional responsibilities. Broad daily coverage also characterises the system in Italy, Germany, Finland and, to a lesser extent, Belgium where facilities are open for 10 hours each day.[15] In three countries (Portugal, Austria, Spain), parents rely on outside public childcare for less than a 'usual' working day (8 hours), meaning that one of them is forced to work short days (or part-time) or that they must seek informal alternatives to cover the time lapse between the closing time of the public facility and the time they get back from work.

Moreover, more or less flexible formulas may be in place with respect to how parents can make use of facilities. In France, for example, crèches are open all day but parents cannot use them on a part-time basis, whereas in the Netherlands, parents are offered the possibility of paying by half days. Given that crèches are quite expensive in the Netherlands, many parents use them only at a part-time rate while they work (part-time).[16]

2.4.2.2 Pre-school-age children   The opening hours of facilities for pre-school-age children show a more time-restricted scheme than for infants in most countries (except for Sweden, Denmark and Finland where the system does not change between the two age groups). Facilities are open around two hours fewer per day in France, Italy, Belgium, the Netherlands, Germany and Portugal, and even up to four hours fewer in Greece, Luxembourg and Ireland. Note that for France, Belgium and Italy, paid childcare outside school hours is provided in most facilities (only a few offer free care), but these provisions are very difficult to measure.[17] The same is true for the Netherlands, but the public share of

---

[14] In France, childcare facilities are usually open 11 hours each day every day but, given that some infants attend nursery schools which are open only for 8 hours each day, weighted average opening hours are somewhat lower (Appendix Table 2.A.2).

[15] The same combination applies to Belgium with crèches and childminders operating for at least 10 hours and nursery schools for 7 hours each day.

[16] This part-time breakdown has been taken into equivalent account in the computation of the coverage rate of Dutch infants. We retained the number of full-time places available.

[17] Note that, in Belgium, the new government of the French-speaking Community (formed in 2004) plans to make substantial efforts to provide free out-of-school childcare for all, in order to supplement the short 7 daily opening hours of schools.

the coverage rate in out-of-school care facilities is below 1% (Berg-Le Clercq *et al.* 2002).

2.4.3   Public share of costs

Besides coverage and opening hours, the third indicator of interest is the share of public funding to cover the cost of childcare. The 'public funding' indicator corresponds to the part of the total cost of a place in childcare that is covered by public funds, first for an infant (Table 2.1, col. 5) and second for a pre-school-age child (Table 2.1, col. 6). For example, when the level of public funding is equivalent to 85% of the cost of childcare, it can be deduced that on average 15% of the cost needs to be covered by parental fees (taking into account possible financial advantages for lower-income families). Therefore, the higher the percentage the less childcare costs weigh on the household budget.[18]

2.4.3.1 Infants   Of note is the finding that Ireland and the UK rely least on parental fees to finance public childcare. However, as mentioned before, public childcare facilities in these two countries play a negligible role compared with private care solutions. Public care is restricted to disabled children or to children of families at risk. As a result, although public childcare is least costly in the UK and Ireland, only a very small number of families benefit from this type of care. Half of the Member States offer public funds amounting to more than 80% of childcare costs. In Sweden, from 2002, a maximum rate has been set up for parental fees as low as 9% for pre-school daycare (from 1–5 year olds). Public funding comes from municipalities for the major part, complemented by government grants. In reality, less than 10% of the population pays higher fees, and the maximum parental fee observed across all municipal centres is 19% (Skolverket 2005b). France and Denmark intervene to a degree of 75%. The Danish maximum for parental fees in any type of childcare is 30%. In Dutch publicly funded childcare centres, parent fees cover more than 35% of the cost.

2.4.3.2 Pre-school-age children   Nine countries fully cover the cost of care in public or publicly funded facilities for this age group. In so far as basic education is free, public childcare for pre-school-age children in the framework of the educational system (public or publicly funded) is free of charge as well, except in Italy where 18% of schools are

---

[18] Yet it does not provide information on the level of these costs (see section 4).

administered by the Church, which although partly subsidised, asks only small participation fees (OECD 2001a). Full public funding of childcare for pre-school-age children does not exist in Finland, Austria, Germany, Denmark and Sweden although public funds do cover between 75% and 90% of the cost of childcare in those countries.

2.4.4   Equivalent of free, full-time childcare coverage

Our purpose is to combine the previous three indicators in order to obtain a more accurate picture of the inclusiveness and affordability of public childcare systems across Europe. Given the assumption of perfect substitution between the three elements, we compute the simple product of each country's scores on all three indicators.[19]

The product of the scores on each of the three indicators can be interpreted as the proportion of children in each age category (infants and pre-school-age children) who are covered by a given country's public and publicly funded care facilities on a fully-funded and full-day basis (11.5 hours per day).

$$FTFECov_i^k = CovRate_i^k + \frac{OpenHours_i^k}{OpenHours_{SE}^k} + PubShare_i^k P \; (k = 0 - 2 \; or \; 3 - 5)$$

With $i = BE, DK, DE, ..., UK$ (EU-15 Member States)

2.4.4.1 Infants   In Figure 2.1 below, the dark bars give the respective position of countries assuming that the combination of the coverage rate, the spread of opening hours, and the share of public funding in the cost measures the real coverage rate of childcare systems for infants across Europe. While the inclusion of more elements to determine the coverage rates of childcare systems decreases the scores (compared with usual coverage rates), it does not significantly change the ranking of countries, because both public funding and opening hours are quite high for most countries or compensate for each other (e.g. Denmark and the UK). Three groups can be distinguished: five countries in the upper part of the ranking with scores above 15% (Denmark, Sweden, France, Belgium, Finland); four countries in the middle part with lower scores of 4–6% (Germany, Portugal, Austria, Italy); and, finally, the last six

---

[19] As far as the indicator on opening hours of care facilities is concerned, we have slightly transformed this indicator in order to express each figure as a percentage of the highest number of opening hours observed. In other words, we have divided each country's opening hours by the Swedish figure (SE).

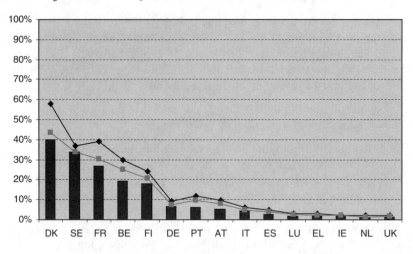

Figure 2.1   Ranking of the EU-15 Member States according to percentage of infants receiving free, full-time public or publicly funded childcare.

Note: Usual coverage is the number of available childcare slots divided by the number of children of this age category.

Free equivalent coverage is usual coverage multiplied by the public share in the average cost of one slot.

Free full-time equivalent coverage is 'free equivalent coverage' multiplied by the average opening hours of facilities (expressed in percentage of the opening hours of the Swedish system).

For explanation of the country abbreviations, see Table 2.1.

How to read the figure: for example, regarding free full-time equivalent coverage (dark bars), in Belgium, 19.5% of children aged 0–2 would be covered by a public or publicly funded facility, free of charge and for 11.5 hours each day if the system were to apply Swedish opening hours and provide free care (compared with the usual coverage rate of 30% and the free equivalent coverage rate of 25%).

Source: Own calculations and Appendix Tables 2.A.2 and 2.A.3.

countries with concentrated scores below 2%. Moreover, the gap is narrowed between Denmark and Sweden and between Belgium and Finland.

2.4.4.2 Pre-school-age children   As far as pre-school-age children are concerned (Figure 2.2 below), the weighting of the coverage rate by full-day equivalent opening hours (11.5 hours each day) and public funding leads to more dramatic changes in the ranking for some countries. Given that

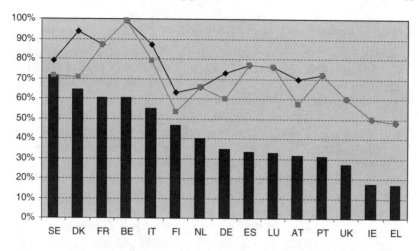

free full-time equivalent coverage ——◆—— usual coverage ——■—— free equivalent coverage

Figure 2.2 Ranking of the former EU-15 Member States according to share of pre-school-age children receiving free, full-time public or publicly funded childcare.

Notes: Usual coverage is the number of available childcare slots divided by number of children of this age category.

Free equivalent coverage is the usual coverage multiplied by the public share in the average cost of one slot.

Free full-time equivalent coverage is the 'free equivalent coverage' multiplied by average opening hours of the facilities (expressed in percentage of opening hours of the Swedish system)

For explanation of the country abbreviations, see Table 2.1.

How to read the figure: e.g., regarding free full-time equivalent coverage (dark bars), in Belgium, 60% of children aged 0–3 would be covered by a public or publicly funded facility, free of charge and for 11.5 hours each day if the system were to apply Swedish opening hours and provide free care (compared with the usual coverage rate of 99% and the free equivalent coverage rate of 99% which is the usual coverage rate multiplied by the public share in the average costs – 100% in this country).

Source: Own calculations and Appendix Tables 2.A.2 and 2.A.3.

coverage for this age group is free in almost all countries (no difference between the two lines except in Nordic and German-speaking countries), the changes in the rankings are due mainly to differences in the opening hours of the educational institutions. Belgium, although it maintains its position in the higher part of the ranking, drops dramatically, which is also the case for Spain, Luxembourg, Portugal and the UK.

2.4.5   *A qualitative approach to childcare coverage*

Several studies have dealt with the issue of evaluating the quality of childcare provision (Fiene 2002; Kamerman 2001). They agree on a range of indicators to assess the different aspects of childcare quality. These consist roughly of health safeguards, the educational content of care and security as well as children's safety. Fiene (2002) proposes fourteen indicators: one child abuse indicator; one immunisation indicator; the child/staff ratio (number of children per carer) and one group size indicator; two staff qualifications indicators; one staff training indicator; one supervision/discipline indicator; one fire drills indicator; one medication indicator; one emergency plan/contact indicator; one outdoor playground indicator; one toxic substances indicator; and one handwashing/diapering indicator. Most of these indicators involve security, safety and health, and many public and publicly funded provisions have to satisfy legislative demands regarding these issues. Therefore, it seems more interesting to compare countries according to aspects concerning staff provision.[20] We focus on the child/staff ratio only, given that qualifications are difficult to harmonise and that staff generally have some degree of higher education in care or education fields.[21]

In our computations, we thus use the number of children per carer as a proxy for the quality of childcare services. Since for both groups of children different forms of formal care exist in different contexts (such as kindergartens, playgroups, crèches, nursery schools and so on), our indicator is often a weighted average number of children per carer over the different types of care solutions.

Most countries adopt some requirements that specify a maximum number of children for whom an adult can be responsible, especially for pre-primary education. This is not the case in Belgium, France, Denmark, the Netherlands and Sweden, where limits are not established at a central level. In the other countries this maximum varies from seven in Finland up to thirty in Ireland and Greece while most of them have ratios of twenty-five (Eurydice 2005).

However, as far as the ideal number is concerned, a consensus is observed in the literature around three or four infants per carer in

---

[20] We deliberately focus on staff indicators because they are expected to differ in greater extent across countries than health or security standards. Nevertheless, we cannot verify this assumption due to a lack of data for the remaining quality indicators for all countries.

[21] More precisely, staff occupied in education-oriented facilities (mostly implemented for preschoolers) have at least some degree of tertiary education (ISCED 5a or 5b) corresponding to three extra study years in all EU-15 Member States (Eurydice 2005).

Table 2.2 *Country rankings according to the child/staff ratio in public and publicly funded childcare for infants and pre-school-aged children*

Child/staff ratio 0–2 (average)		Child/staff ratio 3–5 (average)		Child/staff ratio 3–5 (max. required)	
DK	3.0	DK	6.0	BE	–
IE	3.3	SE	6.0	DK	–
UK	3.7	FI	7.0	FR	–
FI	4.0	AT	8.8	NL	–
AT	4.5	GE	12.0	SE	–
LU	5.0	IT	12.5	FI	7
NL	5.0	FR	12.8	UK	13
PT	5.5	LU	14.3	DE	15
FR	5.8	PT	16.4	ES	25
IT	6.0	BE	18.5	IT	25
SE	6.0	NL	20.0	AT	25
GE	7.5	UK	24.3	PT	25
BE	9.0	ES	25.0	LU	26
ES	13.7	EL	30.0	EL	30
EL	13.8	IE	30.0	IE	30

Note: For country abbreviations, see Table 2.1.
How to read the table: for example in Denmark, there are on average three children aged 0–2 per qualified carer. Countries are ranked in increasing order of the respective ratios.
Source: See Appendix Table 2.A.3 for average ratios and Eurydice (2005) for required ratios.

centres (crèches or family daycare centres) and two staff members per group (Fiene 2002). For preschoolers, the ratio increases to eight children per carer, much less than the maximum required in most European countries. In Table 2.2, we see that for infants, the distribution of child/staff ratios across Europe is much denser than for pre-school-age children. For infants, the ratio ranges between three and fourteen children for every childminder (and in eleven countries even as low as three and six children). For pre-school-age children, the spread is much wider, covering from as few as six to as many as thirty children for each carer.

While Greece and Spain are far from reaching the quality standards for infants – for reasons we were not able to find, other than financial – the low figure for Belgium can, at least partly, be explained by the fact that it includes the share of $2\frac{1}{2}$–3 year olds who attend nursery schools in which the child/staff ratio is much higher (boosting the average figure over all types of care for this age group). As stated above, in the UK and Ireland only infants with special needs have access to public childcare. We observe a ratio of around three children per carer in these latter two countries.

Nordic countries have the highest ratios as far as pre-school-age children are concerned. This is because they have one integrated system for the two age groups, and the differences between both age groups should be interpreted with this in mind. If care is the responsibility of the educational system (the Netherlands, the UK, Greece, Spain and Ireland), the number of children per class and per teacher is much higher, since such care is usually organised in a similar way to primary classes, than when it is provided in kindergartens or daycare centres, as is the case in the Nordic countries, Austria and Germany. Conversely, Italy and France, two countries providing nursery schools for children aged 3–5 – thus falling under the auspices of the Ministry of Education – nevertheless have low ratios, because of the presence of a second childminder in the class.[22]

When we compare this indicator with the free full-time equivalent childcare coverage rate computed previously, child/staff ratios provide complementary information. For example, Belgium and Denmark have the same weighted coverage rate for pre-school children but present a very different picture in terms of staff supervision. Indeed, there are three times as many children per carer in Belgium than in Denmark. This can have a varied impact on child development. This is even clearer in the case of France. Children are admitted to nursery school from as early as 2 years (provided they are born before 31 August). In other words, they can enter early into an education system where groups are larger and where there is just one teacher for about thirteen children. In crèches one carer is responsible for approximately six children whereas a childminder looks after approximately three children in her own home. Parents trade off between different types of provision at this age: on the one hand, free education in larger groups; on the other hand, smaller groups for longer hours but with less educational content and at a higher fee for parents.

2.5   Financial burden of child education and care

The cost of childcare facilities is a factor that cannot be ignored if we aim at understanding incentives to work. The percentage of public intervention in the cost of a slot is part of this analysis, as discussed above. Nevertheless, unless 100% of the cost is covered by public funding, there remain parental fees – especially for younger children. Therefore it is useful to look at the remaining cost for parents and compare the level across countries.

---

[22] These countries are not totally comparable since in Italy both of these carers are qualified teachers while in France one of them is a qualified teacher who is assisted by a trained support agent ('agent qualifié spécialisé en éducation').

2.5.1   Net cost of full-time childcare

Countries can apply different mechanisms to subsidise the market cost of childcare. First, they may subsidise childcare itself so that charges fall below market costs for all parents. Secondly, they may reduce or refund charges for childcare according to income, family type, age or number of children in childcare. Charges for childcare exist everywhere for couples, but for single parents most countries provide free or heavily subsidised childcare places. Third, the extra costs of childcare in some countries are mitigated by higher cash benefits with respect to a child of pre-school age as compared with a school-age child. In Denmark, a non-income-related pre-school subsidy is paid, while in the Netherlands, Luxembourg and Belgium there is a slight reduction in the non-income-related benefit paid for a pre-school age child (Bradshaw and Finch 2002). Countries may offset the market costs of childcare through income tax reductions (see Chapter 4 on tax and cash benefits). Bradshaw and Finch (2002) have computed the average cost of a childcare place for infants in the most prevalent full-time formal pattern available in the country in 2000. However, these figures encompass both private and public facilities so that they are not totally comparable with our data on public and publicly subsidised childcare settings. Yet their results for couples show some similarity with our indicators for the public share in the cost, with Austria, Sweden, Finland, Belgium and Luxembourg performing well (lower cost) while the Netherlands, the UK, Ireland and Greece are found at the bottom of the ranking, due to the prevalence of private arrangements.

2.5.2   Public spending on education for children enrolled in pre-school provisions

Another indicator of the financial aspects of childcare is the amount spent by governments on early childhood education and care. Data for public spending on childcare are difficult to compare across countries because the different kinds of expenditure are mapped differently across statistical institutes and sources (cash and in-kind expenses, subsidies, tax credits, family assistance, etc.). We did not consider the data on social expenditures released by the OECD to be sound enough, harmonised and comparable for our purpose (Math 2003; OECD 2001b).

However, for older children, a substantial share of the public offer of childcare forms part of educational arrangements for children below the age of compulsory school enrolment and thus falls under the responsibility of the ministry of education. This also holds for the Nordic and German-speaking countries where pre-school-age children follow an educational curriculum within the framework of public or publicly funded childcare

Table 2.3 *Public spending per child enrolled in a pre-primary educational programme* (€ *PPP, 2000*)

Public spending per child	
LU	6,682
UK	4,666
AT	4,198
IT	3,832
FR	3,697
DK	3,628
NL	3,529
BE	3,319
GE	3,182
IE	3,084
FI	3,066
SE	2,905
ES	2,663
EL	2,257
PT	2,134

Note: For country abbreviations, see Table 2.1.
How to read the table: for example in Luxembourg, the government spends about € 6,700 per child aged 3–6 enrolled in any educational programme.
Source: OECD Education Database 2003

facilities. As a result, it is easier to gather harmonised financial information for this age group, especially thanks to the OECD Education Database (2003) which provides such data for the year 2000. Public spending on education includes all current and capital expenditures by central, regional or local governments, oriented directly towards institutions providing education (schools and other educational establishments). Our aim here is to compare countries according to their level of spending per child enrolled in an education programme of any kind or form, whether private or public, in order to draw conclusions on various elements such as the quality of care, the earnings level of care staff, capital investment in the sector, material issues, etc. Obviously, public spending per child depends on the public share in the costs of childcare (and also on the coverage rate in public and publicly funded childcare) and, moreover on the child/staff ratio given that the largest share of expenditure on education and care goes to carers' wages. In sum, public expenditure allows us to get a better picture of the level of earnings in the sector as well as of other aspects such as quality (material, infrastructure, etc.) and public involvement in the field.

Table 2.3 shows that some countries are more generous with respect to this indicator compared with their performance regarding the previous ones, especially Austria and the UK. On the other hand, Finland and Sweden fall back to the lower part of the ranking, first, because care for 3–5-year-olds has a smaller educational component in those countries, although children are looked after by qualified staff. A second reason concerns parental fees for childcare for this age group. Similar remarks can be made for Denmark.

2.6 Final results and conclusions

2.6.1 Final score of the countries' childcare systems

Since both age groups (0–2 and 3–5) present very distinct characteristics in terms of enrolment, costs and child/staff ratios, it is interesting to compute a final score for each of these groups in order to assess public involvement regarding the different aspects of child development (Figure 2.3).[23]

For the index of childcare for infants Icc_i^{0-2}, we have used four criteria. The three criteria that compose the coverage rate, expressed in full-time free equivalent coverage $FTFECov^{0-2}$ and then scaled, on the one hand,

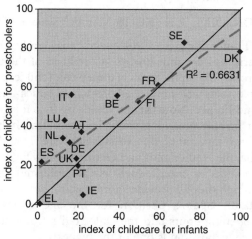

Figure 2.3 Final ranking of the EU-15 Member States' childcare systems.
Note: For explanation of the country abbreviations, see Table 2.1.
How to read the figure: e.g., concerning the final score for children aged 3–5 (vertical axis), France's score is explained as follows: on a scale from 0 (worst performer on all variables) to 100 (best performer), France is located at 61 on average for all underlying scaled criteria (weighted average). See Appendix Table 2.A.4 for the underlying figures and the average score for children aged 0–5.
Source: Own calculations (see sources in Appendix Tables 2.A.2 and 2.A.3).

---

[23] See also Appendix Table 2.A.4 for a combined index of all children aged under 6 (average of the two age-category-specific indicators).

and on the other hand, the inversed child/staff ratio *child/staff* $^{0-2}$, expressed as a percentage of the highest inversed ratio (Denmark) and then scaled. The final index is the weighted average of these two scores (the weight reflecting the number of underlying criteria, three-fourths for the equivalent coverage and one-fourth for the child/staff score). For pre-school-age children Icc_i^{3-5}, the same procedure is followed but we add a fifth criterion, the level of public expenditures *spending*$^{3-5}$. Therefore, the weight is three-fifths for equivalent coverage, one-fifth for the child/staff ratio and one-fifth for public spending.[24]

$$Icc_i^{0-2} = (scaled[FTFECov_i^{0-2}]) \cdot \frac{3}{4} + \left(scaled \left[\frac{\frac{1}{child/staff_i^{0-2}}}{\frac{1}{child/staff_{DK}^{0-2}}} \right] \right) \cdot \frac{1}{4}$$

$$Icc_i^{3-5} = (scaled[FTFECov_i^{3-5}]) \cdot \frac{3}{5} + \left(scaled \left[\frac{\frac{1}{child/staff_i^{3-5}}}{\frac{1}{child/staff_{DK}^{3-5}}} \right] \right) \cdot \frac{1}{5}$$

$$+ (scaled[spending_i^{3-5}]) \cdot \frac{1}{5}$$

With $i = $ BE, DK, DE, ..., UK (EU-15 Member States)

Denmark, Sweden, France, Belgium and Finland consistently score high on all separate criteria and are thus always at the head of the ranking. Italy joins this top group only on the vertical dimension (childcare for the age group 3–5), thanks to its well-developed pre-school education similar to that in Belgium and France. Note that for childcare 0–2, it is of no use commenting further on the remaining countries (including Italy) since they have very low coverage rates, the worst being Greece and Spain. Luxembourg, Austria, the Netherlands and Germany show higher scores for older children, thanks to criteria such as the child/staff ratio and public spending although they all provide short opening hours compared with Nordic standards. Spain's position for the age group 3–5 is explained by short opening hours and the child/staff ratio, although in terms of free coverage its position is one of the highest.

On the basis of this chapter, we can conclude that, even if childcare for infants is somewhat developed (or under way) in only five countries, nevertheless many more children are being socialised as they grow older, although in very different ways as far as opening hours and child/staff

---

[24] In this case, the weight is equally distributed across criteria, both for infants and for preschoolers. Note again that we consider the criteria composing full-time free equivalent coverage as perfect substitutes. For child/staff ratios, we also think that a certain form of trade-off occurs. In a previous version, we had also combined child/staff ratios with the indicator of full-time free equivalent coverage (thus assuming perfect substitution between the four criteria), and it did not lead to a different ranking.

ratios are concerned. Most of the countries provide relatively short hours in pre-school facilities as compared, for example, with their standards in childcare provision for infants (centres are open around five hours a day in Greece, Spain, Ireland, Luxembourg, the Netherlands, Portugal and the UK) and with more crowded classrooms (more than twenty children per member of staff in Greece, Spain, the UK and Ireland, while under ten in the Nordic countries and Austria).

The global picture put forward by Figure 2.3 is in line with other childcare-oriented welfare state typologies (e.g. Gustaffson 1994; Gornick et al. 1997; Letablier 1998). Hence, it seems that our ranking is quite robust and adequately presents the relative positions of each country with respect to the support of their childcare system to achieve a balance between family and professional life for both parents. We have seen that the countries considered have implemented a very diverse provision of public childcare and this exercise has allowed us to systematically compare countries with each other. Note, however, that the linear scaling technique gives relative rankings, meaning that even if a country scores close to 100 (ranked first), it still can be far from any existing maximum of the underlying criterion. For example, Denmark, although its score is close to 100 overall, is far from reaching a 100% free full-time equivalent coverage rate for infants (in fact only around 40% according to Figure 2.1). However, this technique is useful when criteria are not measured relatively to any maximum (mostly given by a percentage), such as public spending per child or child/staff ratios.

Table 2.A.1 *Most prevalent full-time formal pattern of childcare for children under 3 years old*

UK	Childminder
Italy	Day nursery
Luxembourg	Childminder
Belgium	Childminder (*Assistante maternelle*) supervised by public authorities
Finland	Municipal daycare centre
Sweden	Municipal financed daycare centre
Germany	Day nursery
Spain	Private day nursery
Denmark	Crèche
France	Childminder (*Assistante maternelle*)
Netherlands	Subsidised childcare
Austria	Crèche
Greece	Low income: public childcare; high income: private childcare
Ireland	Childminder
Portugal	Private non-profit kindergarten

Source: Bradshaw and Finch (2002).

Table 2.A.2 Coverage and opening hours of childcare according to different sources in EU-15

Country	Coverage		Hours	
	0–2 year olds	3–5 year olds	0–2 year olds	3–5 year olds
Belgium	30%: 20.5% in crèches or Assistantes maternelles and 9.5% in schools (ONE and K&G, 2002)	99% in (a)	9: 68% in crèches for 10 hrs and 32% in schools for 7 hrs (ONE and K&G, 2002)	7 in (f) and (i) (8.30–15.30)
Denmark	58% in Statistics Denmark (2005)	94% in Statistics Denmark (2005)	10.5 in (g) and (h)	10.5 in (a)
Germany	9%: 3% in WG & 36% in EG in (c)	73% in (a)	10 in (c) and (e)	6.7 in (c) (weighted average of FT and PT)
Greece	3% in (d) and (i)	48% in (a)	9 in (e) (full day)	4 in (e)
Spain	5% in (d)	77% in (a) (96% covered but 19% private)	7 in (a)	5 in (c) and (e)
France	39%: 20% Assistantes maternelles, 9% crèches, 10% nursery schools (Leprince, 2003)	87% in (a) (100% covered but 12.5% private)	10.2 in (c) & Leprince (2003) (10–12 hrs in crèches or AM for 75% and 8 hrs in schools for 25%)	8 in (c) (8.30–16.30)
Ireland	2% in (e) and (j)	50% in (a) (75% from age 4 at school)	9 in (e) (full day)	4 in (e) (9.00–13.00)
Italy	7.4% in (d) and (f)	87% in (a) and (e) (98% cov., 11% private, 17% subs. church, 70% public)	10 in (c), (d) and (e)	8 in (c), (d) and (j) (8.30–16.30)
Luxembourg	3% in (f)	76% in (a)	9 in (e)	5 in (e)

Netherlands	2.3% Berg-Le Clercq et al. (2002)	66% in (a) and Berg-Le Clercq et al. (2002) (100% from age 4 at school and 1.7% of 3yrs. in DC)	10.5 in Berg-Le Clercq et al. (2002)	5.5 in Berg-Le Clercq et al. (2002) (8h30–16h30 – 1hr at lunch)
Austria	9.8% in Kytir and Schrittwiezer (2003)	70% in (a)	7.45 in Kytir and Schrittwiezer (2003) (weighted average of FT & PT)	6.3 in Kytir and Schrittwiezer (2003) (weighted average of FT & PT)
Portugal	12% in (d) and (i)	72% in (a)	7.5 in (e) and (i) (between 5 for 55% and 11 for 45%)	5 in (i)
Finland	22% in Ministry of Social Affairs and Health (2004)	63% in Ministry of Social Affairs and Health (2004)	10 in (h)	10 in (h)
Sweden	37% (of which 90% in daycare) in Skolverket (2005a)	72% in Skolverket (2005a)	11.5 in (h)	11.5 in (h)
UK	2% (public) in (f)	60% in (a) (85% but 24% private, excl. play groups)	8 in (c)	5.2 in (c) and (e) (33% in nurseries for 2.5 hrs., 66% in schools for 6.5 hrs.)

Sources: (a) Eurydice (2005), data Eurybase (www.eurydice.org); (c) TSFEPS (2002); (d) OECD (2001a); (e) Eurostat (2002); (f) Gornick and Meyers (2000); (g) Rostgaard and Fridberg (1998); (h) Adema (2001); (i) Bradshaw and Finch (2002); (j) The Clearinghouse on International Developments in Child, Youth and Family Policies (2003).

Table 2.A.3 *Share of costs covered by public funds and child/staff ratio according to different sources*

Country	Share of cost covered by public funds		No. of children per staff member	
	0–2 year olds	3–5 year olds	0–2 year olds	3–5 year olds
Belgium	83% in (c) and (f)	100% in (a)	9 in ONE and K&G 2002 (weighted average of crèches, childminders and school)	18.5 in (a)
Denmark	75% in (f) and (h)	75% in (f) and (h)		
Germany	82% in (f)	82% in (h)	3 in (d) and (j) 7.5 in (k)	6 in (d) and (j) 12 in (k)
Greece	80% (see Spain and Italy)	100% in (a) and (e)	13.75 in (e) (30:2 and 25:2)	30 in (e)
Spain	80% in (c), (e) and (j)	100% in (a) and (j)	13.7 in (c)	25 in (c)
France	77.6% in (a), (f) and (j) (crèches & childminders at 75%, schools at 100%)	100% in (a)	5.8 in (k) (5 in daycare centres, 3 in family daycare centres, 10 in schools for 2yr olds)	12.75 in (a) (25.5 per group with 1 teacher and 1 qualified assistant)
Ireland	100% in (e)	100% in (a) and (e) (primary school)	3.3 (368:111) in Oasis website	30 in (a)
Italy	80% in (k)	100% in (a), (c) and (e)	6 in (e)	12.5 in (a) (public + private subs.)
Luxembourg	82.5% (see Belgium and Germany)	100% in (a), (f) and (e)	5 in (e)	14.3 in (a)

Netherlands	64.5% in Berg-Le Clercq et al. (2002)	100% in (d) (*basisonderwijs*)	5 in (c) and (i)	20 in (i) (*basisschool*)
Austria	82% (see Germany)	82% (see Germany)	4.5 in (a)	8.8 in (a)
Portugal	80% (see Italy and Spain)	100% in (e)	5.5 in (e)	16.4 in (a)
Finland	85% in Ministry of Social Affairs and Health (2004)	85% in Ministry of Social Affairs and Health (2004)	4 in Ministry of Social Affairs and Health (2004)	7 in Ministry of Social Affairs and Health (2004)
Sweden	91.8% (92% in daycare centres, 90% in family daycare) in Skolverket (2005b)	91.8% (92% in daycare centres, 90% in family daycare) in Skolverket (2005b)	6 in (d) and (i)	6 in (d) and (i)
UK	94% in (f)	100% in (d) and (f)	3.7 in (k) (3:1 <2yrs, 4:1 2–3yrs)	24.3 in (c) and (d) (13:1 in nurseries, 30:1 in reception classes)

Sources: (a) Eurydice (2002), data Eurybase (www.eurydice.org); (c) TSFEPS (2002); (d) OECD (2001a); (e) Eurostat (2002); (f) Gornick and Meyers (2000); (g) Rostgaard and Fridberg (1998); (h) Adema (2001); (i) Bradshaw and Finch (2002); (i) The Clearinghouse on International Developments in Child, Youth and Family Policies (2003); (k) Kamerman (2001).

Table 2.A.4 *Final scores of the childcare index for the EU-15 Member States for three age categories*

Final score for childcare (age group 0–2)		Final score for childcare (age group 3–5)		Final score for childcare (age group 0–5)	
DK	100.0	SE	83.4	DK	89.3
SE	72.1	DK	78.6	SE	77.7
FR	59.4	FR	61.4	FR	60.4
FI	49.4	IT	56.3	FI	51.2
BE	39.2	BE	55.8	BE	47.5
IE	22.5	FI	53.1	IT	36.4
AT	22.0	LUX	43.3	AT	29.6
PT	20.1	AT	37.2	LUX	28.4
UK	19.2	NL	34.2	GE	23.9
IT	16.5	GE	31.9	NL	23.3
GE	15.8	UK	23.7	UK	21.4
LUX	13.4	ES	21.6	PT	20.1
NL	12.3	PT	20.1	IE	13.7
ES	2.2	IE	4.9	ES	11.9
EL	1.1	EL	0.5	EL	0.8

Note: For country abbreviations, see Table 2.1.

Key: Concerning the final score for children aged 3–5 (col.2), France's score is explained as follows: on a scale from zero (worst performer on all variables) to 100 (best performer), France is located at 61 on average for all underlying scaled criteria (weighted average). The last column score is the simple average of the former two scores. Note that grouping of countries is purely descriptive (arbitrary) and comes out from a cluster analysis.

Source: Own calculations using Linear Scaling Technique.

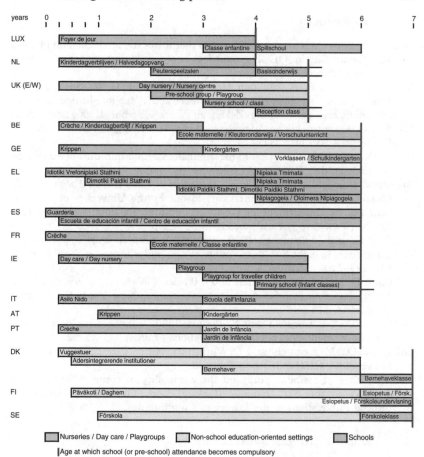

Figure 2.A.1 Types of childcare centres and pre-school education-oriented settings in the EU-15 Member States (2002).

Notes: Belgium: Since 1999, only children aged 3 on 31 Dec. of the ongoing school year have been admitted to pre-primary school.

Germany: In two Länder, Vorklassen are provided for children aged 5 who have not yet reached compulsory school age but whose parents wish them to receive preparation for primary school.

Greece: Since 2001, the former Kratiki stathmi renamed dimotiki paidiki stathmi have become the responsibility of the municipalities.

Spain: Other institutions in the 'play center' category exist alongside the guarderías.

Ireland: The Early Start Pilot Pre-school Project is located in some primary schools in selected disadvantaged areas. It provides an intervention programme for the most needy children from these areas who are between the ages of 3 and 4 and who are most at risk of educational failure.

Italy: Since 2001, the scuola materna have been renamed scuola dell'infanzia.

References

Adema, W. 2001. 'An overview of benefits that foster the reconciliation of work and family life in OECD countries', *Labour Market and Social Policy Occasional Papers*, no. 20.

Berg-le Clercq, L. E, A. van den Heuvel and D. M. E. G. W. Snellen 2002. *Kinderopvang in gemeenten, de monitor over 2001*, Rapport in opdracht van het ministerie van Sociale Zaken en Werkgelegenheid, opgesteld door SGBO, Onderzoeks- en Adviesbureau van de Vereniging van Nederlandse Gemeenten BV, Den Haag.

Boyer, D. 1999. 'Normes et politique familiale: La question du libre choix du mode de garde', *Recherches et prévisions*, no. 57/58.

Bradshaw, J. and N. Finch 2002. *A Comparison of Child Benefit Packages in 22 Countries*. A report of research carried out by the University of York on behalf of the Department for Work and Pensions, Research Report no.174, Leeds. (www.dwp.gov.uk/asd/asd5/rrep174.asp)

Bruning, G. and J. Plantenga 1999. 'Parental leave and equal opportunities: experiences in eight European countries', *Journal of European Social Policy*, 9 (3), 195–210.

Del Boca, D. and M. Repetto-Alaia 2003. *Women's Work, the Family, and Social Policy: Focus on Italy in a European Perspective*, New York: Peter Langs Publishing, 216 pp.

Del Boca, D., M. Locatelli and S. Pasqua 2000. 'Employment decisions of married women: evidence and explanations', *Labour* 14, 35–52.

Del Boca, D., M. Locatelli and D. Vuri 2003. 'Child care choices by Italian households', *CHILD Working Paper 30*.

Eurostat 2002. 'Feasibility study on the availability of comparable childcare statistics in the EU', *Eurostat Working Paper*, Luxembourg: Office for Official Publications of the European Communities.

Caption for Figure 2.A.1 (cont.)

Luxembourg: Pre-school attendance is compulsory from the age of 4. In some municipalities since 1998, the Spillschoul have been able to enrol children aged 3 under an early public childhood education scheme. It will be implemented throughout the country in 2004/05.

Netherlands: Basisonderwijs is compulsory from the age of 5 but 4-year-olds are admitted.

Finland: Since August 2001, municipalities have been obliged to offer free non-compulsory pre-primary education to children aged 6.

United Kingdom (E/W/NI): Since 1997, all 4-year-olds have been entitled to a government-funded early education place, and funded places have since also been made available for many 3-year-olds. Providers can be public sector, voluntary sector and private sector institutions, and include schools, nursery schools and classes, nursery centres and day nurseries, and preschool groups. All institutions in receipt of grants are expected to plan a curriculum that helps children progress towards official early learning goals.

Source: Eurydice (2002).

Eurybase Eurydice Network database (www.eurydice.org/Doc_intermediaires/ indicators/en/fameset_key_data.html)

Eurydice 2002. *Key Data on Education in Europe – 2002 Edition*, Luxembourg: European Commission / Eurostat (www.eurydice.org/Eurybase/frameset_ eurybase.html)

Fagnani, J. 2001. 'Politique d'accueil de la petite enfance en France: ombres et lunmières', *Travail, genre et sociétés*, n. 06 (Paris).

Fenet, F., F. Leprince and L. Périer 2001. *Les modes d'accueil des jeunes enfants*, ed. ASH, Paris.

Fiene, R. 2002. *13 Indicators of Quality Child Care: Research Update*, presented to Office of the Assistant Secretary for Planning and Evaluation and Health Resources and Services Administration/Maternal and Child Health Bureau, US Department of Health and Human Services.

Goldstein, H. 2003. *Analysis of 1997 French Pupil Panel Daga Study*, Report of Ministry of Education (DEP), June.

Gornick, J. and M. Meyers 2000. 'Early childhood education and care (ECEC): cross-national variation in service organisation and financing', paper prepared for presention at A Consultative Meeting on International Developments in Early Childhood Education and Care: An Activity of the Columbia Institute for Child and Family Policy, New York City, 11–12 May.

Gornick, J., M. Meyers and K. Ross 1997. 'Supporting the employment of mothers: policy variation across fourteen welfare states', *Journal of European Social Policy* 7, (1) 45–70.

Gustafsson, S. 1994. 'Childcare and types of welfare states', in D. Sainsbury, *Gendering Welfare State*, London: Thousand Oaks, 45–61.

Gustafsson, S., E. Kenjoh and C. Wetzels 2001. 'A new crisis in european populations: do modern family policies help?', in D. Pieters (ed.), *Confidence and Changes: Managing Social Protection in the New Millennium*, The Hague: Kluwer Law International, 119–41.

Kamerman, S. B. 2001. 'Early Childhood Education and Care: International Perspectives', Testimony prepared for the United States Senate Committee on Health, Education, Labor and Pensions, 27 March.

Kind en Gezin 2002. *Annual Report*. Brussels.

Kytir, J. and K. Schrittwiezer 2002. *Haushaltsführung, Kinderbetreuung, Pflege, Ergebnisse des Mikrozensus*, Vienna: Bundesministerium für soziale Sicherheit, Generationen und Konsumentenschutz, September.

Leprince, F. 2003. *L'accueil des jeunes enfants en france : Etat des lieux et pistes d'amélioration*, Rapport au Haut Conseil de la population et de la famille, January.

Letablier, M.-T. 1998. *Comparing Family Policies in Europe*, Periodic Progress Report no. 1 of the Thematic Network: 'Working and Mothering: Social practices and Social Policies', TSER Programme of the European Commission, Area III: Research into Social Integration and Social Exclusion in Europe, 1st TSER Seminar held in Lund, 26–28 November.

Letablier, M.-T. and G. Rieucau 2001. 'La garde des enfants: une affaire d'Etat ?', Document de travail, Centre d'études de l'emploi, no. 06.

Martin, C. 2003. 'L'accueil des jeunes enfants en Europe: Quelles leçons pour le cas français', in F. Leprince, *L'accueil des jeunes enfants en France: Etat des lieux et pistes d'amélioration*, Rapport au Haut Conseil de la population et de la famille, January.

Math, A. 2003. 'Les politiques publiques d'aide aux familles en Europe occidentale et leurs évolutions depuis le début des années 1990. Une comparaison menée à partir de plusieurs méthodes', Rapport réalisé par l'Institut de Recherches Economiques et Sociales (IRES) avec le soutien de la Caisse Nationale des Allocations Familiales (CNAF), June.

Ministry of Social Affairs and Health 2004. *Early Childhood Education and Care in Finland*, Brochure: 14, Helsinki.

Oasis website (Information on Public Services) (www.oasis.gov.ie/education/)

OECD 2001a. *Starting Strong: Early Childhood Education and Care*, Paris: OECD.

2001b. *Social Expenditures*, Paris: OECD.

2002. *Babies and Bosses*, I, Paris: OECD.

2003a. *Babies and Bosses*, II, Paris: OECD.

2003b. *Education Database*. Paris.

ONE 2002. *Rapport d'activités*, Brussels: Office de la Naissance et de l'Enfance.

Périvier, H. 2003. 'Emploi des mères et garde des jeunes enfants: l'impossible réforme?', *Droit Social*, no. 9–10.

Rostgaard, T. and T. Fridberg 1998. 'Caring for children and older people: a comparison of European policies and practices', *Social Security in Europe 6*. Copenhagen: Danish National Institute of Social Research 98:20.

Salzman, J. 2003. 'Methodological choices encountered in the construction of composite indices of economic and social well-being', Paper presented at the *Annual Meeting of the Canadian Economics Association*, Carleton University, Ottawa, Ontario, 30 May–1 June, 33 pp.

Skolverket 2004. 'Children, pupils and staff: national level', in Official Statistics of Sweden on pre-school activities, school-age child care, schools and adult education, Report 244, part 2.

Statistics Denmark 2005. *Statistical Yearbook 2005*.

The Clearinghouse on International Developments in Child, Youth and Family Policies 2003. http://childpolicyintl.org/

TSFEPS 2002. *Changing Family Structure and Social Policy: Childcare Services in Europe and Social Cohesion*, National Reports. (www/emes.net/en/recherche/tsfeps/etudes.php)

3 Parents' care and career: comparing parental leave policies

Jérôme De Henau, Danièle Meulders and Síle O'Dorchai

3.1 Introduction

The presence of young children in the household makes it necessary for working parents to find ways in which to combine professional responsibilities and care tasks. The externalisation of household chores to the market frees time for parents to spend on their caring duties. Furthermore, public childcare allows for a further externalisation of care tasks and as such is supportive of working parents, because it also secures time for both parents. As stated in chapter 2, a childcare system that meets several conditions (universal access, all-day coverage, high quality and affordability) facilitates an adequate division by parents of their time between childcare and work. However, given the high public cost of an affordable and universally accessible childcare system for children under 6 years of age, some countries have found an alternative in a parental leave system. The state's involvement in parental leave schemes may also be related to the way a country conceives children's early socialisation: through private external care, through public facilities or through parental care (Martin 2003). In many countries, parents are expected to be the primary caregivers when the child is very young (Math and Meilland 2004). Be that as it may, if home parental care is privileged in a given country, it does not necessarily mean that the state intervenes in the family sphere to secure parents' work resumption or substantial replacement of income. Moreover, even if a state sets up legislative regulations to guarantee these two goals, a fact that in principle we would call parental employment supportiveness, it remains to be assessed whether these regulations lead to a gender unbalanced take-up or not, at the expense of mothers. Indeed, Appendix Table 3.A.3 shows that, in all countries, mothers remain by far the primary leave-takers. Therefore, both the causes and the consequences of this gender unbalance are assessed in this chapter.

Two different types of leave are distinguished since their effects on maternal employment are not the same: maternity and paternity leave on the one hand, considered to be 'short' leaves, and parental leave on the other, in particular leave that is longer than four months. Various theoretical frameworks and empirical findings have widely studied the expected or real effects of these types of leaves.

Klerman and Leibowitz (1997) examine the labour supply effects of maternity leave in a static framework. It appears that the impact of maternity leave on mothers' labour supply is very ambiguous. In general, there is agreement on the fact that well-organised maternity leaves offering high replacement incomes strengthen mothers' labour market attachment in the short run. However, as birth leave, be it maternity or parental leave, becomes longer, it risks jeopardising women's long-run employment prospects, particularly in terms of promotion and on-the-job training opportunities, which in turn will decrease their earning capacity.

Ondrich *et al.* (1996) review several studies based on US data on the labour supply effects of maternity leave and conclude that there is only weak evidence for a correlation between the two. Studies based on European data come up with more decisive results. An interesting review of these studies can be found in chapter 7 (this volume). Waldfogel *et al.* (1999) show the positive impact on job continuity of access to maternity leave. Another result is that mandated maternity leave increases mothers' employment in the short run (Winegarden and Bracy 1995; Ruhm 1998) but decreases their relative wages and the quality of their jobs in the long run (Ruhm 1998; Pylkkänen and Smith 2003; Stoiber 1990; Beblo and Wolf 2002; Wetzels and Tijdens 2002). This also holds true in countries such as Sweden where a one-year leave is widespread and well paid (Albrecht *et al.* 1999). It seems there is a vicious circle: allow a woman to take the leave further enhances her unequal treatment in the labour market (Périvier 2004b). Part of the gender wage gap (17% in Denmark, Meilland 2001; 27% in France, Meurs and Ponthieux 2000; 14% in the United Kingdom, Chambaz 2003) can be explained by the more frequent career interruptions of women in the form of parental leave (Pylkkänen and Smith 2003). Taking leave also risks having a reputation effect on the whole of the female population in general:[1] employers may take into account the high probability that young women (as opposed to young men) will take parental leave (Fagnani 1996; Albrecht *et al.* 2003; EIRO 2001b). *De facto*, they may consider women to constitute a less stable workforce than men, which is very likely to be reflected in their relative wages.

---

[1] What Phelps calls statistical discrimination (Phelps 1972) and Arrow the theory of signals (Arrow 1973).

The same circle can be observed for occupational or inter-industry gender segregation, reinforced by the fact that employers of typically male-dominated branches of industry are less likely to be in favour of an employee taking parental leave than employers in typically female-dominated sectors. For example, in Denmark and France, the majority of men taking up parental leave are employed in typically female sectors of activity (Meilland 2001; Boyer and Renouard 2003).

The issue is then to analyse to what extent the state's intervention supports the working parents model and how countries position themselves according to this so-called supportiveness. Following the methodology used in chapter 2, we compare a comprehensive set of policy instruments and discuss their expected impact on parents' labour market attachment. Equality between fathers and mothers in comparison with non-parents is at stake.

We will first analyse maternity leave regulations as well as paternity leave, followed by a section dedicated to parental leave.

3.2 Main features of maternity and paternity leave schemes

We have compared different regulatory settings for maternity leave in the private sector[2] according to three basic criteria: the length of the qualification period, the length of job-protected leave and the replacement rate of earnings (Table 3.1). The right to maternity leave (mostly payment) is in some countries made conditional upon a former period of employment or payment of social contributions. Therefore, the longer this period, the more limited the access to maternity leave. Countries such as France, Ireland and Greece score low on this indicator.

The length of the leave is necessarily equal to or above 14 weeks, the minimum period required by the European Commission (EC);[3] this is believed to be the necessary minimum in medical terms to allow mothers fully to recover after childbirth. All EU-15 Member States except Germany offer a longer leave than that required by the EC. If mothers' labour market attachment is privileged in a given country, the maternity leave period is not expected to be extended beyond the period that is actually needed from a medical perspective. As a benchmark, we have chosen to neglect any maternity leave period exceeding 18 weeks,

---

[2] Data for the public sector were too difficult to gather and to harmonise.
[3] Council Directive 76/207/EEC of 9 February 1976 on the implementation of the principle of equal treatment for men and women as regards access to employment, vocational training and promotion, and working conditions.

Table 3.1 *Maternity and paternity leave, duration and payment in the EU-15 Member States (2003)*

Qualification period (days)		Maternity leave period (weeks)		Average replacement rate (%)		Paternity leave period (working days)		Average replacement rate (%)	
AT	0	IT	21.7	DE	100	FI	18	EL	100
FI	0	DK	18	EL	100	FR	14	ES	100
IT	0	IE	18	ES	100	BE	10	FR	100
NL	0	SE	18	FR	100	DK	10	LU	100
UK	0	UK	18	LU	100	SE	10	NL	100
DK	21	FI	17.5	NL	100	PT	5	PT	100
DE	84	PT	17.1	AT	100	ES	2	FI	100
ES	180	EL	17	PT	100	LU	2	BE	87
BE	183	ES	16	IT	80	NL	2	SE	80
LU	183	FR	16	SE	80	EL	1	DK	51
PT	183	LU	16	BE	77	DE	0	DE	0
SE	183	NL	16	IE	70	IE	0	IE	0
EL	200	AT	16	FI	66	IT	0	IT	0
IE	273	BE	15	DK	62	AT	0	AT	0
FR	304	DE	14	UK	49	UK	0	UK	0

Notes: For explanation of the country abbreviations, see Table 2.1.

In the UK, all female employees are entitled to 18 weeks but those women who have been employed for one year by the same employer are entitled to 29 weeks compensated at 90% of their earnings for 6 weeks and at a flat rate for a further 12 weeks (Moss and Deven 1999). How to read the table: e.g. in Belgium, in 2003, maternity leave lasted 15 weeks during which wages were replaced at 77% on average; there is a 10-day paternity leave paid at 87% of the father's wage.

Source: See Appendix Table 3.A.1.

which corresponds to the length of leave in Denmark, Finland, Ireland and the UK.[4]

The length of the maternity leave period needs to be compared with the level of wage replacement available to working mothers. The

[4] Note that for Sweden, there is no paid postnatal maternity leave because it is integrated in the general parental leave scheme. However, since we must take into account that Swedish working women are protected during this period and receive a wage replacement rate of 80%, we have considered 18 weeks of paid leave as the duration of maternity leave to make comparison with the other countries possible. Swedish fathers are entitled to 10 days of temporary cash benefits around the birth of their child, and are also entitled to parental leave. We separated the two in order to compare the Swedish situation with other countries. Therefore Sweden will appear less generous than Finland as far as paternity leave is concerned, but catches up when parental leave policy for fathers is considered.

replacement rate is quite high in most countries, except in the UK where it reaches only around 50%. In Denmark, maternity leave in the private sector is compensated at the full-rate unemployment insurance benefit as is the case for parental leave (62% of average national female earnings).[5]

Therefore, both the length of leave and the replacement rate have been combined to obtain a new indicator that expresses maternity leave as an equivalent number of working days that are fully paid (Table 3.2). Now Denmark, the UK and Finland see their ranking fall compared with that for length of leave; this is due to their relatively lower wage replacement rate (less than 80%).

Note that Southern European countries offer mothers a generous leave that is of substantial length and fully paid. It is perhaps the only dimension of family policies in which these countries appear somewhat effective as regards women's labour market attachment (see other chapters and discussion on parental leave).

For fathers, only a few countries offer a real paternity leave, between 5 days in Portugal and 18 working days in Finland, the famous 'father's month'.[6] In Denmark, low compensation possibly explains why only 58% of eligible men took paternity leave (2003). In France, Finland and Sweden, where the system is more generous financially, respectively 68%, 68% and 75% took leave in 2002, while in Belgium virtually all eligible fathers took up their right in 2005 (see Appendix Table 3.A.3 for details and sources).

As for maternity leave, information regarding the length of paternity leave and the wage replacement rate were combined to obtain the equivalent of leave in fully paid working days.

Three country rankings were established, one for each type of leave separately and one for both combined. Again we use the linear scaling technique to construct the indicators (see chapter 2).

The maternity leave index ($Imat_i$) is the weighted average of the scaled number of fully paid working days ($MatDays_i \cdot ReplRate_i$ – weight of two thirds because based on two sub-criteria) and the reversed scaled qualification period (weight of one third). The paternity leave index

---

[5] Though we focus on the private sector for purposes of harmonisation and available data, we should note that in Denmark more than half of all working women are employed in the public sector, offering replacement rates of 100% (Statistics Denmark 2005).

[6] Note that in Sweden, an extra two months of paid leave are available for fathers under the parental leave scheme. However, we have not considered this period in our paternity leave indicator as we did for mothers given that most fathers take this leave when the child is aged between 11 and 15 months and mostly during holiday periods (Rostgaard 2002). Parental leave is discussed in the next section.

Table 3.2 *The equivalent of fully paid maternity/paternity leave and ranking of the EU-15 Member States (2003)*

Maternity leave fully paid working days		Paternity leave fully paid working days		Final score for maternity leave		Final score for paternity leave		Final score for birth leaves	
PT	86	FI	18	NL	92.2	FI	100.0	FR	80.8
EL	85	FR	14	AT	92.2	FR	77.8	FI	78.1
ES	80	BE	9	IT	80.9	BE	48.6	PT	73.9
FR	80	SE	8	PT	80.0	SE	44.4	NL	71.0
LU	80	PT	5	EL	77.4	PT	27.8	AT	66.5
NL	80	DK	5	ES	72.5	DK	27.0	SE	63.7
AT	80	ES	2	LU	72.2	ES	11.1	EL	63.7
IT	72	LU	2	DE	68.8	LU	11.1	ES	61.1
SE	72	NL	2	SE	60.9	NL	11.1	LU	61.0
DE	70	EL	1	FI	60.7	EL	5.6	IT	56.9
IE	63	DE	0	FR	58.9	DE	0.0	DE	49.9
BE	58	IE	0	DK	52.5	IE	0.0	BE	49.8
FI	58	IT	0	BE	40.7	IT	0.0	DK	43.9
DK	54	AT	0	IE	38.2	AT	0.0	IE	31.2
UK	38	UK	0	UK	33.3	UK	0.0	UK	16.7

Note: For explanation of the country abbreviations, see Table 2.1.

How to read the table: the maternity leave index is computed as follows: three original criteria are considered (qualification period, number of weeks – transformed in working days – and average rate of replacement income). To illustrate countries' positions, we first combine the latter two variables (multiplication of their values) to obtain an 'equivalent of fully paid maternity leave days' indicator. We now have two variables we would like to scale using Linear Scaling Technique. Separately for each variable, we grant the country obtaining the maximum (minimum) value a score of 100 (0) and we scale all other countries' values according to the formula below. Then, a final indicator is obtained as the arithmetic average of both scaled variables, the scaled 'equivalent of fully paid maternity leave days' indicator being given a double weight, since it is based on two original criteria. The paternity leave index follows the same computation rules (we do not consider the qualification period).

The birth leave index is the average of six units, the first four related to the combined length of maternity and paternity leave expressed in a number of fully paid working days (representing four units because there are four underlying criteria), the fifth being the number of paid days of paternity leave expressed as a percentage of the ideal number of 90 days of maternity leave (one unit), and the sixth measuring the qualification period.

Source: Own calculations based on Appendix Table 3.A.1.

$(Ipat_i)$ gives the scaled equivalent number of fully paid working days $(PatDays_i \cdot ReplRate_i)$.

The birth leave index $(Ibirth_i)$ takes into consideration the huge difference between each type of leave in terms of length. It is the average of six units, the first four related to the combined length of maternity and paternity leave expressed as a number of fully paid working days (representing four units because there are four underlying criteria), the fifth being the number of paid days of paternity leave expressed as a percentage of the ideal number of ninety days of maternity leave ($\frac{PatDays_i \cdot ReplRate_i}{90}$ – even in those countries where maternity leave is shorter) and the sixth measuring the qualification period.

$$Imat_i = (scaled[MatDays_i \cdot ReplRate_i]) \cdot \frac{2}{3} + (scaled^{-1}[QualPeriod_i]) \cdot \frac{1}{3}$$

$$Ipat_i = (scaled[PatDays_i \cdot ReplRate_i])$$

$$Ibirth_i = (scaled[MatDays_i \cdot ReplRate_i]) \cdot \frac{2}{6} + (scaled[PatDays_i \cdot ReplRate_i]) \cdot$$

$$\frac{2}{6} + \left(scaled\left[\frac{PatDays_i \cdot ReplRate_i}{90}\right]\right) \cdot \frac{1}{6} + (scaled^{-1}[QualPeriod_i]) \cdot \frac{1}{6}$$

With $i = $ BE, DK, DE, ..., UK (EU-15 Member States)

Table 3.2 shows that Finland and France stand out quite clearly at the top of the ranking from the other countries while Ireland and the UK share the lowest ranks, resulting from the absence of paternity leave and the low level of replacement income for mothers. Unlike many other countries that offer full replacement rates for mothers, the Nordic countries seem to focus support more on long leaves (parental leave, see below), childcare facilities or paternity leaves (also important in France and Belgium). Besides these relative rankings, let us recall that, overall, most EU-15 Member States offer quite generous maternity leave schemes.

3.3   Discussing parental leave systems

The European Commission has emphasised that parental leave is a key component of a strategy aimed at facilitating the work/life balance. Indeed, in 1996, the EC issued a Directive (EC/34/EC) requiring Member States to offer at least 3 months (following the birth of a child) of parental leave to all employees. Such leave is to be added to a minimum of 14 weeks of maternity leave. This forms part of the directive concerning equal opportunities for men and women that is concerned with mothers' integration in the labour market and men's in the family sphere. The EC definition provides enough room for each state to implement its own rules in terms of leave duration, payment, flexibility, etc. Table 3.3 and Table 3.4 provide quantitative information on the different legal frameworks for parental leave in Europe (see Appendix Table 3.A.2 for a description of parental leave). Note that we focus

Table 3.3 *Features of parental leave schemes throughout the EU-15 (2003)*

Total leave duration (months)		Job-protected period (% of total leave)		Seniority-protected period (% of total leave)		Paid period (% of total leave)		Fathers' period (months)		Transferable months		Min. leave to be taken as % of usual working time		Child age limit (years)	
FI	36	BE	100	BE	100	BE	100	IT	7	BE	0	DK	8	DK	9
DE	36	DK	100	DK	100	FR	100	LU	6	EL	0	IE	10	DE	8
FR	36	DE	100	DE	100	LU	100	AT	6	IE	0	NL	10	IT	8
AT	36	EL	100	IT	100	AT	100	UK	4.15	IT	0	SE	13	NL	8
ES	36	FR	100	LU	100	FI	100	EL	3.5	LU	0	FI	15	SE	8
SE	18	IE	100	PT	100	SE	79	IE	3.23	NL	0	BE	20	PT	6
LU	12	IT	100	FI	100	DK	70	BE	3	PT	0	FR	20	IE	5
IT	11	LU	100	SE	100	DE	67	NL	3	UK	0	UK	20	LU	5
DK	10.6	AT	100	FR	50	IT	55	PT	3	DK	10.6	DE	25	UK	5
UK	8.3	PT	100	AT	50	PT	8	SE	2	SE	11.8	IT	25	BE	4
EL	7	FI	100	ES	33	EL	0	DK	0	AT	24	ES	33	EL	3.5
IE	6.5	SE	100	EL	0	ES	0	DE	0	FI	36	PT	33	ES	3
BE	6	UK	100	IE	0	IE	0	ES	0	DE	36	LU	50	FR	3
NL	6	ES	33	NL	0	NL	0	FR	0	FR	36	AT	50	AT	3
PT	6	NL	0	UK	0	UK	0	FI	0	ES	36	EL	100	FI	3

Note: For explanation of the country abbreviations, see Table 2.1.
How to read the table: e.g. in Belgium in 2003, the total period of parental leave available for both parents is 6 months. The whole leave is paid, and one's job is protected, thus safeguarding a parent's return to his/her post (or equivalent job) after the end of the leave. Moreover, pension and seniority rights are safeguarded as opposed to the Dutch scheme, e.g., where they are suspended. Fathers, like mothers, are each entitled to a 3 month leave. Given that parental leave is an individual right, none of it can be transferred between parents. Leave does not need to be taken at a full-time rate but can be taken by reducing working hours by $\frac{1}{5}$ in which case total leave covers a period of 15 months (minimum leave of 20%). Leave has to be taken up before the child reaches 4 years.
Source: See Appendix Table 3.A.2.

Table 3.4 Monthly wage replacement rates during parental leave by sex in the EU-15 Member States (2003)

Average male replacement rate during first 3 mts.		Average female replacement rate during first 3 mts.		Ratio of household income if father takes leave instead of mother (first 3 mts.)		Average male replacement rate during paid father period		Average female replacement rate during mother and/or transferable periods	
SE	80	SE	80	SE	97	SE	80	LU	63
PT	75	FI	66	PT	96	LU	52	SE	53
FI	66	LU	63	FI	95	IT	30	DK	41
LU	52	DK	60	IT	92	PT	23	BE	27
DK	49	IT	30	LU	89	BE	22	AT	26
IT	30	BE	27	DK	88	NL	0	FR	26
BE	22	AT	26	BE	85	DK	0	FI	23
FR	21	FR	26	FR	84	DE	0	DE	9
AT	16	DE	14	EL	80	EL	0	NL	0
DE	10	NL	0	DE	77	ES	0	EL	0
NL	0	EL	0	ES	75	FR	0	ES	0
EL	0	ES	0	UK	75	IE	0	IE	0
ES	0	IE	0	AT	66	AT	0	IT	0
IE	0	PT	0	IE	66	FI	0	PT	0
PT	0	UK	0	NL	65	UK	0	UK	0
UK	0								

Note: For explanation of the country abbreviations, see Table 2.1.

How to read the table: e.g. in Belgium, in 2003, replacement income during the first 3 months amounted to €547 monthly which corresponds to 22.1% of average male earnings and 27% of average female earnings (cols. 1, 2); if the father takes the leave instead of the mother, total household earnings are only 85% of what they would be if the mother was taking the leave (col. 3). During the whole paid period available for fathers, they are granted the same amount, corresponding to 22.1% of their monthly average earnings, and the same holds true for mothers since there is no transferable period in this country (cols. 4 and 5).

Source: Appendix Table 3.A.2 and own calculations.

primarily on private sector employees for the same reasons as for maternity leave. Parental leave can be described by the following criteria: duration; job protection and the guarantee of pension and seniority rights during the leave; the proportion of leave that can be transferred between parents, and the part reserved for the father only; the possibilities for dividing the leave; and the child's upper age limit at which the right to parental leave expires (Table 3.3). The indemnification rate is also a key criterion (Table 3.4).

3.3.1   Elements related to the lack of supportiveness of parental work

As we have seen from the empirical and theoretical findings, parental leave is believed to be characterised by a gender bias that strengthens the traditional role models of mothers and fathers and, as such, may have a negative impact on mothers' participation and career prospects. Different features of parental leave are related to this issue.

3.3.1.1 Available period of leave   The length of parental leave substantially differs across countries: from the minimum period required by the EC directive of three months per parent (Belgium, Portugal and the Netherlands) to a longer leave, until the child reaches the age of 3 years (France, Germany, Spain, Austria and Finland).

The way in which leave is available to each parent plays a key role through potential incentives for fathers to take up part of the leave (Table 3.3). The right to leave can be individual (Benelux, Anglo-Saxon and Mediterranean countries) or family-based (Nordic countries, France, Germany and Austria). In the former case, each parent is entitled to a period of leave that is not transferable to the spouse. In other words, if a parent does not take the leave to which he/she is entitled, it is lost to the family. In the latter case, parental leave is a family right and can be shared by both parents more or less freely depending on the country. In France, if one parent takes advantage of the child-raising allowance,[7] he/she as such assumes the right for the entire family. In Germany, where parental leave can be just as long as in France, it is possible for parents to alternate in taking leave. In Germany, parental leave takes the form of a 'parental' wage because it is open to all parents, whether at work or not (or only work 'short' part-time[8]), who take care of their children (Moss and Deven 1999).

---

[7] *Allocation parentale d'éducation* (APE), replaced by the *Prestation d'accueil du jeune enfant* from 2004 (PAJE).

[8] Up to 19 hours a week or 30 hours for children born after 1 January 2001.

Besides these two particular cases, some countries have introduced a mixture of individual and family-based rights. In Italy, each parent is entitled to 6 months with a maximum of 10 months per family but, as soon as the father takes at least 3 months, he is entitled to an additional month bringing his total leave right up to 7 months. However, the right to benefits is limited to 6 months and is family-based. The same holds for Sweden where 480 days can be shared between parents while 60 days are reserved for each parent separately. In Austria, a leave of 6 months is offered as an individual right, while the rest is transferable between parents. In Denmark, a parental leave of 10 weeks was introduced in 1984 and extended to 12 weeks in 1999, with the last two weeks being exclusively available to fathers. This father quota was abolished in 2002 when the leave was extended to 32 weeks, fully transferable between parents (Pylkkänen and Smith 2003).

3.3.1.2 Wage replacement policy Another important issue is the payment policy during the various available periods of leave. Some countries do not grant any replacement income during leave (Greece, Spain, Ireland, the Netherlands, Portugal and the UK). Most of the remaining countries pay a flat-rate amount (Germany, France, Austria, Belgium, Denmark and Luxembourg), which, except for Denmark and Luxembourg, is lower than half national average female earnings.

Table 3.4 summarises the countries' relative wage replacement rates during parental leave, expressed as percentages of national average monthly earnings by gender, and evaluated from two different angles. The first two columns show replacement income during the first three months of parental leave. The amounts are more or less maximum amounts, given the different arrangements for parental leave payment (mostly regressive in time) across the countries (especially Sweden and Finland). Portugal applies an unusual type of father incentive. Fathers on leave are paid 100% of their earnings during the first 15 working days (3 weeks), while mothers receive no benefits at all when on leave.

Although flat-rate payments are the same for men and women, the figures in the table differ by gender because of gender wage gaps in the countries. This is particularly clear in Luxembourg and Denmark, and it illustrates the impact flat-rate payments are bound to have on the attractiveness of parental leave to fathers with an average wage. A wage-related payment, as in Sweden or Finland, helps to weaken the effect of the wage differential between women and men which weighs negatively on mothers' employment when households decide which partner should take parental leave. The same logic underlies the Italian system, but there, the wage replacement rate is much lower (although, on average, higher than in other countries). To measure the intra-household differential as a proxy to illustrate the non-attractiveness of leave for fathers, column 3 of Table 3.4 shows the ratio of average total household earnings if the father takes the leave to total earnings if it is the mother.[9] An outcome of 100% means that no matter who takes the leave, no loss of income arises for the household. This would be the case if replacement rates were 100% for each partner or if one of the partners was sufficiently compensated to overcome the existing average gender wage differential (as is almost the case for Portugal). The country ranking shows that wage-related payments are quite effective in weakening the effect of gender wage differentials.

The last two columns in the table present not the maximum but the average replacement rates seen over the whole period of paid and unpaid leave available to each of the parents separately after having split it between them: men are considered to take all the leave available to them provided it is paid, and mothers take what is left (leave that is available for the mother only, as well as the transferable period, if it exists, whether paid or unpaid). For example, for Italy, this means that fathers take 6 months (the whole period of paid leave available to the family) but not the seventh month to which they are entitled, given that it is not paid, while mothers are left with five months of parental leave all of which is unpaid. In Sweden, we have assumed that fathers take up their right to 60 days of leave paid at the maximum rate (80%), while mothers take the remaining period of paid leave available (excluding maternity leave), as well as the unpaid leave.[10] Note that, with this method, the impact on Finland's relative ranking of its very long and transferable leave, which is paid at a flat rate, is significant (the wage replacement rate for mothers drops from 66%, when only the first month of payment is concerned, to 23% when the whole length of leave is considered).

Table 3.4 thus shows that, in any case, since the woman is often less well paid than her partner, intra-household financial motivations are generally at the expense of the woman's activity rate, although this effect is weakened in countries where parental leave is wage-related. In France, fathers receiving the child-raising allowance ('APE') most often form part of atypical couples in which the female has the highest

---

[9] Considering an average dual-earner couple (the man earns AME – average monthly male earnings; the women AFE – average monthly female earnings).

[10] For mothers, 49 days of postnatal leave paid at 80% need to be subtracted from the total, which means that 291 days are paid at 80%, 90 days at a flat rate while the two remaining months are unpaid. In sum, the average replacement rate based on average earnings equals 53%.

earnings. Moreover, in this country, their unemployment rate is three times as high as that of other men (Boyer and Renouard 2003). The issue of the intra-household gender wage gap is linked to that of the 'general' gender wage gap: if the first gap partly explains why women take up leave more often than their partners (on top of other reasons), their more prevalent career interruptions then form part of the causes of the second gap as shown by the empirical studies presented in the introduction to this chapter and as such reinforce the incentive for families to let leave take-up be gender unbalanced.

3.3.2   Elements supportive of parents' labour market attachment

Besides the elements that may hinder women's position in the labour market, other elements of the parental leave system are worth mentioning since they are likely to support working mothers (and fathers in general). Three important criteria enter the picture here: (i) the level of protection with respect to work resumption and pension/seniority rights; (ii) flexibility in the timing of leave; and (iii) the level of replacement income (see Tables 3.3 and 3.4).

3.3.2.1 Level of job protection   The European Directive requires that a job guarantee be offered, that is the right to return to the same or an equivalent job. In Spain, job protection covers only the first year of parental leave and, in the Netherlands, an employment guarantee is included only in some collective agreements, especially in the social services sector. In the other countries, the whole leave is protected. However, France and Austria offer guarantees for pension and seniority rights only for half of the leave, while in Ireland, the Netherlands and the UK these rights are not legally safeguarded but left to the discretion of the employer. Regarding qualification conditions, some parental leave schemes impose employment and seniority conditions, usually one year of work, most often with the same employer (Belgium, Greece, France, Ireland, Luxembourg, the Netherlands and the UK).

3.3.2.2 Flexibility in the timing   The flexibility of the leave is analysed by means of three criteria: the age limit of the child, fractionability and reduction of working hours.

In France, Spain, Austria and Finland, parental leave policies are targeted at parents of young children (up to 3 years of age). Leave needs to be taken immediately following childbirth. In Sweden, Italy, the Netherlands and Germany, it can be taken before the child reaches the age of 8.

Most leaves are fractionable (that is they can be split into different periods across time) but to different degrees. For example, in France, leave has to be taken in periods of at least one year while in Sweden, the UK and Ireland, leave can be taken by the day (although the employer needs to agree in the latter two countries). In Germany, if only one year is taken instead of two or three, the monthly flat-rate payment for leave is higher (by around 50%), which provides parents with quite an incentive to opt for shorter leave, although no childcare is available afterwards.

In all countries but Greece, leave can be taken on a part-time basis with a proportional extension of its duration, except for Austria and France where leave is bounded by a low child age limit. This part-time possibility exists in order to avoid parents becoming totally disconnected from the labour market. Nevertheless, the extent of flexibility varies greatly across countries. In Luxembourg, it is only possible to take half-time leave (i.e. in half days), and in Austria, the protective measures implemented through the parental leave legislation (dismissal, etc.) do not extend to part-time work/leave. By contrast, countries such as Sweden, Ireland and the UK, and also Denmark, provide a flexible system of working hours and leave arrangements, allowing for half days to be taken or for a proportional reduction of working hours on all working days (Sweden), sometimes in agreement with the employer. In Denmark, parental leave could initially be taken only on a part-time basis in order to ensure that parents continuously stayed in touch with the labour market. In 1997, this measure was revised and hence it is possible to take periods of full-time leave provided the employer agrees (Bruning and Plantenga 1999).

3.3.2.3 Level of replacement income   Much has already been said above about this criterion through its differential effect on women and men. But whatever the gender differences arising, it is also important to take into account the level of replacement income, by sex. As for maternity leave, the higher the replacement level, the more attractive the system. If we consider maximum rates for mothers working in the private sector (Table 3.4, column 2), huge differences between countries are revealed, from 80% of wage replacement in Sweden to no paid leave in Portugal, the Netherlands, Spain, the UK, Ireland and Greece. In the Netherlands, leave indemnification is to be negotiated with the employer. For example, in the public sector, parental leave beneficiaries receive 75% of their wages (NIDI 2003). However, in the private sector, which is the focus of our analysis, only few collective agreements (6% in 2000) include payment of parental leave (with a replacement rate of up to 30%).

3.3.3 Building synthetic legislative indicators

From the above discussion it should be clear that parental leave is, to say the least, a very ambiguous form of public support to facilitate the work/life balance for both parents. However, if it is a country's policy to implement leave in order to allow working parents to take care of their child – either while simultaneously relying on childcare provisions or before turning to outside facilities, or even much later, when the child has grown up a little – an effective system for working mothers would imply that parental leave takes the form of a short and fully job-protected period of leave (with seniority and pension rights accounted for) that is individually granted and equally shared between parents, with flexible timing possibilities and a high and wage-related replacement rate. However, this ideal picture needs to be considered in the context of existing budget constraints (well paid short leaves versus lower paid long leaves) taking into account the provision of childcare following the leave.

We have built two indicators, one to assess the attractiveness of a country's leave system, and the other its incentive to achieve a potentially more gender-balanced take-up (in the sense of a reduced female employment trap). Again, we use the linear scaling technique to make our different criteria comparable.

The first indicator ($Iattrc_i$) is the arithmetic average of three synthetic and scaled criteria (the X-axis of Figure 3.1): (i) the average of the scaled job-protected proportion of the leave ($JobProtShare_i$), the scaled seniority-protected share ($SeniorProtShare_i$), and the scaled paid part ($PaidShare_i$); (ii) the average of the scaled degree of flexibility in the timing of take-up ($Flex_i$) and of the scaled child age limit ($ChildAge_i$); and (iii) the scaled level of replacement income expressed as a percentage of average female earnings ($ReplRate_i$). Recall that the higher the indicator, the more attractive the system.

$$Iattrac_i = \left(\frac{scaled[\,JobProtShare_i] + scaled[SeniorProtShare_i] + scaled[PaidShare_i]}{3} \right) \cdot \frac{1}{3}$$
$$+ \left(\frac{scaled[Flex_i] + scaled[ChildAge_i]}{2} \right) \cdot \frac{1}{3} + (scaled[ReplRate_i]) \cdot \frac{1}{3}$$

With $i = $ BE, DK, DE, ..., UK (EU-15 Member States)

The second indicator ($Ibalance_i$) is the arithmetic average of two indicators (the Y-axis of Figure 3.1): (i) the reversed scaled total period of leave minus the share reserved for the father ($TotPeriod_i - FathPeriod_i$), and (ii) the scaled ratio of total average household earnings if the father takes the leave instead of the mother. This is completely in line with the

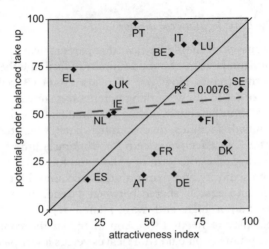

Figure 3.1   Parental leave policies: scores on attractiveness and potential gender balance in the take-up for the EU-15 Member States (2003)

Note: For explanation of the country abbreviations, see Table 2.1.

How to read the figure: for example in 2003, the attractiveness score of Finland's parental leave is 76, meaning that on average on all underlying criteria (job protection, flexibility and wage replacement), Finland is positioned at three quarters of the best performer's score on each criterion.

Source: Appendix Table 3.A.2 and own calculations.

discussion above about the main features of parental leave schemes that are associated with potential gender-balanced take-up. Recall that the higher the score, the less gender biased the system.

$$Ibalance_i = scaled^{-1}[(TotPeriod_i - FathPeriod_i)] \cdot \frac{1}{2}$$
$$+ \left(scaled\left[\left(\frac{AFE_i + ReplInc_i^{father}}{AFE_i + ReplInc_i^{mother}}\right)\right]\right) \cdot \frac{1}{2}$$

With $i = BE, DK, DE, \ldots, UK$ (EU-15 Member States).

AFE_i stands for National Average Female Earnings, AME_i for National Average Male Earnings.

The figure shows a high level of disparity between systems as regards their achievement of both gender balance in take-up and attractiveness. The Nordic countries seem to have the most attractive leave schemes but differ greatly in terms of gender balance. Sweden scores somewhat higher than Finland and Denmark because of the proportional wage

Table 3.5 *Combined index of attractiveness
and gender balance in take-up for EU-15
Member States, 2003*

Final index of the parental leave's supportiveness of working mothers	
LU	80.5
SE	79.5
IT	77.3
BE	71.5
PT	70.8
FI	61.6
DK	61.5
UK	47.8
EL	43.0
IE	42.0
FR	40.9
DE	40.7
NL	40.1
AT	32.9
ES	17.6

Note: For country abbreviations, see Table 2.1.
Source: Appendix Table 3.A.2 and own calculations.

replacement rate and because some part of the leave is reserved to the father. Belgium, Italy and Luxembourg, and to a lesser extent, Portugal, score relatively high on both indices (short, individual, paid, protected leave). The remaining countries can be split into two groups: the first includes countries with a low level of attractiveness, mostly because leave is not paid (the UK, the Netherlands, Ireland and Greece) although they score somewhat higher in terms of potential equal sharing since their leave is granted individually. The second group has quite opposite features, with long leave that is fully transferable, so that they score very low on the vertical axis while their degree of attractiveness varies (Spain, France, Austria and Germany).

The combination of the two indices synthesises a leave system's supportiveness of working mothers. We simply take the average of the two scores to compute such a parental leave index (Table 3.5).

3.3.4   Policy outcomes: leave take-up and work resumption

The above indices should be compared with the real outcomes in terms of take-up and return to one's job after leave. Indeed, the set of financial arrangements and incentives for fathers described above has a varied impact on leave take-up rates across the countries studied.[11]

3.3.4.1 Take-up rates and shares   The proportion of eligible fathers who actually take parental leave is very low in Germany, France and Austria (2% at most). In comparison, more than 90% of eligible mothers take up their right to leave in Germany and Austria.[12] In these countries, as discussed above, traditional family norms are still extremely binding and parental leave continues to be a woman's affair. Indeed, in France and Germany, not even a small part of parental leave is reserved exclusively for the father. By contrast, in Austria, a 6-month father period exists and is fully paid. The low leave-taking rate by fathers might therefore be explained by the length of the transferable period, which makes it possible for mothers to take 30 months leave so that families do not really rely on fathers taking their 6 months. Another reason for the low score of these countries is that leave is very long (36 months), but has to be taken during the first 3 years of the child's life so that no flexibility is offered to parents (except for Germany, where the third year of leave can be taken up until the child's eighth birthday). It seems that, although few fathers make use of their right to parental leave, those who do, take leave for a very long period of time. In 2001, of all male users of parental leave in West Germany, 63% took between two and three years off resulting in an average length of leave for all male users of 33 months (24 months in East Germany).

In Greece, apparently no father takes parental leave. In Italy, although leave is short and conceived as an individual right, the fact that replacement income is granted to the family and remains low (30%) probably explains why only fewer than 5% of entitled fathers take at least part of their leave.

Although the three Nordic countries score high as far as the attractiveness index is concerned, they differ with respect to the gender balance

---

[11] All figures in the next paragraphs are taken from Appendix Table 3.A.3 which summarises leave take-up rates and average leave durations found in different sources. Note, however, that outcomes and regulatory settings may not be fully comparable for countries where regulatory settings have changed since take-up rates have been measured. This is the case for Denmark in particular. In other countries no major changes have occurred between the years in which take-up was last measured (between the end of the 1990s and 2003) and the reference year for the legislative criteria, 2003.

[12] In France, only mothers (or fathers) of at least two children are eligible; having a single child does not entitle the parent to the child-raising allowance (APE). According to Leprince (2003), 27% of children under 3 years were taken care of by a parent at home within the framework of this allowance (APE) in 2001. However, note that since 2004 mothers of a single child can claim a parental leave allowance for 6 months.

index and this is also illustrated by the gender differences in the take-up of parental leave. In Denmark and Sweden, around the turn of the century, just 3% and 2% of eligible fathers, respectively, took up the whole period of their parental leave entitlement. These figures contrast sharply with the large share of eligible women who fully use the parental leave to which they are entitled (93% in Denmark and 99% in Finland). It should be said, however, that more men take part of the leave than in the other countries mentioned above. In Denmark, fathers have made up around 16% of leave takers since 2002 (after the suppression of the father period). However, on average, they took just 5.7 weeks of leave in 2004 which corresponds to roughly 19% of the total parental leave to which they are entitled, whereas women took up 22.6 weeks or 72% of the total leave to which they are entitled. Therefore, fathers' actual share in the take-up of the total number of leave weeks available to parents amounted to 4% in 2003 and 2004.[13] On the other hand, one could get the impression that a much greater gender balance in taking leave is achieved in Sweden: 78% of first fathers compared with 90% of mothers. However, these figures are put in a somewhat different light when the actual length of leave taken by fathers is analysed. In Sweden, although approximately three quarters of eligible fathers take parental leave (accounting for 42% of leave takers in 2002), on average they only take one month (28 days) which corresponds to a mere 16% of the total number of claimed days since mothers on average take 109 days.[14]

Take-up of parental leave is on average lower in the Netherlands, Ireland and the UK than in the Nordic countries, even for mothers. Disincentives may be the absence of a legal framework for wage compensation and job protection, as well as the discretionary power of employers in the practical organisation of parental leave. This is also stated by EIRO (1999) for the UK: 'According to an opinion poll

---

[13] The Danish system is different for parents employed in the public sector and those employed in the private sector. The leave scheme being much more generous in the public sector, one would expect relatively more men and women to take leave in this sector. However, this seems to hold true only for fathers: while 18% of fathers of a child aged less than 6 years work in the public sector, the proportion of male leave-takers working in the public sector was 33.4% in 2004, while for women, the respective proportions were 54% and 48%. The length of leave taken does not seem to change significantly for either sex across the two sectors (Statistics Denmark 2005).

[14] This contrasts with figures of Hong and Corman (2005) who found that for births delivered during the period 1995–2000, only 30% of new mothers ever returned to work after 12 months, 60% after 18 months, 80% after 36 months. This is not totally comparable to official statistics of leave takers as these figures consider all mothers, whether employed prior to birth or not (80% were employed), and whether having taken up leave or not (92% of those employed). However, it gives significant insight into the length of labour market withdrawal.

commissioned by the Trade Union Congress, 34% of parents report they will not be able to afford taking unpaid parental leave. Furthermore, 13% of respondents said that they were unlikely to take leave except in emergencies because they were worried that their employer would hold it against them.' In the Netherlands, only 40% of entitled mothers actually make use of their right compared with 9% of entitled fathers, and in the UK, 20% of eligible women and 9% of eligible men take the full 3 months of unpaid leave open to them.[15] The length of parental leave in the Netherlands is proportional to previous working hours so that men, more frequently working full-time, are likely to be entitled to longer leave than women. Indeed, fathers on leave take on average 11 months, while mothers take up an average 8 month period. Yet mothers take more hours of leave, viewed on a weekly basis, thus remaining the primary caregivers. In both countries, women's labour market attachment is weak and discontinuous with a large share of (short) part-time employment and numerous career interruptions related to important family events. In Ireland, of the 6.74% of the workforce eligible, 20% used parental leave of whom 84% were women.

Fathers' share among leave beneficiaries accounts for 19% of the total in Luxembourg and 12.5% in Belgium. In Luxembourg, an equal share of male users take leave on a part-time and on a full-time basis, while 63% of women take full-time leave. Therefore, in 2002, men's share among full-time leavers was 15.6%, but it rose to 25.1% among parents taking leave at a part-time rate. Men's preference for part-time leave is even more pronounced in Belgium where more flexible part-time arrangements are available: only 13% of men (33% of women) take full-time leave compared with 74% (48% of women) taking leave for one-fifth of working time (2003). As a result, men account for only 5% of full-time leave takers, for 7% of half-time leavers and for up to 18% of those taking leave for one fifth of their working time. In Luxembourg, the somewhat stronger participation of fathers might be explained by the quite generous level of wage replacement compared with Belgium or other countries. Nevertheless, it seems that fathers prefer to preserve their ties with the labour market and therefore rely on their wives to take care of the children full-time. Part of the explanation might be found in employer practices and prejudices or in the reigning ideas regarding early socialisation of children in the society. Note that in these two countries, despite flat-rate replacement of earnings, higher-educated mothers are more likely to take leave than lower-educated (Devisscher 2004; KPMG 2002).

---

[15] The proportion of women taking up their right to parental leave rises when taking at least some of the leave is considered instead of taking the entire leave available.

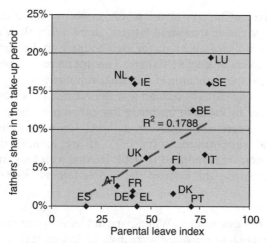

Figure 3.2 Parental leave supportiveness compared with fathers' share in the whole take-up period in the EU-15 Member States

Note: For explanation of the country abbreviations, see Table 2.1.

How to read the figure: e.g. in Sweden, of the whole number of days of parental leave claimed by both parents, 16% are used by fathers (Y axis). Scores on the X axis are those from Table 3.5 above (leave's supportiveness of working mothers).

Source: Appendix Tables 3.A.2 and 3.A.3 and own calculations.

So it is clear that the effect of the different types of father incentives is rather small.[16] In fact, the most decisive feature seems to be the level of replacement income as demonstrated by the examples of Sweden and Luxembourg. However, from the discussion above, it appears more attractive for men to have leave which is granted as an individual right, which is not transferable between partners, which offers parents greater flexibility in terms of working time reduction, and the payment of which is wage related. Furthermore, each adjustment of the parental leave scheme in this sense sends out an important political signal towards an increased integration of fathers in family life.

Figure 3.2 shows the link between the index of the leave's relative supportiveness of parents' labour market attachment in legislative terms

---

[16] Although we have not included Norway in our study, the father quota, introduced in 1993, pushed fathers' take-up rate up from 3% to 70% in 1995. This measure consists in four additional weeks of parental leave reserved for the father or else lost (Bruning et Plantenga 1999). The Icelandic example is also striking. Mothers and fathers are entitled to 3 months of leave each (and a further 3 months to either parent) with a replacement rate of 80% (with a ceiling of €7,700 a month). From the beginning of this new scheme (implemented about five years ago), almost all fathers have taken up the leave option (Jepsen 2006).

and the actual share of fathers in the whole period of leave taken by parents. Note that we have measured fathers' share rather than fathers' take-up due to a lack of available data for each country on the number of either male leave takers or eligible fathers. This measure is expected to correspond better to our indicator of potential supportiveness.

If we exclude the two cases of Ireland and the Netherlands (they have a high fathers' share in the take-up but a low take-up by both sexes), there is a positive correlation between fathers' share and the leave scheme's potential supportiveness (r = 0.7). If we include the two countries, the correlation is reduced to 0.42. Be that as it may, it seems that the more supportive the system, the higher fathers' share in the take-up.

3.3.4.2 Mothers' work resumption   When parental leave compensation is flat-rate, it is expected to be more attractive to low-qualified women because of the lower wage level (compared with their partners) that they can expect on the labour market. In France, the parental leave system has been shown to have had a negative effect on labour market participation of mothers of two children, especially those who are unskilled, for whom it is likely to be more difficult to work again after parental leave has ended (Battagliola 1998; Afsa 1999; Piketty 2003). In the Nordic countries, work resumption after leave seems much easier. Swedish women are backed up by a wide range of policy initiatives to enhance labour market participation. As a result, they tend not to withdraw completely from the labour market but rather to reduce their working time. The problem is that working part-time still results in poor career prospects in terms of wage and responsibilities which reinforce the glass ceiling effect (Albrecht *et al.* 2003; Périvier 2004b). In Germany, according to a study published in June 2001, more than 60% of German women who had one child and were employed beforehand had returned to their previous or an equivalent job three years after the birth of their child but mostly at a part-time rate (West Germany), whereas more than 16% were registered as unemployed (Eiro 2001b). Note that work resumption is not the only way to assess mothers' success in developing a satisfactory professional life since the effects of career interruptions are often delayed in time, translating for instance into wage differentials and slower promotions, as discussed in the introduction to this chapter.

Swedish parental leave offers an interesting illustration of this latter issue. From our analysis, Sweden appears as having implemented one of the most work/life friendly parental leave schemes in the EU-15. However, Albrecht *et al.* (1999) showed that, controlling for individual unobserved heterogeneity, the duration of past career interruptions taken up as parental leave had a significant negative impact on actual wages similar to other types of time out of work (unprotected and not wage-replaced), with the exception of unemployment spells. The effect is particularly strong for fathers (perhaps signalling their lower labour market attachment) and for higher-educated mothers.

3.4   Conclusion

We have analysed how countries' implementation of birth and parental leave can either help or hinder mothers' labour market integration. Maternity leave is more or less well designed across Europe, except in Ireland and the UK where it is less well paid. However, paternity leave does not really exist in many countries. It is important to note that those countries that have implemented a paternity leave of more than one week coincide with those that have developed public childcare facilities for infants (Denmark, Sweden, Finland, France and Belgium). Both theory and empirical findings have shown that a good childcare setting combined with job-protected, relatively short, and paid maternity leave is likely to keep working mothers in the labour market and secure their career opportunities. On the other hand, parental leave is shown to have an important gender dimension and as such risks creating indirect discrimination: it affects women and men differently, in the sense that most beneficiaries are women, sometimes for a very long period of time when other options such as childcare facilities are absent (Spain, Germany and Austria). Consequently, it is impossible for mothers to be as integrated as fathers in the labour market. It is noteworthy that in countries where the leave period is shorter but with no childcare available at the end of the leave period, many mothers have no other choice but to totally withdraw from the labour market, unless they can work out an informal solution.

To conclude on these issues, we have observed that public childcare and parental leave policy principles and regulations may be implemented in order to address the following issues: allowing parents to spend time with their children; promoting their active participation in the labour market and a successful career; achieving a gender balanced sharing in both of the former spheres; and securing children's socialisation. If a given country aims at achieving these four objectives altogether, an effective way would be in two steps. First, priority should be given to encompassing childcare provisions following paid maternity leave (alongside paternity leave) in order to promote equal opportunities for women and men in the pursuit of their professional careers as well as children's early socialisation. Such a policy increases mothers' labour market attachment and secures their financial independence because they maintain full career opportunities, and hence are subject to less pressure by their labour market conditions when realising their desired family plans. Second, if this first step can be fulfilled, it would be possible to conceive parental leave schemes from a completely different point of view, no longer as a means for parents to *take care of* their children, but rather as one that allows them to *make time for* their children. The second step involves making parental leave less of a forced choice but rather a means by which parents, both mothers and fathers, can choose more freely with respect to the time they spend with their children. From such a perspective, parental leave would be short, flexible, well paid, involve special incentives for fathers and not be especially directed at very young children.

Again, a simultaneous choice of the four dimensions is subject to budget constraints which should be further investigated, at least on theoretical grounds.

However, recall that we are not interested in determining whether young children should be taken care of by their family or in a collective system. But, if parental leave is designed to promote parental care while at the same time securing work resumption, a necessary condition is to promote care by both parents through instruments that favour an equal sharing of parental leave, and these do not exist in any country. In sum, none of the countries studied, not even those with the most attractive birth leaves, can be cited as good practice examples for care leave policy in Europe.

Table 3.A.1 *Maternity and paternity leave arrangements in the EU-15 Member States (2003)*

	Prenatal duration (weeks)	Postnatal duration (weeks)	Total duration (weeks)	Employment period to qualify for maternity leave (days)	Indemnification rate or level (% of earnings)	Paternity leave (days)	Indemnification rate or level (% of earnings)
BE	7 (1 compulsory)	8	15	182.5 (6 m)	82% without ceiling during first 30 days after birth (and mandatory week before) and 75% during the rest of the leave (100% for civil servants during the whole leave)	10 (within 30 days after delivery)	82% (100% first 3 days) with ceiling around €102/day
DK	4	14	18	21 (120 hrs.)	100% of unemployment benefits	10 (2 wks. uninterrupted)	100% of unemployment benefit
DE	4	8	14	84 (12 weeks between 10th and 4th month before confinement)	100% of average net wage	0	–
EL	8 (56 days)	9 (63 days)	17	200 (during last 2 yrs.)	100	1 (private sector)	100
ES	–	6 (+10 shared)	16	180	100	2 (+ up to 10 wks. if mother transfers)	100

Table 3.A.1 (*cont.*)

	Prenatal duration (weeks)	Postnatal duration (weeks)	Total duration (weeks)	Employment period to qualify for maternity leave (days)	Indemnification rate or level (% of earnings)	Paternity leave (days)	Indemnification rate or level (% of earnings)
FR	6	10	16 (26 if 3rd child)	304 (10 m)	100	14 (3 + 11)	100
IE	4 compulsory	4 compulsory	18	273 (39 wks.)	70	0 (some trade unions have negotiated a short leave around birth)	n.a.
IT	1 or 2 m	3 or 4 m	21.7 (5 m)	0	80% (some collective agreements require employers to pay the remaining 20%; 100% for civil servants)	0	–
LU	8	8	16	182.5 (6 m)	100	2	100
NL	4–6 compulsory	10–12	16	0	100	2	100
AT	8	8	16	0	100% of net average income of the last 13 weeks or 3 m	0	–
PT	30 days	90 days (6 weeks reserved for the mother)	17.1 (120 days uninterrupted)	182.5 (6 m)	100% of average daily wage	5 (fractionable) during first month	100

FI	30–50 days compulsory	free choice	17.5 (105 days excluding Sundays)	0	70% max. (income-tested, average 66%)	18 (can be extended by 1 to 12 weekdays if father takes last 1 to 12 weekdays at the end of parental leave)	100
SE	7	7	14	Being employed	80% (pregnancy benefit for 50 days leave before birth)	10 (2 weeks)	80
UK	up to 11	free choice	18 (if worked for 1 year, total is 29)	No conditions (for 18-week leave) and having worked 1 year before 11th week preceding birth (for 29-week leave).	90% for first 6 weeks, €115 weekly for the remaining 12 weeks	0	–

Note: For explanation of the country abbreviations, see Table 2.1.
Source: MISSOC (2003) and Table 3.A.4.

Table 3.A.2 Parental leave arrangements in the EU-15 Member States (2003)

	Parental leave duration	Transferability	Compulsory duration and fractionability	Part-time leave arrangements	Child age limit	Qualification conditions	Job and pension guarantees	Monthly benefit level
BE	3 mths. for each parent if full-time leave (6 if PT and 15 if 1/5 time)	Individual right (not transferable); no changes allowed in take-up mode	Full-time leave in 3 times, half-time leave not fractionable or 1/5 leave in 5 periods of 3 mths.	Full-time leave for 3 months, part-time leave for 6 mths. or 1/5 leave for 15 mths.	4	Worked 12 mths. during the 15 mths. before leave (private sector); excluded are the public sector, apprentices and trainees	Job guaranteed and social rights maintained	FT: €547 (gross and taxable), proportional to amount of working time reduction
DK	32 paid weeks to be shared between parents (for the mother to be taken after the 14 wks. of maternity leave, for the father after childbirth) + 14 wks. unpaid but job-protected leave	Family right (transferable between parents); take-up together or one after the other	Possible to split in weeks	Part-time leave with proportional extension of duration	8–13 wks. may be postponed until child's 9th birthday (32 if employer OK)	being employed	guarantee of tenure, social rights and return to the same or an equivalent job	€1755 (full unemployment benefit) during the 32 wks. that are to be shared

	Duration	Right	Flexibility		Part-time	Eligibility	Job protection	Payment
DE	up to 3 yrs. (2 yrs. paid at flat rate)	Family right, take-up together is possible	3rd yr. taken before child's 8th birthday, 1st 2 yrs. taken before the 3rd birthday; If only 1 yr. is taken, the flat-rate benefit is higher; Possible to take a shorter period (multiples of 1mths.)	8	Possibility to work part-time up to 30h	all employees, persons in vocational training, those working at home and pieceworkers	Job protection, right to resume previous working hours and social rights maintained during leave	€300 during 1st 2 yrs. €450 if only 1 yr. (2004), paid only once per child (even if both parents take leave)
EL	3.5 mths. each but 7 mths. for lone parents	individual right (not transferable); no changes allowed in take-up mode	Civil servants: fractionable	3.5	not possible	Both parents must work, the claimer for at least 1 yr. with the same employer	right to return to the same or an equivalent job, pension and seniority rights suspended (unless employee pays all SS contributions)	unpaid
ES	Up to 3 yrs. following childbirth for each parent. Also 1 h (or 2 half-hours) of breastfeeding leave each workday until the child is aged 9 mths.	Individual right (both can take leave at the same time); the right expires if another leave is claimed (e.g. for the 2nd child)	No compulsory duration (less than 1 yr. may be taken); if 1 yr. is taken, this can be done before the child's 3rd birthday	3	PT leave until child aged 6 (hours reduced between 1/3 min and 1/2 max)	being employed	job guaranteed during 1 yr. of leave (tenure, social rights and participation in training courses at return)	unpaid

Table 3.A.2 (cont.)

	Parental leave duration	Transferability	Compulsory duration and fractionability	Part-time leave arrangements	Child age limit	Qualification conditions	Job and pension guarantees	Monthly benefit level
FR	1 yr. parental leave renewable twice for each child. Allowance: 3 yrs. of APE (PAJE since 2004) from the 2nd child and 6 mths. PAJE (since 2004) for 1st child	Family right (APE); individual right (unpaid parental leave) which both can take up together or one after the other	1 yr. renewable twice and transition from PT to full-time leave or inversely is allowed; no changes during the year unless employer agrees	Reduction of hours worked by at least 1/5 (but min 16h of work)	3	seniority of at least 1 yr. (parental leave & APE)	right to return to the same or an equivalent job, guarantee of wage, half of leave counted for pension & seniority issues, right to training at return	€502 (2004) paid only once per child or to each parent if PT take–up but with a max equal to the FT benefit per family
IE	14 wks. each	Individual right (not transferable)	Take-up as a continuous block or, in agreement with employer, spread over a max of 5 yrs. by means of reduced working hours or by breaking down the time into individual days/wks. or as a combination of the previous two; a max. of 14 wks. of parental leave per year except when employer agrees with a different scheme		5	continuously employed for at least 1 yr.	rights related to pay/pensions/ superannuation benefits are not legally guaranteed but left to the discretion of the employer; the right to return to one's job is guaranteed	unpaid

	Duration	Type of right	Form of leave	Part-time		Eligibility	Job protection	Payment
IT	Mother max 6mths., father max 7mths., for a total of max 11mths.; lone parents can take up to 10mths.	Individual right, not transferable and not possible to take up at the same time	No compulsory duration (if father takes at least 3mths., the total rises from 10 to 11mths.). The whole leave is fractionable	part-time take-up possible (1/2 or 1/4)	8	excluded from the right to parental leave: atypical industry branches and liberal professions	contract remains applicable during the whole leave period (employment guarantee + social rights)	30% of earnings for 6 mths. (remaining period unpaid, unless low-income); self-employed women taking parental leave and who are replaced at work receive tax relief
LU	6 mths. each if FT or 12 mths. each if PT	Individual right but one parent has to take leave right after maternity leave, otherwise it is lost, exc. if other parent is not entitled (lone parents excl.)	Whole leave to be taken in one draw	Part-time possible for 12 mths. each	5 (for 2nd leave)	continuously employed for at least 1 yr. (min 20h/w) with the same employer	same contract, type of job and earnings; pension rights not affected	€1693 (2004)
NL	13 times the amount of hours regularly worked per week	Individual right for each parent and for each child	Possible to split leave in 3 periods of at least 1 mth.; parents can go on leave together or one after the other; legally, leave	the length of leave and the number of leave days per week (with a max. of half the number of weekly working hours) are fixed in	8	private and public sector (regular waged workers employed for at least 1 full year by the same employer)	contract, seniority and pension guaranteed by some collective agreements only, especially in the social services sector	Civil servants: 70–75% paid; private sector: only 6% of collective agreements (in 2000) pay the leave (up to 30%)

Table 3.A.2 (cont.)

	Parental leave duration	Transferability	Compulsory duration and fractionability	Part-time leave arrangements	Child age limit	Qualification conditions	Job and pension guarantees	Monthly benefit level
			can be taken over a max. period of 6 mths. but if there is an agreement with the employer, leave can be spread over a period >6 mths.	advance in agreement with employer; full-time leave is possible if employer agrees	8			
AT	36 mths. if each parent takes 6 mths., otherwise 30 mths.	Family right, 24 mths. transferable	Parents can alternate twice at most (max. 3 blocks of at least 3 mths.)	part-time take-up possible	3	All parents providing they are entitled to family allowances	18 mths. of the *kinderbetreuungs-zeit* enter into the calculation of pension entitlements; if part-time work during parental leave, then no protection against dismissal	*kinderbe-treuungsgeld* of €436 for all (incl. self-employed, housewives, etc.)
PT	3 mths. each if FT or 6 mths. each if PT, up to 6th birthday (parental leave); 2 yrs. unpaid (special leave) or 3 yrs. in case of a 3rd child	Individual right (not transfer-able)	Take-up in one draw or in 3 blocks (or alteration between part-time and full-time leave periods)	6 mths (half-time) or alternation of full-time and part-time leave periods summing up to a FTE period of 3 mths.	6	both parents employed	Job-protected parental leave is recognised for pension calculations	the father's 1st 15 days after mat. or pat. leave are fully paid, what is left for the father & the mother is unpaid as is special leave

FI	158 weekdays (excl. Sundays) at a max. of 70% of earnings; afterwards, long leave up to child's 3rd birthday with flat-rate home care allowance	Family right (transferable), take-up only possible one after the other, min. take-up of 12 days for 1st leave. Childcare leave also transferable but taken up one after the other with a min. of 1 mth. per child	Fractionable (see transferability)	the long childcare leave can be taken up on a part-time basis (with proportional allowance)	3	being employed	Job security during both leaves and both are considered as time in employment (pensions, seniority, etc.)	max. 70% of earnings (income-related, average 66%) for 158 days; flat-rate allowance of around €252.28 monthly during child-rearing leave; €70/month if part-time leave
SE	FT leave until child aged 18 mths. and FT leave as long as full-rate parental benefit is received (granted for 480 days to be taken before child's 8th birthday, including paid postnatal leave of 7 wks.)	Of the paid leave, 60 days are for the mother and 60 for the father, what is left is transferable	Each leave can be split in blocks but only 3 periods max. can be taken per year. An employee may choose a number of full-time leave days or can opt for part-time take-up spreading leave over all or some working days. An employee may return to work before the end of leave (min. 1 mth's. notice)	Reduced hours to 1/2, 1/4, 1/3 or 1/8 with corresponding benefit, or uncompensated reduced hours up to 1/4 (until child's 8th birthday)	8	being employed for 6 mths. before leave or for a total of 12 mths. during the last 2 yrs.	job and social rights protected (no dismissal possible)	80% for 1st 390 days (min. €16.5/day), flat-rate for 90 days (€6.6/day)

Table 3.A.2 (*cont.*)

	Parental leave duration	Transferability	Compulsory duration and fractionability	Part-time leave arrangements	Child age limit	Qualification conditions	Job and pension guarantees	Monthly benefit level
UK	18 times the amount of hours regularly worked per week	Individual right (not transferable)		leave can be taken up at once, by means of reduced working hours or in blocks depending on workplace agreement (if parental leave is negotiated, blocks are multiples of 1 day; if not, a default scheme defines blocks as multiples of 1 week with a max. of 4 weeks/yr.)	5	continuously employed for at least 1 yr. with the same employer	Guaranteed return to the same job if leave for max. 4 weeks and to an equivalent job if for more than 4 wks. (mat. and par. leave counted together). In both cases, pension & seniority rights are suspended	No statutory right to paid leave but left to employer's discretion

Note: For explanation of the country abbreviations, see Table 2.1.
Source: See Table 3.A.4.

Table 3.A.3 *Take-up rates of parental leave by sex according to different sources in the EU-15 Member States*

	Female take-up	Male take-up	Average female duration of leave	Average male duration of leave	Source
BE	16,720 (of which 80% in private sector)	2,398 (of which 80% in private sector) All fathers took up their right to paternity leave in 2005	48% take 1/5 leave	74% take 1/5 leave	ONEM (2003) Computed from INAMI
DK	93%	3%			Lourie (1999); www.childpolicyintl.org/ Wehner & Abrahamson (2003)
	42,166 ('94)	3678 ('94)	1990–2000: 85% of women (47,978) on leave for 7–10 wks., 2% for 1–6 wks. (1,129) and 8% (4516) for more than 11 wks.	1990–2000: 47% of men (713) on par. leave for 1–4 wks., 17% for 5–8 wks (258) and 36% (546) for 9–10 wks	
	62,307 concluded cases in 2004 (common leave) whose 10% less than 8 wks., 19% 9–13 wks., 24% 14–26 wks., and 47% 27–39 wks.	11,738 concluded cases in 2004 (common leave) whose 50% less than 14 days and 90% less than 14 wks. 58% of entitled fathers took their 2-week paternity leave in 2002 and 2003.	22.6 wks. in 2004 (concluded cases)	5.7 wks in 2004 (concluded cases). Men accounted for 4% of weeks claimed by the parents (common leave) in 2003 and 2004.	All info (persons, cases, weeks, amounts, by type of benefit, region, years, etc.) from Statistics Denmark (www.statbank.dk)
DE	95%	1%			Lourie (1999); www.childpolicyintl.org/

Table 3.A.3 (cont.)

	Female take-up	Male take-up	Average female duration of leave	Average male duration of leave	Source
		1–2% for some parental leave	estimated duration 2001: West Germany: 63% for 2–3 yrs., 12% up to 1yr., 15% for 1–2 yrs. and 12% for more than 3 yrs, so average of 33 mths; estimated duration 2001: East Germany: 38% for 2–3 yrs., 25% up to 1yr. and 37% for 1–2 yr., so average of 24 mths.		Ostner et al (2003)
EL	(n.a.)	no fathers take leave	Not applicable (not fractionable)	Not applicable (not fractionable)	Stancanelli (2003) (data 1998)
ES	100%		n.a.	n.a.	Stancanelli (2003) (data 1998); www.childpolicyintl.org/
FR	555,700 APE, nearly all women; 98% of leave taken by women	100% for 3-day paternity leave and 59% for the 11-day leave; 2% for parental leave	n.a.	n.a.	Hermange et Steck (2003); Clément et Strasser (2003); Drees (2003)
IE	Of the 6.74% of the workforce eligible, 20% used par. leave of which 84% are women (2002)		n.a.	n.a.	Stancanelli (2003) (data 1998); Eiro (2002)
	5% continuous block of 14 wks.; 8% blocks of full wks.; 9% other; so, total take-up rate of 22%; 85% of leave-takers are full-time workers				MORI MRC (2001)
IT		<5% take any of the leave offered	n.a.	n.a.	Hennech (2003) (data 1998)
LU	1313 full-time; 760 half-time	243 full-time; 255 half-time	whole leave compulsory	n.a.	CNPF (2003)

								Source
NL	40%	9%	8 mths.	11 mths. (but women more hours per week)	25% of all parents (50% of women and 75% of men get paid while on leave)	take-up rates average 13% for part-time leave	The Netherlands is the only country in the EU where fathers do not take shorter leaves than mothers	Lourie (1999); www.childpolicyintl.org/ Knijn (2003); Stancanelli (2003) (data 1998); NIDI (2003) (data 2000)
	44%							
AT	49% (public sector)	90%	1%	12% (public sector)	1%	2% (2002)	n.a.	Lourie (1999); www.childpolicyintl.org/ Stancanelli (2003) (data 1998); The Clearinghouse (2002)
							n.a.	
PT	100%						n.a.	www.childpolicyintl.org/
							n.a.	
FI	99%	99%	2%	64% (par. leave)	67.6% (pat. leave) and 2.6% for par. leave	47,000 take the 158-day leave	n.a.	Lourie (1999); www.childpolicyintl.org/ Ministry of Social Affairs and Health (2003), p. 111; Ministry of Social Affairs and Health (2002)
						2500 take the 158-day leave	n.a.	

Table 3.A.3 (cont.)

	Female take-up	Male take-up	Average female duration of leave	Average male duration of leave	Source
	107,060 children (69,640 families) receive a home care allowance (57% of children under 3),				Ministry of Social Affairs and Health (2003), p.113
SE	295,287 women and 210,456 men receive parental leave allowance, i.e. fathers' share of 42% of beneficiaries but only 16% of the total claimed days; 75% of fathers take paternity leave (on average 9.6 days)		109 days	28 days	The National Social Insurance Board (2003) (data 2002)
UK	20% (estimated in 1999) take full 3 mths. unpaid leave	9% (estimated in 1999) take full 3 mo. unpaid leave			Lourie (1999)
	35% (estimated in 1999) of eligible women	2% (estimated in 1999) of eligible men			Lourie (1999)

Note: For explanation of the country abbreviations, see Table 2.1.

Table 3.A.4 Parental leave provisions in the EU-15 Member States, *legal sources*

AT	Kinderbetreuungsgeldgesetz of 07/08/2001. Additional Information: (WWW.WIF.WIEN.AT/WIF_SITE/ WIF_PAGES/SE_IPOL_13_DOWN_EN.HTML)
BE	Royal Decree of 29/10/1997 Modified by Royal Decree of 20/1/1998, 10/8/1998, 8/6/1999 and 24/01/2002. Additional Information: WWW.ONEM.BE/
DK	Ministry of Employment in Wehner and Abrahamson (2003).
EL	Art. 5 ACT 1483/1984 as amended by Art. 25 Act 2639/1998, Art. 6 Act 1483/84, Art. 53 (1) in combination with art. 51 (2) act 2683/1999 of the Greek civil servants' code, Art. 3 Decree 193/1988(WWW.KETHI.GR/ENGLISH/ MELETES/GUIDE_GOOD_PRACTICES/ GREEKper cent20REPORT/IA.HTM)
ES	Code du Travail (Estatuto de los Trabajadores), updated edition 23/4/2003 (based on 1995 law) Art. 37.4, 37.5 AND 46.3.
FI	Ministry of Social Affairs and Health website (WWW.STM.FI); the Social Insurance Institution of Finland website (Kela) (HTTP://193.209.217.5/IN/INTERNET/ENGLISH.NSF/) Additional Information: Forssén, Laukkanen and Ritacallio (2003)
FR	*APE: Hermange, M.-T. and P. Steck* (2003); parental leave and *P4JE : ART.L122-28-1 TO 7. (Code du Travail on–line:* WWW.LEGIFRANCE.GOUV.FR/)
DE	Gesetz zum Erziehungsgeld und zur Elternzeit (Bundeserziehungsgeldgesetz-Berzg) in der Neufassung der Bekanntmachung vom 09/02/2004, Art.1–24. Additional information: Ostner *et al.* (2003)
IE	Irish Parental Leave Act 1998. Additional Information: parental leave in ireland (WWW. SOFTWORKSCOMPUTING.COM/APR_04/PARENTALLEAVE_PRINT.HTML). Communications Workers' Union (WWW.CWU.IE/HTML/PARENTAL.HTM)
IT	Law of 10/03/2000 (WWW.GIUSTIZIA.IT/CASSAZIONE/LEGGI/153 00.HTML)
LU	Law of 12/02/1999 (WWW.CNPF.LU)
NL	Wet Arbeid en Zorg 16/11/2001. Additional Info: Ouderschapsverlof in Nederland (WWW.KINDERINFO.NL/ PERIODEN/PAPIERWINKEL/JURIDISCH/ALGEMEEN/) AND KNIJN (2003).

Table 3.A.4 (cont.)

PT	DEC.-LEI N°70/2000 (04/05/2000), DEC.-LEI N°230/2000 (23/09/2000), DEC.-LEI N°154/1988 (29/04/2000). (WWW.CITE.GOV.PT/LEGISNAC.HTM)
SE	Parental Leave Act (SFS 1995: 584) including amendments up to 2001 and including SFS 2001:144. Additional information: Ministry of Health and Social Affairs (2003), the National Social Insurance Board (RFV) (2004) and Björnberg & Dahlgren (2003)
UK	Maternity and Parental Leave (Amendment) Regulations 2002; Additional Sources: GMB (Britain's General Union) (WWW.GMB.ORG.UK/DOCS/VIEWADOCUMENT_SEARCH.ASP?ID=25); Department of Trade and Industry (United Kingdom), Section Employment Relations, Parental Leave – A Short Guide for Employers and Employees (WWW.DTI.GOV.UK/ER/PARENTAL.HTM) and Finch (2003).

Note: For explanation of country abbreviations, see Table 2.1.

References

Afsa, C. 1999. 'L'allocation parentale d'éducation: entre politique familiale et politique de l'emploi', *Données Sociales*.

Albrecht, J. W., P. A. Edin, M. Sundstrom and S. B. Vroman 1999. 'Career interruptions and subsequent earnings: a reexamination using swedish data', *Journal of Human Resources* 34 (2), 294–311.

Albrecht, J. W., A. Björklund and S. Vroman 2003. 'Is there a glass ceiling in Sweden?', *Journal of Labor Economics* 21(1), 145–77.

Battagliola, F. 1998. 'Les trajectoires d'emploi des jeunes mères de famille', *Recherches et Prévision* no. 52: 87–99.

Björnberg, U. and L. Dahlgren 2003. 'Policy: the case of Sweden', *Third Report* for the project 'Welfare policy and employment in the context of family change', drafted for the meeting, 8–9 October, Utrecht, the Netherlands.

Boyer, D. and S. Renouard 2003. 'Les pères bénéficiaires de l'allocation parentale d'éducation', *L'essentiel* no. 17: 1–4.

Bruning, G. and J. Plantenga, 1999. 'Parental leave and equal opportunities: experiences in eight European countries', *Journal of European Social Policy* 9 (3), 195–210.

Chambaz, C. 2003. 'L'accueil des jeunes enfants au Royaume-Uni', *Etudes et résultats*, no. 234: 1–8.

Choné, P., D. Le Blanc and I. Robert-Bobée 2003. 'Female labor supply and childcare in France', *CESinfo Working Paper*, no. 1059, http://ssrn.com/abstract=462429.

Clément, M. and A. Strasser 2003. 'Rapport du Groupe de Travail', *Rapport du Groupe de Travail 'Familles et Entreprises'*, Tome 1, rapport remis au Ministre délégué à la famille.

CNPF 2003. *Statistiques sur les familles: L'indemnité de congé parental. Situation au 31 décembre 2002*, Caisse Nationale des Prestations Familiales (www.cnpf.lu)

CREDOC 1997. *Enquête sur les conditions de vie des ménages*, Paris.

2003. *Enquête sur les conditions de vie des ménages*, Paris.

De Henau, J. and D. Meulders 2003. *Alma mater, Homo sapiens? Quel genre pour la recherche universitaire?*, Brussels Economic Series, Brussels: Editions du Dulbea, 220 pp.

Del Boca, D. and M. Repetto-Alaia 2003. *Women's Work, the Family, and Social Policy: Focus on Italy in a European Perspective*, New York: Peter Lang Publishing, 216 pp.

DREES 2003. 'Les pères bénéficiaires du congé de paternité en 2002', *Etudes et Résultats no. 266*, October: 1–4.

EIRO 1999. 'United Kingdom: TUC poll highlights case for parental leave to be paid', European Industrial Relations Observatory On-line, European Foundation for the Improvement of Living and Working Conditions, March (www.eiro.eurofound.eu.int)

2001a. 'Denmark: fathers fail to use full parental leave entitlement', European Industrial Relations Observatory On-line, European Foundation for the Improvement of Living and Working Conditions, February (www.eiro.eurofound.eu.int)

2001b. 'Germany: study examines the employment situation of women after taking parental leave', European Industrial Relations Observatory On-line, European Foundation for the Improvement of Living and Working Conditions, August (www.eiro.eurofound.eu.int)

2002. 'Ireland: Take-up of unpaid parental leave reaches 20%', European Industrial Relations Observatory On-line, European Foundation for the Improvement of Living and Working Conditions, March (www.eiro.eurofound.eu.int)

EUROSTAT 2003. The European labour force survey: Methods and definitions – 2001. Luxembourg: European Commission.

Fagnani, J. 1996. 'Retravailler après une longue interruption': Le cas des mères ayant bénéficier de l'allocation parentale d'éducation', *Revue Française des Affaires Sociales*, no. 3.

1999. 'La politique familiales, flexibilité des horaires de travail et articulation travail/famille', *Droit social*, no. 3.

Fagnani, J. and M.-T. Letablier 2003. 'S'occuper des enfants au quotidien: Mais que font donc les pères?', *Droit social*, no. 3.

Finch, N. 2003. 'Family policy in the UK', *Third Report* for the project 'Welfare policy and employment in the context of family change', drafted for the meeting, 8–9 October, Utrecht, the Netherlands.

Forssén, K., A.-M. Laukkanen and V.-M. Ritacallio 2003. 'Policy: the case of Finland', *Third Report* for the project 'Welfare policy and employment in the context of family change', drafted for the meeting, 8–9 October, Utrecht, the Netherlands.

Gornick, J. C., M. K. Meyers and K. E. Ross 1997. 'Supporting the employment of mothers: policy variation across fourteen welfare states', *Journal of European Social Policy* (7), 45–70.

Gustafsson, S., E. Kenjoh and C. Wetzels 2001. 'A new crisis in european populations: do modern family policies help?', in D. Pieters (ed.), *Confidence and Changes: Managing Social Protection in the New Millennium*, The Hague: Kluwer Law International, 119–41.

Henneck, R. 2003. 'Family policy in the US, Japan, Germany, Italy and France: parental leave, child benefits/family allowances, childcare, marriage/cohabitation, and divorce', Briefing Paper Prepared for the Council on Contemporary Families, May (www.contemporaryfamilies.org)

Hermange, M.-T. and P. Steck 2003. 'La PAJE en propositions', *Rapport du Groupe de Travail 'Prestation d'Accueil du Jeune Enfant'*, Tome I, rapport remis au Ministre délégué à la famille, February.

Hong, Ying and Diana Corman 2005. 'Women's return to work after first birth in Sweden during 1980–2000', *Arbetsrapport no. 19*, Swedish Institute for Futures Studies.

Klerman J. A. and A. Leibowitz 1997. 'Labor supply effects of state maternity leave legislation', in F. D. Blau and R. G. Ehrenberg (eds.), *Gender and Family Issues in the Workplace*, New York: Russell Sage Foundation.

Knijn, T. 2003. 'Social and family policy: the case of the Netherlands', *Third Report* for the project 'Welfare policy and employment in the context of family change', drafted for the meeting, 8–9 October, Utrecht, the Netherlands.

Leprince, F. 2003. *L'accueil des jeunes enfants en France: Etat des lieux et pistes d'amélioration*, Rapport au Haut Conseil de la population et de la famille, January.

Letablier, M.-T. and I. Jönsson 2003. 'Caring for children: the logics of public action', in U. Gerhart, T. Knijn and A. Weckwert (eds.), *Erwerbstätige Mütters: Ein europäischer Vergleich*, Munich: Beck.

Letablier, M.-T. and G. Rieucau 2001. 'La garde des enfants: Une affaire d'Etat?', Centre d'études de l'emploi, *Document de travail*, no. 6.

Lourie, J. 1999. Family leave. House of Commons, *Library Research Paper 99/89*, 11 November.

Martin, C. 2003. 'L'accueil des jeunes enfants en Europe: Quelles leçons pour le cas français', in F. Leprince, *L'accueil des jeunes enfants en France: Etat des lieux et pistes d'amélioration*, Rapport au Haut Conseil de la population et de la famille, January.

Martin, J. 1998. 'Politique familiale et travail des femmes manées en France. Perspective historique: 1942–1982', *Population* (French Edition), 53ème année no. 6, pp. 1119–1153.

Math, A. and C. Meilland 2004. Congés pour raisons familiales et négociation collective, report for the European Industrial Relations Observatory On-line, European Foundation for the Improvement of Living and Working Conditions, Dublin (www.eiro.eurofound.ie/).

Meilland, C. 2001. 'Danemark: L'égalité hommes–femmes sur le marché du travail mise à mal par les congés parentaux', *Chronique Internationale de l'IRES*, no. 71.

Meurs, D. and S. Ponthieux 2000. 'Une mesure de la discrimination dans l'écart de salaire entre hommes et femmes', *Economie et Statistique*, nos. 5. 337–8.

Ministry of Health and Social Affairs 2003. 'Swedish family policy', *Factsheet n°14* (www.sweden.se/upload/Sweden_se/english/factsheets/RK/PDF/RK_Swedish_family_policy.pdf)

Ministry of Social Affairs and Health 2002. *Finnish Social Protection in 2002*, Helsinki, 28 pp.

2003. *Trends and Social Protection in Finland 2003*, Helsinki.

MISSOC 2003. (http://europa.eu.int/comm/employment_social/missoc2003/missoc_89_fr.htm)

MORI MRC 2001. *Up-take of Parental and Force Majeure Leave*, Department of Justice, Equality and Law Reform, Report December 2001, Appendix B.

Moss, P. and F. Deven 1999. 'Parental leave in context', in P. Moss and F. Deven, *Parental Leave: Progress or Pitfall ? Research and Policy issues in Europe*, The Hague/Brussels: NIDI/CBGS Publications, xxxv.

NIDI 2003. 'Arbeid, zorg en beleid', Netherlands Interdisciplinary Demographic Institute, The Hague, *Demos*, no.8, series 19, September.

Ondrich, J., C. K. Spiess and Q. Yang 1996. 'Barefoot and in a German kitchen: federal parental leave and benefit policy and the return to work after childbirth in Germany', *Journal of Population Economics* 9(3), 247–66.

ONEM 2003. *Annuaire statistique 2003*, Office National de l'Emploi, Brussels (www.onem.be/)

Ostner, I., M. Reif, C. Schmitt and H. Turba 2003. 'Family policies in Germany', *Third Report* for the project 'Welfare policy and employment in the context of family change', drafted for the meeting, 8–9 October, Utrecht, the Netherlands.

Périvier, H. 2003. 'Emploi des mères et garde des jeunes enfants: L'impossible réforme?', *Droit Social*, no. 9–10.

2004a. 'Emploi des mères et garde des jeunes enfants en Europe', *Revue de l'OFCE*, June.

2004b. 'Synthèse de la journée OFCE. Emploi des femmes et charges familiales: Repenser le congé parental en France à la lumière des expériences étrangères', *Revue de l'OFCE*, June.

Piketty, T. 2003. 'L'impact de l'allocation parentale d'éducation sur l'activité féminine et la fécondité, 1982–2002', *Working paper CEPREMAP*, no.9.

Pylkkänen, E. and N. Smith 2003. Career interruption due to parental leave: a comparative study of Denmark and Sweden, OECD, DELSA/ELSA/WD/SEM 1.

Rostgaard, Tine 2002. 'Setting time aside for the father: fathers' leave in Scandinavia', *Community, Work and Family* 5(3), 343–64.

Ruhm, C.J. 1998. 'The economic consequences of parental leave mandates: lessons from Europe', *Quarterly Journal of Economics* 112, 1, pp. 285–317.

Stancanelli, E. 2003. 'Do fathers care?', OFCE, *Working Paper n° 2003–08*, December (www.ofce.sciences-po.fr/pdf/dtravail/wp2003-08.pdf).

Stoiber, S. 1990. 'Family leave entitlements in Europe: lessons for the United States', *Compensation and Benefit Management 6*.

The Clearinghouse on International Developments in Child, Youth and Family Policies 2003. (http://childpolicyintl.org/)

The Clearinghouse on International Developments in Child, Youth and Family Policies 2002. *Mother's Day: More than Candy and Flowers, Working Parents Need Paid Time Off. Issue Brief on Parental Leave*, Spring (http://childpolicyintl.org/issuebrief/issuebrief5.htm)

The National Social Insurance Board (RFV) 2004. *Social Insurance in Sweden 2003*, Stockholm, 132 pp.

Waldfogel, J., Y. Higuchi and M. Abe 1999. 'Family leave policies and women's retention after childbirth: evidence from the United States, Britain and Japan', *Journal of Population Economics* 12, 523–45.

Wehner, C. and P. Abrahamson 2003. 'Policy: the case of Denmark', *Third Report* for the project 'Welfare policy and employment in the context of family change', drafted for the meeting, 8–9 October, Utrecht, the Netherlands.

Wetzels, C. and K. Tijdens 2002. 'Dutch mothers' return to work and the re-entry effect on wage', *Brussels Economic Review (Cahiers Economiques de Bruxelles)* 45(2), 169–89.

Winegarden, C.R. and P.M. Bracy 1995. 'Demographic consequences of maternal leave programs in industrial countries: evidence from fixed-effects models', *Southern Economic Journal*, 61, 1020–35.

4 Support for market care: comparing child cash and tax benefits

Jérôme De Henau, Danièle Meulders and Síle O'Dorchai

4.1 Introduction

Besides public childcare provision and maternity/paternity leave arrangements, a third way for the state to intervene in the childcare sphere is to grant benefits to families with young children. These could help them finance the cost of childcare purchased on the market or cover part of their child-related expenses. However, the problem with this support is the broad use that parents can make of it. On the one hand, financial support can help families buy care time on the market and thus allow both parents to work (e.g. Del Boca *et al.* 2003; Viitanen 2005). On the other hand, when benefits are not issued for the specific purpose of purchasing market care, they can and are used to pay for other needs (food, clothes, etc.). A possible effect, which is very important from the gender point of view, is that, if financial support is perceived as being too generous, it risks inducing mothers to quit the labour market (e.g. Lewis and Ostner 1994; Naz 2004). The effect of such support on the work/family balance is then less clear. In the following sections we will present indicators that measure purely financial generosity, knowing that it should be kept in mind that 'general' cash or tax benefits have an ambiguous effect.

Huge differences exist between countries in terms of the means available to fund this type of family support, which usually takes one of the following forms:

- support through the tax system: family support may be granted through the income taxation system in the form of tax allowances (Germany, Spain), tax credits (the UK, Belgium, Luxembourg, Italy, Portugal) or a system of tax shares such as the French family ratio ('quotient familial'), or
- direct support in the form of a cash allowance granted to each child, sometimes means-tested (in Portugal, Italy, Spain and, partially, in Greece).

The purpose of this chapter is to compare countries on this third dimension in two major steps. First, we investigate the level of financial support granted to families, through either cash or tax benefits. Secondly, we compute differences in levels to retain only those cash or tax benefits that can be used for childcare purposes (difference of support granted to families with children aged less than 6 years and to families with children aged more than 6 years). Both analyses are necessary to assess childcare support. The index of 'difference' allows us to identify how a given country targets families with *very young* children, while the index of 'level' is more designated to evaluate how a given country targets families *with* children. Even if the latter support can be used for broader purposes, it is useful to incorporate it in our analysis, not only to allow the computation of the index of 'difference', but also to provide information on policy instruments that can have an impact on women's labour market attachment (see Part III).

In the next sections, we split the analysis of the generosity of direct support between cash benefits (section 4.2) and tax benefits (section 4.3), and then we consider a combination of the two. Next, we narrow the focus on childcare-related support as a third field of policies targeted at working mothers (section 4.4). Section 4.5 concludes.

4.2   Building a child cash benefit indicator

In all countries, except in Southern Europe, cash benefits are universally granted to all families with children under a certain age. This means that all (resident) children, whatever their parents' or relatives' employment status, are entitled to family allowances (MISSOC 2003). In Southern countries, this right is open only to salaried workers' children.[1]

The amount of cash benefits varies according to the age and rank of the children in the household and to the type of family (lone parents, dual-earner and one-earner couples, etc.). All countries except Southern European ones apply a system of flat-rate monthly payments made to each family or to each child independently of parents' income. In Italy,

---

[1] Another exception is Belgium. In this country, family allowances are associated with the occupational status of the beneficiary, namely, wage-earner, self-employed, civil servant and not employed or social contributor. In practice, however, most of the legislation is common to the four types, though amounts differ slightly for self-employed parents. Bearing in mind this exception, we consider Belgium as a quasi-universalist system. Besides this, and for purposes of data harmonisation for the whole EU-15, we will focus on wage-earners only, in order to include the main Southern European schemes. Note that given the very low amounts granted in these countries, with the exception of Greece, this restriction does not change the overall picture of the EU-15 systems.

Spain and Portugal, cash benefits are means-tested and thus vary according to families' income level. In these countries, family policy relies on the idea of vertical redistribution in order to concentrate available means on the neediest. In Greece, on the other hand, employers proportionally raise the wages of those employees who are heads of family.

The pursuit of universalism in their systems of family cash benefits by most countries serves a particular cause. Indeed, non-means-tested cash benefits granted to all children, whatever the situation of their parents (whether employed or not), are considered an important tool in the fight against child poverty (Atkinson 1999). First, they avoid stigmatising specific vulnerable groups, they are easy to take up given the absence of eligibility conditions, and, as a result, they efficiently reach all families concerned. Second, since benefits are granted on a monthly basis, simultaneously with earnings, they are more easily perceived by parents as a regular financial aid to cover the expenses of everyday life, whereas tax relief, given that it is collected with a year's time lag, is tied much less to the expenses that it is supposed to cover and seen more as a bonus. A third reason arises from the fact that fathers and mothers tend to spend the benefits they individually receive as parents very differently. Many studies have shown, using household budget surveys (mostly in the UK), that mothers are more inclined to spend on behalf of the children, while fathers often use the money for personal purposes, especially in the case of a yearly payment. By contrast, the fact that cash benefits are directly linked to the child and mostly granted to the mother increases the probability of their effective use (see Lundberg et al. 1997; Phipps and Burton 1998; Bradbury et al. 2000; UNICEF 2000; Micklewright 2003; Blow et al. 2005). This is known as the *wallet to purse* phenomenon (Lundberg and Pollak 1993, 1996).

At the outset of our exercise to rank countries according to their score on a synthetic indicator representing the generosity of child cash benefits in a given country, note that we focused on children who are neither disabled nor students above the standard age limit applied in the country. We studied the systems for different types of households in order to reflect all possible sources of variation in the benefit systems (according to age and number of children, and to account for the presence of two parents versus one parent in the household).

4.2.1   Income variation

Only in the Southern European countries is cash support influenced by the level of household income (Tables 4.1, 4.2 and 4.3). Portugal and

Table 4.1 Monthly cash benefits per child for working mothers at 0.5 AFE (+ 0.5 AME for couples) in the EU-15 Member States (percentage of the corresponding wage, 2003)

Lone parent with 1 child aged 11 months (%)		Lone parent with 1 child aged 6 years (%)		Lone parent with 2 children aged 12 & 6 years (%)		Couple with 1 child aged 11 months (%)		Couple with 1 child aged 6 years (%)		Couple with 2 children aged 12 & 6 years (%)		Couple with 3 children aged 16, 12 & 6 years (%)	
PT	26.5	AT	19.2	AT	21.8	PT	9.7	AT	7.3	AT	8.3	LU	9.5
AT	18.4	DK	15.1	LU	17.3	AT	7.0	LU	6.3	LU	7.9	AT	9.1
DK	16.1	IE	14.5	IE	14.5	GE	6.0	GE	6.0	GE	6.0	BE	6.4
IE	14.5	GE	14.1	GE	14.1	LU	5.8	IE	5.8	IE	5.8	IE	6.2
GE	14.1	LU	13.8	FI	13.9	IE	5.8	SE	4.2	BE	5.0	GE	6.0
FI	12.9	FI	12.9	DK	12.6	DK	4.4	FI	4.1	FI	4.6	FR	5.2
LU	12.7	IT	11.9	BE	11.2	SE	4.2	DK	4.0	SE	4.2	FI	5.1
IT	11.9	SE	9.6	IT	11.1	FI	4.1	BE	3.8	DK	3.6	SE	4.6
SE	9.6	BE	8.4	SE	9.6	UK	3.4	UK	3.4	NL	3.3	IT	4.4
UK	8.0	UK	8.0	NL	8.4	BE	3.2	EL	2.9	EL	3.2	EL	3.7
BE	7.2	PT	8.0	PT	8.0	EL	2.9	NL	2.9	IT	3.1	NL	3.6
NL	6.0	NL	7.2	UK	6.7	IT	2.4	PT	2.6	UK	2.9	DK	3.4
EL	5.5	EL	5.5	EL	6.2	NL	2.4	IT	2.4	PT	2.6	PT	3.0
ES	3.6	ES	3.6	FR	5.7	ES	0.0	ES	0.0	FR	2.5	UK	2.7
FR	0.0	FR	0.0	ES	3.6	FR	0.0	FR	0.0	ES	0.0	ES	0.0

Notes: AFE = National Average Female Earnings; AME = National Average Male Earnings (Bradshaw and Finch 2002).
For country abbreviations, see Table 2.1.
How to read the table: e.g. in Austria, in 2003, a lone parent (mother) earning half average female earnings, with a single child aged 11 months received each month a cash allowance equivalent to 18.4% of her monthly earnings.
Source: Own calculations based on Appendix Table 4.A.1.

Table 4.2 *Monthly cash benefits per child for working mothers at 1 AFE (+ 1 AME for couples) in the EU-15 Member States (as a percentage of the corresponding wage, 2003)*

Lone parent with 1 child aged 11 months (%)		Lone parent with 1 child aged 6 years (%)		Lone parent with 2 children aged 12 & 6 years (%)		Couple with 1 child aged 11 months (%)		Couple with 1 child aged 6 years (%)		Couple with 2 children aged 12 & 6 years (%)		Couple with 3 children aged 16, 12 & 6 years (%)	
PT	11.6	AT	9.6	AT	10.9	AT	3.5	AT	3.6	AT	4.1	LU	4.8
AT	9.2	DK	7.6	LU	8.7	GE	3.0	LU	3.1	LU	3.9	AT	4.6
DK	8.0	IE	7.2	IE	7.2	LU	2.9	GE	3.0	GE	3.0	BE	3.2
IE	7.2	GE	7.0	GE	7.0	IE	2.9	IE	2.9	IE	2.9	IE	3.1
GE	7.0	LU	6.9	FI	7.0	EL	2.6	EL	2.6	EL	2.8	GE	3.0
FI	6.4	FI	6.4	DK	6.3	PT	2.6	SE	2.1	BE	2.5	EL	3.0
LU	6.4	EL	4.9	BE	5.6	DK	2.2	FI	2.1	FI	2.3	FR	2.6
EL	4.9	SE	4.8	EL	5.2	SE	2.1	DK	2.0	SE	2.1	FI	2.5
SE	4.8	BE	4.2	SE	4.8	FI	2.1	BE	1.9	DK	1.8	SE	2.3
UK	4.0	UK	4.0	NL	4.2	UK	1.7	UK	1.7	NL	1.7	NL	1.8
BE	3.6	NL	3.6	UK	3.3	BE	1.6	NL	1.4	UK	1.4	DK	1.7
NL	3.0	PT	3.1	PT	3.1	NL	1.2	PT	1.0	FR	1.3	UK	1.3
IT	1.4	IT	1.4	IT	3.1	ES	0.0	ES	0.0	PT	1.0	PT	1.1
ES	0.0	ES	0.0	FR	2.8	FR	0.0	FR	0.0	IT	0.3	IT	0.7
FR	0.0	FR	0.0	ES	0.0	IT	0.0	IT	0.0	ES	0.0	ES	0.0

Notes: AFE = National Average Female Earnings; AME = National Average Male Earnings (see Bradshaw and Finch 2002).
For explanation of the country abbreviations, see Table 2.1.
How to read the table: e.g. in Austria, in 2003, a lone parent (mother) earning average female earnings, with a single child aged 11 months received each month a cash allowance equivalent to 9.2% of her monthly earnings.
Source: Own calculations based on Appendix Table 4.A.1.

Table 4.3 *Monthly cash benefits per child for working mothers at 1.5 AFE (+ 1.5 AME for couples) in the EU-15 Member States (percentage of the corresponding wage, 2003)*

Lone parent with 1 child aged 11 months (%)		Lone parent with 1 child aged 6 years (%)		Lone parent with 2 children aged 12 & 6 years (%)		Couple with 1 child aged 11 months (%)		Couple with 1 child aged 6 years (%)		Couple with 2 children aged 12 & 6 years (%)		Couple with 3 children aged 16, 12 & 6 years (%)	
PT	7.7	AT	6.4	AT	7.3	EL	2.5	EL	2.5	AT	2.8	LU	3.2
AT	6.1	DK	5.0	LU	5.8	AT	2.3	AT	2.4	EL	2.6	AT	3.0
DK	5.4	IE	4.8	EL	4.9	GE	2.0	LU	2.1	LU	2.6	EL	2.8
IE	4.8	GE	4.7	IE	4.8	LU	1.9	GE	2.0	GE	2.0	BE	2.1
GE	4.7	EL	4.7	GE	4.7	IE	1.9	IE	1.9	IE	1.9	IE	2.1
EL	4.7	LU	4.6	FI	4.6	PT	1.7	SE	1.4	BE	1.7	GE	2.0
FI	4.3	FI	4.3	DK	4.2	DK	1.5	FI	1.4	FI	1.5	FR	1.7
LU	4.2	SE	3.2	BE	4.2	SE	1.4	DK	1.3	SE	1.4	FI	1.7
SE	3.2	BE	2.8	SE	3.7	FI	1.4	BE	1.3	DK	1.2	SE	1.5
UK	2.7	UK	2.7	NL	3.2	UK	1.1	UK	1.1	NL	1.1	NL	1.2
BE	2.4	NL	2.4	UK	2.8	BE	1.1	NL	1.0	UK	1.0	DK	1.1
NL	2.0	PT	2.1	PT	2.2	NL	0.8	PT	0.7	FR	0.8	UK	0.9
ES	0.0	ES	0.0	FR	2.1	ES	0.0	ES	0.0	PT	0.7	PT	0.7
FR	0.0	FR	0.0	IT	1.9	FR	0.0	FR	0.0	ES	0.0	ES	0.0
IT	0.0	IT	0.0	ES	0.7	IT	0.0	IT	0.0	IT	0.0	IT	0.0

Notes: AFE = National Average Female Earnings; AME = National Average Male Earnings (see Bradshaw and Finch 2002).
For explanation of the country abbreviations, see Table 2.1.
How to read the table: e.g. in Austria, in 2003, a lone parent (mother) earning one and a half times average female earnings, with a single child aged 11 months received each month a cash allowance equivalent to 6.1% of her monthly earnings.
Source: Own calculations based on Appendix Table 4.A.1.

Italy provide lower amounts as income increases. Spanish policy is quite similar: only households with an income below a fixed ceiling receive benefits. This ceiling – although increasing with the number of children – is so low that only households earning at most half of average female earnings qualify for child benefits. They are granted €24.25 per child. It follows that Spain holds a position at the lowest end of the ranking.[2] Greece has adopted a flat-rate benefit. Moreover, given that almost all employers grant gross wage rises to employed married fathers and lone parents, we have treated these wage supplements as taxable cash benefits that derive from the presence of children.

4.2.2   Lone parent allowances

Supplements for lone parents are explicitly granted only in Denmark and Finland, i.e. an additional amount of benefits per household in the former country and per child in the latter. Given that Italy has an income-related system that is based on the number of household members, lone parents necessarily receive different amounts of benefit than couples. In Ireland, it is possible for lone parents to draw extra money from social assistance although, properly speaking, this is not a supplement for lone parents since the main goal of this measure is to guarantee a minimum income for families in need. A similar point of view is reflected in the French system which guarantees a minimum of €521.52 per lone parent plus €173.54 per child. The Single Parent Allowance (API) is paid out if the beneficiary's income is below this threshold and it covers the difference between the guaranteed minimum and his/her income.

4.2.3   Variation with the child's age

Some countries grant supplements (or lower the benefit amount) according to the child's age (applied either to all children or only to the first qualifying child, as in Belgium). A cross-country comparison is quite difficult because of both the differences in the systems that are in place and the reforms that are in progress. For example, in France, the age supplement depends on the number of children: it is granted for the

---

[2] In Spain, lump-sum birth allowances are granted in addition to these 'basic' periodic benefits, but only from the third child on. Various types of birth allowances are granted in some of the other EU-15 countries (see Appendix Table 4.A.1). Note that we do not consider those birth allowances in our calculations given their great heterogeneity, resulting in major harmonisation complexities.

first child but only if there are at least three children in the family. In the Netherlands and Belgium, the amount of child benefit is gradually changed according to children's date of birth.

In order to reflect these differences in the design of systems across the countries considered we focus on four ages. They are chosen in order to encompass all age-specific (and country-specific) adjustments of the amount of benefit. Although most countries that apply variation with age (Austria, Belgium, the Netherlands, France and Luxembourg) raise the amount with the age of the child, Denmark and Portugal do the opposite, privileging the youngest child.

4.2.4   Combined effect of number and age of children

The greatest changes in family cash benefits are generated by the number of children, not only because of proportionally increasing amounts but also because, in most countries, an additional child (up to or from a certain number of children) provides an extra amount of benefit per child. Our tables show the total amount per family, divided by the number of children, and take into account the age supplement for those countries that apply it. It can be seen that countries' rankings change dramatically as the number of children (and therefore the age of the eldest) rises. Belgium and Denmark are opposite cases, as the former sees its rank improved as number and age of children rise while the latter drops (due to age variation only). Note also that although France grants benefits only from the second child onwards, it becomes quite generous from the third child. This special feature of the French system is inherited from the past when the key issue was not to encourage women to have their first child but rather to provide them with incentives to have three children or more (Martin 1998). As a result, family allowances in France are conceived so as to cover the cost of children. This conception contrasts sharply with what is now being put forward as the main objective of family cash support by numerous experts: the fight against child poverty, starting with the first child. Moreover, nowadays, it has also become an important challenge to provide women with enough incentives to have at least one or preferably two children.

4.2.5   Final score for cash benefits

We have built a final indicator that summarises the information for the seven types of families we studied. For each income level, we have weighted these types according to their share in the overall population of each country.

Table 4.4 *Final indicator for cash benefits according to three income levels (family type weighted by country) and overall, for the EU-15 Member states (2003)*

Final score 0.5 AFE + 0.5 AME (population weighted)		Final score 1 AFE + 1 AME (population weighted)		Final score 1.5 AFE + 1.5 AME (population weighted)		Final indicator all incomes (non-income weighted)	
AT	92.6	AT	98.9	AT	96.2	AT	95.9
LU	87.0	LU	91.2	EL	94.6	LU	89.2
GE	70.0	GE	74.2	LU	89.4	GE	72.2
IE	67.2	IE	69.3	GE	72.5	IE	68.3
BE	56.3	EL	67.6	IE	68.6	EL	66.4
FI	54.0	BE	58.4	BE	57.7	BE	57.4
SE	47.5	FI	56.3	FI	55.5	FI	55.2
DK	44.6	SE	50.5	SE	49.8	SE	49.3
PT	41.7	DK	47.5	DK	46.4	DK	46.2
EL	37.1	NL	38.5	NL	38.0	NL	37.7
NL	36.6	UK	36.7	UK	35.9	UK	35.3
IT	35.6	PT	31.5	PT	30.5	PT	34.6
UK	33.4	FR	26.0	FR	26.0	FR	25.8
FR	25.4	IT	6.1	IT	0.1	IT	14.0
ES	0.3	ES	0.0	ES	0.0	ES	0.1

Notes: AFE = National Average Female Earnings; AME = National Average Male Earnings (see Bradshaw and Finch 2002).
For explanation of the country abbreviations, see Table 2.1.
How to read the table: e.g., Austria obtains the highest score for each income level. This means that its score on cash allowances (expressed as a proportion of corresponding earnings) is on average close to 100 for all types of households. Note that the average score of one household type is weighted by its proportion in the population.
Source: Own calculations based on Appendix Table 4.A.1.

Final income-specific indicators $Icash_i^y$ are the weighted average of the linearly scaled cash benefits granted to each of the seven types of families (Table 4.4). A combination of the three income-specific indices is obtained by taking their arithmetic average (last column of Table 4.4).

$$Icash_i^Y = \sum_{j=1}^{7} \left(w_{i,j} \cdot scaled\left[Cash_{i,j}^Y \right] \right)$$

With $w_{i,j}$ = proportion of each household type in the population (country-specific)

With j = each of the seven household types

With i = BE, DK, DE, ..., UK (EU-15 Member States)

With Y = each of the three income levels

Except for the Southern European countries and especially Greece, rankings do not change according to the level of family income given that cash benefits are mostly universal. At the top we find Austria and Luxembourg which are very generous for all family types, as are Germany and Ireland, although to a lesser extent (the benefit amount per child is lower for larger families in Germany). A second group of fairly generous countries includes Belgium and Finland, both of which grant supplements to larger families, and Finland also to lone parents. Denmark and Sweden follow, with lower amounts that are quite constant across family types, the former giving a supplement to lone parent families and the latter to larger families. The amount granted by the UK is low compared with the average level of earnings in that country. France lags behind because benefits are granted only from the second child on and become very generous only from the fourth child.

4.3   Building a child tax benefit indicator

In some countries, cash benefits are not the only form of financial public support for families with children. In addition, we have been careful not to neglect tax benefits as part of our analysis of monetary transfers to families with children, even though they do not immediately increase the amount of cash available to families and do not have the same universal character as standard family allowances. Tax benefits are granted in one of two forms: tax allowances or tax credits. Tax allowances allow for deductions to be made from taxable income and thus reduce the final amount of tax to be paid. Tax credits directly affect the amount of tax due. They are subtracted after gross tax has been calculated.

Tax benefits raise a very important redistributive question. Households not paying taxes, because they do not have sufficient resources, are excluded from any public support the government decides to offer through the tax system, and, as a result, only better-off families take advantage of such measures. For example, a tax allowance to cover childcare costs is of no use to parents who, although active, do not pay taxes (or not enough). Such parents cannot, or not entirely, benefit from any government support in this form. On the contrary, refundable tax credits,[3] such as those implemented in the UK and Belgium, function as negative taxes and do allow help to be extended to families not liable to pay taxes. Indeed, in this case, if the amount of support offered turns out to be greater than the amount of taxes due by the household in question, then not only are no taxes paid but the tax administration reimburses the difference to the household. The tax system is thus effectively used to pass on support to families. Moreover, in the UK, the tax credit is paid out monthly at the same time as family allowances.

Tax benefits in the form of tax allowances raise another problem in terms of fairness, especially in France, Spain and Germany. They tend to increase with family income, although in a limited way, thanks to the existence of ceilings on the support offered. Nevertheless, this means that the richer the family, the more help it receives. Such a system based on the principle of horizontal fairness – which requires a household's standard of living to be constant regardless of the presence of children – has therefore been the subject of fierce criticism (Atkinson 1999). The French family ratio system (*quotient familial*) was designed completely in line with this idea that the cost of children *stricto sensu* increases with family income: better-off children receive more and more expensive leisure and consumer goods compared with children from less-well-off families (Olier 1999).

If a given country's aim is to target children effectively and directly, family allowances present a number of advantages compared with tax benefits. They are direct and simultaneous whereas tax measures necessarily refer to last year's income and thus at best have a lagged effect. Moreover, a system based entirely on family allowances offers a very high level of transparency compared with the more complicated nature of mixed systems or those transiting via the tax system. It is also important to note that family allowances can be conceived as deriving from the child's own right rather than from that of the surrounding family. The Nordic welfare states highly value the principle of individual rights. Each person is individually granted a set of social rights. Moreover, the fact that the child does not depend on its parents, but is itself entitled to benefits, safeguards its rights in the event of divorce, shared custody, etc. By contrast, on the continent, for example in France, the family is considered to be the unit which has the right to public support.

---

[3] Refundable tax credits are to be understood as credits granted even though the individual is not liable to tax or whose tax due is lower than the credit expected. They are also called non-wastable credits (as opposed to wastable credits which are limited to the amount of tax due).

In sum, direct cash allowances seem to be the most appropriate, transparent and fair means for the state to help families with children financially.

4.3.1   Simulation of tax benefits

We have considered only those tax elements that are likely to influence differently all of our seven family types (see Appendix Table 4.A.2 for more details). The detailed procedure to compute tax benefits is as follows.[4]

First we define hypothetical earnings for men and women. A sample of 1,000 men is computed, the yearly earnings of whom range from zero to €100,000, and are ranked from least to highest.[5] For female partners, we compute their respective wages by applying the average national gender wage ratio (AFE/AME) to each male income. This procedure allows us to easily aggregate the earnings of the couple in those countries where taxation is joint, while conserving our three 'reference' income levels. Note that for lone parents we only consider the earnings computed for women. Secondly, we apply the country-specific systems of taxation:

(i)   separate computation of taxable income for each sex (deduction of social security contributions, work-related expenses and so forth) – joint taxable income in some countries
(ii)   computation of tax due for a childless couple (single woman)
(iii)   computation of taxable income and tax due for each type of household with children, considering all relevant elements that may result in differences with taxes due by childless adults (increase in gross earnings, tax allowance, tax credit, etc.)
(iv)   computation of the difference in final tax due (after credits) for each earnings level between a particular couple (single) with children and the childless couple (single).

Note that the tax system of the three Nordic countries does not distinguish between different family types. Therefore, we do not have to run this exercise for these countries. Austria and Ireland make a distinction only between singles and lone parents, regardless of the number of children, Austria granting a non-wastable tax credit of €364 per family and Ireland a wastable credit of €1,520. In the Netherlands, there is no distinction between couples and singles, but for parents, regardless

---

[4] The complete procedure is available upon request from the authors (the computation is processed through Microsoft Office Excel 2003).
[5] Each man thus earns €100 more than his predecessor.

of the number of children they have, a refundable (means-tested) credit exists. In neighbouring countries, the amount of the benefit per child increases with family size (France, Germany and Belgium).

Results of our computations are illustrated in Appendix Figure 4.A.1 for ten countries (excluding Denmark, Finland, Sweden, Austria and Ireland). The amounts of benefits are shown only for couples and are in current euros.[6] Note that the first value on the X-axis represents corresponding half average earnings of a couple (0.5 AME + 0.5 AFE), the second, average earnings and the third, one and a half average earnings. This does not hold for Portugal, for which the first value represents average earnings.

From Appendix Figure 4.A.1, we can see (*inter alia*) that the average level of national earnings differs greatly across countries, so that the figure is rather a tool for understanding how benefits evolve with gross income and according to type of family within each country. In order to improve comparisons between countries (which is our main objective), we have been careful to express the benefits per household as a percentage of corresponding gross earnings, for our three reference income categories, but also per child and in monthly terms, also in order to compare them later with cash benefits. Results are displayed per income level for all EU-15 Member States (Tables 4.5, 4.6 and 4.7 below).

4.3.2   Low-earning families

Table 4.5 shows that, at this level of income, the UK clearly stands out from the other countries because of its generous child and working tax credits, both of which are refundable. Note that the advantage for lone parents with very young children stems from the generous childcare element of the working tax credit. This element amounts to a maximum of €7,126 a year for one child if registered forms of childcare are used, compared for example with the similar credit of maximum €575 in France.

The existence of a tax allowance for young children (for childcare) in Spain and Belgium explains why, at the same income level, families with a single child aged 11 months receive a more substantial tax benefit than families with one child aged 6 years. Note that, since a childcare allowance is a reduction of taxable income, the resulting benefit

---

[6] Results for lone parents are available upon request from the authors, as are the results of the whole procedure of tax computation for each country (except for Northern European countries for which it is not relevant).

Table 4.5 Monthly tax benefits per child for working mothers at 0.5 AFE (+ 0.5 AME for couples) in the EU-15 Member States (percentage of the corresponding wage, 2003)

Lone parent with 1 child aged 11 months (%)		Lone parent with 1 child aged 6 years (%)		Lone parent with 2 children aged 12 & 6 years (%)		Couple with 1 child aged 11 months (%)		Couple with 1 child aged 6 years (%)		Couple with 2 children aged 12 & 6 years (%)		Couple with 3 children aged 16, 12 & 6 years (%)	
UK	82.7	UK	32.2	UK	22.8	UK	14.2	IT	2.4	IT	2.3	BE	2.6
BE	10.1	BE	5.3	BE	5.0	BE	5.7	UK	2.1	BE	1.5	IT	1.9
ES	7.4	IT	4.7	IT	2.3	ES	4.2	NL	1.6	UK	1.1	UK	1.3
IT	4.7	AT	3.6	AT	1.8	IT	2.4	BE	1.1	ES	0.8	ES	0.8
AT	3.6	LU	1.3	LU	0.6	NL	1.6	ES	1.0	NL	0.8	NL	0.5
LU	1.3	ES	1.1	ES	0.5	FR	1.3	FR	1.0	FR	0.7	FR	0.5
FR	0.6	FR	0.6	FR	0.4	LU	0.7	LU	0.7	LU	0.4	LU	0.2
DK	0.0	DK	0.0	DK	0.0	PT	0.5	PT	0.5	PT	0.2	PT	0.2
GE	0.0	GE	0.0	GE	0.0	DK	0.0	DK	0.0	DK	0.0	DK	0.0
EL	0.0	EL	0.0	EL	0.0	GE	0.0	GE	0.0	GE	0.0	GE	0.0
IE	0.0	IE	0.0	IE	0.0	EL	0.0	EL	0.0	EL	0.0	EL	0.0
NL	0.0	NL	0.0	NL	0.0	IE	0.0	IE	0.0	IE	0.0	IE	0.0
PT	0.0	PT	0.0	PT	0.0	AT	0.0	AT	0.0	AT	0.0	AT	0.0
FI	0.0	FI	0.0	FI	0.0	FI	0.0	FI	0.0	FI	0.0	FI	0.0
SE	0.0	SE	0.0	SE	0.0	SE	0.0	SE	0.0	SE	0.0	SE	0.0

Notes: AFE = National Average Female Earnings; AME = National Average Male Earnings (see Bradshaw and Finch 2002).
For explanation of the country abbreviations, see Table 2.1.
How to read the table: e.g. in Belgium, in 2003, the difference between the amount of tax due (computed on a monthly basis) by a childless single woman with half average monthly earnings and that due by a lone mother of a child aged 11 months, and at the same earnings level, amounts to 10.1% of these earnings.
Source: Own calculations based on Appendix Table 4.A.2.

Table 4.6 Monthly tax benefits per child for working mothers at 1 AFE (+ 1 AME for couples) in the EU-15 Member States (as a percentage of the corresponding wage, 2003)

Lone parent with 1 child aged 11 months (%)		Lone parent with 1 child aged 6 years (%)		Lone parent with 2 children aged 12 & 6 years (%)		Couple with 1 child aged 11 months (%)		Couple with 1 child aged 6 years (%)		Couple with 2 children aged 12 & 6 years (%)		Couple with 3 children aged 16, 12 & 6 years (%)	
UK	22.9	LU	8.9	LU	4.4	ES	4.4	FR	1.5	FR	1.4	FR	1.7
ES	13.5	IE	7.8	IE	3.9	BE	3.4	LU	1.3	LU	1.3	BE	1.3
LU	8.9	ES	5.3	ES	3.8	FR	2.6	IT	1.2	IT	1.2	LU	1.3
IE	7.8	FR	3.1	FR	2.6	UK	2.0	UK	1.0	ES	0.9	IT	1.2
BE	7.2	BE	2.7	IT	2.6	LU	1.3	ES	0.9	BE	0.7	ES	1.1
FR	5.5	PT	2.6	BE	2.5	IT	1.2	PT	0.7	PT	0.7	PT	0.7
PT	2.6	IT	2.6	PT	2.2	PT	0.7	NL	0.7	UK	0.5	EL	0.4
IT	2.6	UK	2.5	UK	2.1	NL	0.7	BE	0.5	NL	0.4	UK	0.3
AT	1.8	AT	1.8	AT	0.9	EL	0.3	EL	0.3	EL	0.3	NL	0.2
NL	0.9	NL	0.9	NL	0.5	GE	0.1	GE	0.1	DK	0.0	DK	0.0
DK	0.0	DK	0.0	DK	0.0	DK	0.0	DK	0.0	GE	0.0	GE	0.0
GE	0.0	GE	0.0	GE	0.0	IE	0.0	IE	0.0	IE	0.0	IE	0.0
EL	0.0	EL	0.0	EL	0.0	AT	0.0	AT	0.0	AT	0.0	AT	0.0
FI	0.0	FI	0.0	FI	0.0	FI	0.0	FI	0.0	FI	0.0	FI	0.0
SE	0.0	SE	0.0	SE	0.0	SE	0.0	SE	0.0	SE	0.0	SE	0.0

Notes: AFE = National Average Female Earnings; AME = National Average Male Earnings (see Bradshaw and Finch 2002).
For explanation of the country abbreviations, see Table 2.1.
How to read the table: e.g. in Belgium, in 2003, the difference between the amount of tax due (computed on a monthly basis) by a single woman with average monthly earnings and that due by a lone mother of a child aged 11 months, and at the same earnings level, attains 7.2% of these earnings.

Source: Own calculations based on Appendix Table 4.A.2.

Table 4.7 Monthly tax benefits per child for working mothers at 1.5 AFE (+ 1.5 AME for couples) in the EU-15 Member States (as a percentage of the corresponding wage, 2003)

Lone parent with 1 child aged 11 months (%)		Lone parent with 1 child aged 6 years (%)		Lone parent with 2 children aged 12 & 6 years (%)		Couple with 1 child aged 11 months (%)		Couple with 1 child aged 6 years (%)		Couple with 2 children aged 12 & 6 years (%)		Couple with 3 children aged 16, 12 & 6 years (%)	
ES	10.2	LU	5.8	LU	3.8	ES	3.5	FR	1.7	FR	1.7	EL	2.1
LU	5.8	IE	5.2	ES	2.8	FR	2.4	LU	0.9	LU	0.9	FR	1.9
IE	5.2	ES	4.0	FR	2.8	BE	2.3	IT	0.8	IT	0.8	BE	0.9
FR	5.1	FR	3.5	IE	2.6	LU	0.9	ES	0.7	ES	0.7	LU	0.9
BE	4.8	BE	1.8	IT	1.7	IT	0.8	GE	0.6	GE	0.5	ES	0.9
UK	3.4	PT	1.8	BE	1.7	GE	0.6	PT	0.5	BE	0.5	IT	0.8
PT	1.8	IT	1.7	PT	1.5	PT	0.5	NL	0.5	PT	0.5	PT	0.5
IT	1.7	UK	1.7	UK	0.8	NL	0.5	BE	0.4	NL	0.2	GE	0.5
AT	1.2	AT	1.2	AT	0.6	EL	0.1	EL	0.1	EL	0.1	NL	0.2
NL	0.6	NL	0.6	NL	0.3	DK	0.0	DK	0.0	DK	0.0	DK	0.0
DK	0.0	DK	0.0	DK	0.0	IE	0.0	IE	0.0	IE	0.0	IE	0.0
GE	0.0	GE	0.0	GE	0.0	AT	0.0	AT	0.0	AT	0.0	AT	0.0
FI	0.0	FI	0.0	FI	0.0	FI	0.0	FI	0.0	FI	0.0	FI	0.0
SE	0.0	SE	0.0	SE	0.0	SE	0.0	SE	0.0	SE	0.0	SE	0.0
EL	-1.1	EL	-1.1	EL	-1.2	UK	0.0	UK	0.0	UK	0.0	UK	0.0

Notes: AFE = National Average Female Earnings; AME = National Average Male Earnings (see Bradshaw and Finch 2002).
For explanation of the country abbreviations, see Table 2.1.
How to read the table: e.g. in Belgium, in 2003, the difference between the amount of tax due (computed on a monthly basis) by a single woman with one and a half average monthly earnings and that due by a lone mother of a child aged 11 months, and at the same earnings level, amounts to 4.8% of these earnings.
Source: Own calculations based on Appendix Table 4.A.2.

increases with income and does not apply to earnings lower than the taxable threshold (Appendix Figure 4.A.1.e and g).

Table 4.5 also shows that most countries do not grant any tax benefits at this low level of income. Families in Greece, Ireland, the Netherlands and Portugal do not earn enough to benefit from the existing refundable child tax credits.

In Germany the explanation is different: the €154 cash benefit per child is the only benefit granted to families with children, at least up to a certain level of income. In fact, in the German system a trade-off continuously takes place between this cash benefit (formally it is a tax credit) and a tax allowance which is computed according to the number of children and parents' marital status. Both types of support are considered and the most advantageous is retained and offered to the family in question. As already mentioned, up to a very high level of income, the cash benefit is always preferable. However, at a certain income thresholds the reduction in tax payable brought about by the tax allowance becomes greater than €154. As soon as this happens, parents can choose to trade in their cash benefits for this new form of support, a tax allowance that reduces their taxable income. Keep in mind that this allowance concerns only the richest families, whereas, in all other cases, the standard cash benefit remains the most generous option. Only those couples who both earn 1.5 times the corresponding average wage begin to reach the point where it becomes genuinely interesting to trade in their cash benefits for the existing tax allowance.

4.3.3   Average-earning families

Table 4.6 shows that this average income level falls in the range within which the UK's child tax credit no longer varies with income or remains constant (family element) (see Figure 4.A.1.a). At this level, the child element of the tax credit, which is paid according to the number of children, and the family supplement, paid if there is a child under 1 year of age, are no longer granted (they are means-tested, based on joint income). The same holds for extra advantages for lone parents. As a result, the UK's system for couples is no longer the most generous (and also because the number of children is no longer taken into account). Spain, Belgium, Ireland, Italy, France and especially Luxembourg (despite its relatively higher level of average earnings) turn out to offer substantial support to couples with children and to lone parents. Austria, the Netherlands, Ireland and Luxembourg grant an equal amount to lone parents with one or two children. With a system based mostly on tax allowances, Spain and France become very generous as income increases, while Italy and the UK, where tax credits are means-tested, show the opposite trend. However, in this range of earnings, Italy holds on to its generous position (the threshold for the maximum credit is based on individual income as opposed to the UK where it is based on joint income).

4.3.4   Higher-earning families

Table 4.7 shows that nothing has changed in the amount of benefits compared with the previous level in a certain number of countries since credits have reached their full effect (Luxembourg, the Netherlands, Belgium, Austria, Portugal). This also seems to hold true in Italy but only because this level of income is under the first threshold above which the credit is reduced. In France and Spain benefits keep rising, while German couples start to benefit from the tax allowance for children. British couples no longer benefit from the child credit and lone parents in this country have reached the floor for the family element of this same credit. Finally, Greece stands out as very atypical at this level (in fact, already also at the previous level). In that country, the effect of taxation of the benefits granted by employers to family heads is negative for singles with one or two children, despite the tax exemption applied to their income (the same holds true for couples with fewer than three children although the effect remains closer to zero). By contrast, couples with at least three children benefit greatly from the tax exemption applied individually on earned income as it is much higher per capita than for two children (see Appendix Table 4.A.2).

4.3.5   Final score for tax benefits

The final scores[7] in Table 4.8 (col. 4) draw a relatively clear picture: only a few countries rely on the tax system to support families with children (the UK, Belgium, Italy, France, Spain and, to a lesser extent, Luxembourg). The UK, Italy and Belgium by far outperform other countries as far as families at lower income levels are concerned but they have to make way for other countries such as Spain, Luxembourg and especially France, with respect to higher income families.

---

[7] Computation of the indices is exactly the same as for cash benefits. The only exception is col. 5. The indicator is the arithmethic average of the three income-specific indexes and of the difference between benefits received by low income families (0.5 average earnings) and those received by high-income families (1.5 average earnings).

Table 4.8 Final indicator for tax benefits, in general and according to three income levels (family type weighted by country) in the EU-15 Member States (2003)

Final score 0.5 AFE + 0.5 AME (population weighted) (%)		Final score 1 AFE + 1 AME (population weighted) (%)		Final score 1.5 AFE + 1.5 AME (population weighted) (%)		Final indicator all incomes (non-income weighted) (%)		Final indicator all incomes + regressiveness index (non-income weighted) (%)	
IT	75.4	FR	89.0	FR	90.3	FR	67.9	IT	63.8
UK	69.4	LU	75.3	ES	53.9	IT	60.6	BE	58.3
BE	65.4	ES	71.7	LU	45.7	BE	54.0	FR	52.1
ES	35.1	IT	66.5	IT	39.9	ES	53.6	UK	52.0
NL	28.7	BE	58.7	BE	37.8	LU	45.1	ES	49.5
FR	24.3	PT	44.4	GE	26.4	UK	38.7	LU	39.0
LU	14.4	UK	39.9	PT	26.3	PT	26.6	NL	29.7
PT	9.1	NL	22.3	EL	22.8	NL	22.1	PT	27.2
AT	0.6	EL	18.1	NL	15.3	EL	13.6	EL	15.7
DK	0.0	IE	5.1	UK	6.8	GE	9.1	IE	12.8
GE	0.0	AT	1.3	IE	5.2	IE	3.4	GE	11.3
EL	0.0	GE	0.8	SE	3.9	AT	1.4	FI	9.7
IE	0.0	DK	0.0	AT	2.4	SE	1.3	SE	9.2
FI	0.0	FI	0.0	FI	1.6	FI	0.5	DK	9.0
SE	0.0	SE	0.0	DK	1.0	DK	0.3	AT	8.6

Notes: AFE = National Average Female Earnings; AME = National Average Male Earnings (see Bradshaw and Finch 2002).
For explanation of the country abbreviations, see Table 2.1.
How to read the table: e.g., Italy's average score for low earners is at 75.4 on a scale from zero (the relative minimum) to 100 (the relative maximum) over the seven types of households. This average score is weighed by the relative proportion of each household type in the population.
Source: Own calculations based on Appendix Table 4.A.2.

However, the main problem with our aggregated indicator in col. 4 is that it does not account for the strong degree of regressiveness that is built into the tax systems of some countries (mainly Spain and France but also Germany) given that it is a simple average over all income levels (col. 1–3). From Appendix Figure 4.A.1, the picture of regressiveness for Spain, Germany and France is clear, as opposed to the UK (and to some extent, Italy and the Netherlands) that promote progressive taxes. Belgium, Portugal and Luxembourg, from a certain level of income support flat-rate tax benefits (which, in proportion of gross earnings, favour lower-income families).

We have built a second indicator that does take into consideration the regressive character of the system in those countries that rely on tax allowances or wastable tax credits. The UK comes out at the top of this new ranking while France and Luxembourg, due to their tax allowances for lone parents, move slightly downwards. At the opposite end of the ranking, countries such as Austria, Ireland and the Nordic countries, given that they do not distinguish between income levels, obtain improved scores.

4.3.6   *Final score for combined tax and cash benefits*

A combination of tax and cash benefit systems across the EU-15 allows us to compare countries as to their financial generosity towards families with children, keeping in mind that both systems have different advantages and drawbacks, as discussed above. The result of such an assimilation should be interpreted with great caution: by adding both indicators we obtain a total amount which ignores the time lag that affects most tax benefits. A final indicator accounting for all family types at different income levels has been computed in the exact same way as above, based on total monthly amounts of benefits (cash + tax) paid out in the different countries (Table 4.9). This allows us to take into account the difference in the level of benefits granted to families either through cash allowances or the tax system.

Three countries lead the overall ranking (col. 5), Luxembourg, Austria and Belgium, all of which offer very generous cash benefits or tax reductions (childcare relief or support specifically targeted at lone parents). The UK, Germany, Ireland and Greece form part of a second group, the UK offering extremely generous tax cuts to low and average earners (and lone parents), while the other three focus more on cash benefits. France's position reflects the fact that it does not grant cash benefits to families with only one child. Southern European countries, except Greece, systematically hold positions at the bottom end of the

Table 4.9 *Final indicator for cash and tax benefits, in general and according to three income levels (family type weighted by country) in the EU-15 Member States (2003)*

Final score 0.5 AFE + 0.5 AME (population weighted) (%)		Final score 1 AFE + 1 AME (population weighted) (%)		Final score 1.5 AFE + 1.5 AME (population weighted) (%)		Final indicator all incomes (non-income weighted) (%)		Final indicator all incomes + regressiveness index (non-income weighted) (%)	
LU	84.0	LU	95.6	LU	91.3	LU	90.3	LU	80.3
AT	81.3	AT	70.5	EL	78.2	AT	73.3	AT	67.1
BE	71.8	BE	60.6	AT	68.0	BE	62.9	BE	64.0
UK	61.8	EL	48.1	GE	61.6	GE	56.1	GE	50.6
GE	59.6	GE	46.9	FR	59.9	EL	51.4	IE	47.6
IE	59.0	IE	45.9	BE	56.2	IE	48.7	EL	47.2
IT	51.4	FR	39.7	IE	41.3	FR	41.9	UK	43.3
FI	44.3	UK	32.2	FI	26.5	UK	35.2	FR	36.6
NL	37.5	FI	29.6	SE	21.3	FI	33.5	FI	34.0
SE	36.7	PT	23.2	PT	20.7	SE	27.0	NL	30.3
DK	33.7	SE	22.9	ES	19.9	NL	26.5	IT	28.4
PT	30.9	NL	22.2	NL	19.9	PT	24.9	SE	27.8
EL	27.9	DK	21.0	DK	18.8	DK	24.5	DK	26.0
FR	26.1	ES	16.5	UK	11.7	IT	20.9	PT	25.5
ES	3.8	IT	9.5	IT	1.7	ES	13.4	ES	16.8

Notes: AFE = National Average Female Earnings; AME = National Average Male Earnings (see Bradshaw and Finch 2002).
For explanation of the country abbreviations, see Table 2.1.
How to read the table: e.g., Italy's average score for low earners is at 51.4 on a scale from zero (the relative minimum) to 100 (the relative maximum) over the seven types of households. This average score is weighed by the relative proportion of each household type in the population.
Source: Own calculations based on Appendix Table 4.A.1 and 4.A.2.

ranking. And as far as low income families are concerned, France scores no better. Italy, on the other hand, turns out to be much more generous towards these, thanks to means-tested cash benefits. Finally, the Nordic countries do not score particularly high, and neither does the Netherlands, because of the absence of tax relief and the lower average benefit amount compared with the relatively high level of average earnings (especially in Denmark and Sweden).

4.4   Building a childcare-related direct support indicator

From the discussion in the introduction to this chapter, it follows that direct support to families as it was measured in sections 4.2 and 4.3 is not easy to evaluate in terms of the degree to which it actually helps purchase childcare on the market by providing financial means for families with young children.

Therefore, if we consider the instruments that are likely to be designed as a way of helping families cover the expenses that are directly related to childcare, only a few countries have set up such measures, and all are tax-based (if we ignore the French and Finnish allowances that were included in the public childcare discussion above). France, Belgium, Luxembourg and the UK grant tax relief explicitly for any kind of registered childcare service – public, publicly subsidised or private – through either an allowance or a credit, refundable or not. Spain grants a tax allowance for each child under the age of 3 years but also a non-refundable tax credit to working mothers with a child under 3 years. Similarly, Denmark grants child benefit supplements for children under 3 years, although they are not explicitly labelled to purchase external care.

In order to focus as much as possible on those benefits that are implemented to help with the care of a young child, we have compared child-benefit packages (childcare and more generally labelled benefits) received by a family with one child aged 2 years (representative of a preschool child aged under 6) and a family with one child aged at least 6 years. In this sense, we do not consider benefits in the presence of multiple children, nor those received for older children, because the latter are not directly linked to pre-school care and education expenses. Recall that previous sections have analysed the level of support and this has to be kept in mind alongside the analysis of differences.

Since we are careful to consider representative situations of households and account for the different institutional settings in place according to household type, we have computed our direct support index for the same three income levels (half average earnings, average earnings and one and a half times average earnings) and two family types (lone mothers and couples), this for both possible child ages (under 6 years and 6 years or above). Each amount has been expressed as a percentage of the corresponding earnings level, as in the previous sections.

Our indicators were computed for each income level as follows. We first compute for each household type (lone parents and couples) the difference in total cash and tax benefits between a situation where there is just one child aged 11 months and one where there is a child of around 6 years. Secondly, we scale these two variables (LST, see Chapter 2), and then we compute an income-specific indicator which is the arithmetic average of both household indices, taking into account the proportion of lone parents in the population according to Lehmann and Wirtz (2004). Third, a final index is obtained as the non-weighted average of the three income-specific indices (Table 4.10). This 'difference index' gives an idea of how policy is oriented in the different countries via the extent of differentiation in direct support between pre-school and school-age children.

The main result of this table is that the majority of countries do not consider pre-school and school-age children differently. Therefore, only five countries are to be considered, if we exclude Denmark, which provides low cash benefit supplements to infants. The five countries of interest have all implemented direct support through their tax system with a different impact according to income and household type. The childcare tax credit in France is wastable, so that low-income parents do not benefit much from it. The same holds true for the Belgian and the Luxembourg childcare tax allowance and the Spanish young child tax allowance, all of which reduce taxable income and thus disadvantage lower income families. By contrast, the UK has implemented a childcare tax credit (family-based) that is means-tested. A lone mother with half average earnings and childcare expenses is granted up to 50% of her income, while couples who both earn one and a half times average earnings and also have childcare expenses are no longer granted any tax relief. Moreover, in the UK, the childcare tax credit is granted each month to compensate for actual expenses that were encountered in that period, while, in the other countries, support comes with a lagged effect of about two years. In France and Belgium, childcare tax relief is a real supplement to further reduce the cost of existing facilities, most of which are publicly organised or subsidised, and could therefore have been included in the index of public childcare. On the other hand, in Spain, Luxembourg and the UK, it seems that because there is limited public childcare provision, this direct support serves more to purchase private

Table 4.10 Index of childcare-related direct support to families with pre-school children in the EU-15 Member States (2003)

Final score 0.5 AFE (population weighted) (%)		Final score 1 AFE (population weighted) (%)		Final score 1.5 AFE (population weighted) (%)		Final indicator all incomes (non-income weighted) (%)	
UK	100.0	ES	98.3	ES	100.0	ES	75.2
BE	33.8	BE	69.3	BE	64.5	UK	64.2
ES	29.2	UK	46.3	LU	44.7	BE	57.5
DK	7.2	LU	34.9	FR	30.7	LU	26.5
FR	6.7	FR	33.8	DK	10.7	FR	24.8
EL	4.0	DK	12.0	UK	10.2	DK	10.4
IT	4.0	EL	6.6	SE	5.9	EL	5.7
PT	4.0	IT	6.6	FI	5.8	IT	5.7
IE	3.9	PT	6.6	GE	5.8	IE	5.6
GE	3.9	IE	6.5	IE	5.8	GE	5.6
FI	3.9	GE	6.4	PT	5.8	FI	5.6
SE	3.7	FI	6.4	EL	5.8	PT	5.4
AT	1.4	SE	5.9	IT	5.8	SE	5.2
LU	0.0	AT	2.3	AT	2.1	AT	2.0
NL	0.0	NL	0.0	NL	0.0	NL	0.0

Notes: AFE = National Average Female Earnings (see Bradshaw and Finch 2002).
For explanation of the country abbreviations, see Table 2.1.
How to read the table: e.g. Belgium's average score for low earners is at 33.4 on a scale from zero (the relative minimum) to 100 (the relative maximum) over the two types of households. This average score is weighed by the relative proportion of each household type in the population.
Source: Own calculations based on Appendix Table 4.A.1 and 4.A.2.

care, as is the case for the Finnish private care allowance. In the UK, the condition to be granted relief is that childminders are registered, while in Spain and Luxembourg all informal solutions are possible. From this discussion we conclude that state interventions in the third dimension of the childcare field, i.e. support to purchase care on the private market (only), were almost non-existent in the pre-2004 European Union, except in the UK.

4.5   Conclusion

All countries implement some form of financial support for families with children, through either cash allowances or tax relief. A very wide range of systems can be found across Europe. For example, Sweden seems to have one of the least complex systems (in terms of the number of instruments involved) with universal child cash benefits (with supplements only according to the number of children), no childcare support, and no tax relief for families with children given its totally individualised taxation system. At the other extreme, we find Belgium, for example, with a most complex system of cash benefits that vary according not only to age, rank and number of children but also to job status; a tax allowance for childcare expenses; partially refundable tax credits for children, varying according to their number; tax relief for lone parents; and a still not totally individualised tax system. France also provides a whole variety of tax and cash instruments.

Clearly, the Nordic countries support working mothers through the public provision of childcare to follow maternity and parental leaves, although they also grant some kind of universal cash benefits. The Southern European countries do not favour universal cash benefits, but instead use means-tested allowances (which are proportional to wages in Greece). Although tax relief is privileged in Spain and Italy, these countries remain at the lower end of the final overall ranking because only low amounts are granted (cash and tax). In these countries, only very little support is available for working parents in any of the three fields of childcare policy, although credit should be given to Italy for its substantial childcare provision for pre-school age children and its well-organised maternity leaves. France and Belgium have set up a very complex mixture of policies although most efforts concentrate on the development of public childcare, but also on the provision of childcare tax relief to reduce the cost of childcare for households.

Austria, Germany, Luxembourg and, to a lesser extent, Ireland, seem to rely on maternal care at home during the early years of life of the child, providing generous cash allowances alongside paid leave (very long in Germany and Austria), while little is done to provide childcare solutions outside the home. In these countries, mothers are expected to take care of the child in the early years on a full-time basis at home (Letablier and Barbier 1998). Note that, for Ireland, market options are available but without any direct support. Nevertheless, although cash benefits are not explicitly granted to help purchase market care (e.g. they do not vary according to the child's age), they could be used to do so.

The Netherlands could be considered part of this group although neither cash nor tax benefits for families are especially generous. In this country, childcare options and parental leave are not very well developed; the focus is much more on privileging mothers' part-time work/full-time care model.

Finally, the only country that really concentrates all its efforts on helping working parents (low earners) purchase care on the market is the UK, while little is done there in the other policy fields.

As a result of our discussion, if the goal of a country is to guarantee fairness between families, effectiveness in reaching all family types and support for working parents in their childcare expenses, an ideal system of cash and tax benefits should be designed as follows: Such a country is expected to implement a generous system of universal cash benefits that are granted independently of parents' work status and their level of income. These benefits would be conceived as an individual right of each child, since it is the political challenge to encourage working women in the pursuit of the simultaneous goals of developing a career and raising a family. Countries should be encouraged to increasingly provide support in the form of direct cash benefits instead of through the tax system when the budget cost is held constant. This because cash support is more simple and transparent and comes closer to the idea of social justice and children's proper rights than tax benefits. The individualisation of the tax and social security system follows this logic but also helps to avoid employment traps for spouses (Jepsen *et al.* 1997).

Table 4.A.1 Cash benefit features in the EU-15 Member States (2003)

	Age limit conditions	Monthly amounts	Variation with income	Variation with age	Child raising allowances (different from parental leave schemes)	Birth and adoption grants	Childcare allowances	Allowance for single parents
BE	usual: 18 years / vocational training or education: 25 years / serious infirmity: 21 years	1st child: €72.61 / 2nd child: €134.35 / 3rd child and subsequent: €200.59	no	child 1st rank born since 1st Jan. 1991: 6–12yrs: +€12.65, 12–18 years: +€19.26 child 1st rank born before 1 Jan. 1991: 85–90: +25.22 up to 18 years, +27.09 older / before 85: +€40.41 child becoming 1st rank and born 91–96: 6–18 years: +€25.22, 18+: +€38.54	no special	€983.68 for 1st birth and each adopted child / €740.10 for next births	no special	no special
DK	18 years for all children	each child 0–3: €145 / 3–7: €131 / 7–18: €103	no (special means-tested allowance only if parents are retired)	see monthly amounts	education allowance	multiple births or adoption: €75 per month until children's 7th birthday / adoption of foreign child: €5,159 (one shot)	no special	+€45 per month per child and +€46 per month per household

Table 4.A.1 (cont.)

	Age limit conditions	Monthly amounts	Variation with income	Variation with age	Child raising allowances (different from parental leave schemes)	Birth and adoption grants	Childcare allowances	Allowance for single parents
DE	usual: 18 years / education or vocational training: 27 years / handicapped: no limit	1st–3rd child: €154 / 4th and subsequent: €179	no	no	no special	no special grants (see maternity benefits scheme)	no special	no special
EL	usual: 18 years / education: 22 years / serious infirmity: no limit	1 child-family: €5.87 / 2 children: €18 / 3 children: €40 / 4c: €48 / more: +€8.07 / child	Employer provides 10% gross wage rise if married and 5% per child to husbands (or lone parent). Taxable benefit	no	no special	no special grants (see maternity benefits scheme)	no special	+€3.67 per child for parent widow/er
ES	usual: 18 years / serious infirmity: no limit	€24.2–5 / child	household income ceiling to receive child benefits: €8,264.28 per year (raised by 15% per child from 2nd)	no	no special	€451 for 3rd and each subsequent child	no special	no special

					APJE	AGED	API
FR	20 years for all (at 55% of minimum wage, max for child income)	1 child: 0/2 children: €111.26 total / each subsequent child: +€142.55	no (only min guaranteed if lone parent with 1c+)	11+: +€31.29/16+: +€55.63 (except for 1st child in families with fewer than 3 children)	no special	APJE (cash allowance if young child): €159.76 (means-tested) per month per child (also adopted) from 4th month of pregnancy until 3 years or from adoption and for 21 months. Replaced by PAJE (Young child's benefits – from 2004): €808.31 (income related)	AGED (child home care allowance): income tested and age variable benefit until child's 6th birthday / AFEAMA (private childcare allowance) child < 6 and income tested / all replaced by PAJE from 2004	API (single parent allowance): monthly income of €521 and €173.84 per child less than 3 years is guaranteed (allowance equal to this amount minus parent's income).
IE	usual: 16 years / education: 19 years / serious infirmity: 19 years	1st & 2nd child: €117.6 each / 3rd and further: €147.3	no	no	n/a	€635 for all multiple births with further grants of €635 paid at ages 4 and 12	n/a	income tested, max. €124.8 per week +€19.3 per week per child but seems to be min. income guaranteed for low-income parents

Table 4.A.1 (*cont.*)

	Age limit conditions	Monthly amounts	Variation with income	Variation with age	Child raising allowances (different from parental leave schemes)	Birth and adoption grants	Childcare allowances	Allowance for single parents
IT	usual: 18 years / serious infirmity: no limit	means-tested benefit and proportional to no. of family members		no	no special	families with 3+ children or adopting a child: €775 per child, income related and taxed allowance	no special	increased family allowances for lone parent
LU	usual: 18 years / education training: 27 years / serious infirmity: no limit	1st child: €172.36/2 children: €409.28/3 children: €745.44/ further: €335.99 each	no	6+: +€15.02 / 12+: +€45.06	child raising allowances for those not entitled to parental leave schemes	total amount of €1,615.89 per mother/ maternity allowance in case of no loss of income during maternity leave	no special	no special
NL	usual: 17 years	children born since 01/1995: 0–5 years: €58.11 each / 6–11 years: €70.57 each / 12–17 years €82.02 and those born before	no	see monthly amounts	no special	no special benefit	no special	no special

		1995 it is according to no. of children (1 child: 82.02; 2 children: 93.78; 3 children: 97.36; 4 children: 105.25, etc., each per child aged 12–17, 85% of each amount if aged 6–11yrs.)			no special	no special benefit	no special / tax credit for single parent: annual tax reduction of €364
AT	usual: 18 years / education or vocational training: 26 years / earning incapacity: unlimited	€105.4 / child < 3 years / €112.7 if 3–10 / €130.9 if 10–19 / €152.7 19+ / if 2 children, amount increased by 12.8 each and from the 3rd child,	Income ceiling of €40,320 to perceive supplement for large families of €36.4 for 3rd and each subsequent child	see monthly amounts	no special		no special

Table 4.A.1 (*cont.*)

	Age limit conditions	Monthly amounts	Variation with income	Variation with age	Child raising allowances (different from parental leave schemes)	Birth and adoption grants	Childcare allowances	Allowance for single parents
		amount increased by €25.5 per child / + tax credit of €50.9 per child assimilated as benefit						
PT	usual: 16 years / education or vocational training: 24 years / serious infirmity: +3 years		income-related (4 earnings levels related to minimum wage) and according to age and number of children: 1st level: income <1.5 min. wage: children <12 months: €89.04 for 1st–2nd, €133.65 for next 2nd level: 1.5 min. W < income < 4 min. W.: children <12 months: €77.74 for 1st–2nd, €112.74 for next	children >12 months: €26.76 for 1st–2nd, €40.15 for next children >12 months: €20.86 for 1st–2nd, €30.58 for next	no special	no special benefit	no special	no special, but since benefit is income related, it can change from 2 earnings

	3rd level: 4 min. W < income < 8 min. W.: 4th level: income >8 min. W.:	children <12 months: €66.49 for 1st–2nd, €89.39 for next children <12 months: €41.16 for 1st–2nd, €53.57 for next	children >12 months: €17.86 for 1st–2nd, €24.21 for next children >12 months: €15.72 for 1st–2nd, €20.45 for next				
FI	17 years for all children	1st child: €90 / 2nd–5th child: + €20.5 per child / 6th and following: same amount each than for the 5th child	no	no	no special	maternity grant for pregnant woman whose pregnancy has lasted at least 154 days and with health examination: €140 per birth or adopted child / adoption grant for foreign child according to country of origin: from €1,900 to €4,500	child home care allowance (see parental leave schemes) / private childcare allowance of €117.73 per month and per child paid to private care provider directly (+ means-tested supplement) / partial	+€33.6 per child (supplement of the child allowance)

Table 4.A.1 (*cont.*)

	Age limit conditions	Monthly amounts	Variation with income	Variation with age	Child raising allowances (different from parental leave schemes)	Birth and adoption grants	Childcare allowances	Allowance for single parents
							childcare allowance (parent reducing hours max 30h) of €63.07 per month per child < 3 yrs. paid to the parent	
SE	16 years for all children	each child: €104 / additional amount 3rd child: +€28 / for 4th child: +€83 / for 5th and subsequent: +€104	no	no	no special	no special benefit in case of birth/ adoption grant for foreign child: €4,383	no special	no special

UK	usual: 19 years / education: 19 years	1st qualifying child: €105 / each other child: €70.	no	no	no special	€767 for each birth or adoption (born or expected)	no special but some children under the scheme of working families tax credits (now WTC) for low-income workers	higher benefit rate withdrawn from 1998, a few remain in payment

Notes: For explanation of the country abbreviations, see Table 2.1.
French abbreviations: APJE (Allocation parentale du jeune enfant); PAJE (Prestation d'accueil du jeune enfant); AGED (Allocation de garde d'enfant à domicile); AFEAMA (Allocation pour l'intervention d'une assistante maternelle agréée); API (Allocation pour parent isolé).

Source: MISSOC (2003).

Table 4.A.2 *Tax benefit features in the EU-15 Member States (2003)*

	Tax unit retained	Relief for marital status	Relief for children	Relief for lone parents	Relief for childcare or education costs
BE	Earnings are taxed individually and application of marital quotient (if earnings < 30% of total earnings after deduction for soc. sec. contributions and work-related expenses)	Tax rebate for single person: €5,570 / married individuals: €4,610 each, applied at the basis of the tax schedule (refundable credit)	1 child: €1,180 / 2 children: €3,050 / 3 children: €6,830 / 4 children: €11,040 / each subsequent : +€4,220 (also at the base of the tax schedule combined with previous relief, but refundable credit up to €340 per child)	€1,180 (at the basis of tax schedule and combined with latter two reliefs, refundable credit)	Childcare tax allowance on taxable earnings up to €11.2 per day (computed as €2,464 per year), relief applied to each parent according to share of hh earnings. Age limit 3 years
DK	Spouses are taxed separately for earned income	no	no	no	no
DE	Spouses are taxed jointly (option of separate taxation).	Other specific reliefs are doubled. Tax schedule for spouses is applied on half joint taxable income and tax due is then multiplied by two	Tax credit considered as cash benefit of €1,848 per child (non-refundable). If relief from tax allowance (€5,808 per child) > credit, then former applied to tax schedule instead of latter.	Tax allowance of €2,340	no

EL	Spouses are taxed separately	no	1st band of tax schedule (non-taxable income) is raised by €1,000 for each of 1st and 2nd child, €8,000 more for 3rd child and €1,000 for each subs. child	no	no
ES	Spouses are taxed separately	Basic allowance of €3,400 for each spouse or individual	<25 years: tax allowance of €1,400 for 1st child, €1,500 for 2nd child, €2,220 for 3rd child and €2,300 for 4th child	The basic allowance for individual is raised to €5,550	Additional tax allowance of €1,200 for each child <3yrs. / maternity credit (non-refundable) up to €1,200 for working females with children <3yrs. (limited by SSC due)
FR	Household (spouses taxed jointly with dependent children)	Tax schedule is applied to joint taxable income divided by number of shares (1 per parent, 0.5 per dependent child, 0.5 more from 3rd child), then tax due is multiplied by the number of shares (quotient). For married couples, advantage from quotient is limited to €2,086 for each half share exceeding 2 shares (i.e. from 3rd child) for married couples (or PACS). For lone parents advantage from first two half shares is limited to €3,609 (i.e. from 2nd child).'Prime pour l'emploi': refundable tax credit for low earners with supplement for dependent children: €33 / child for married/cohabiting couples / €66 for 1st child for lone parents and €33 / child from 2nd.			Tax credit (refundable) for children cared for outside home or at school (under 7): 25% of real costs up to a max. of €2,300 per year. Costs for secondary or tertiary education are also deductible from tax: €61 / child in college, €153 / child in school and €183 /c in higher education

Table 4.A.2 (*cont.*)

	Tax unit retained	Relief for marital status	Relief for children	Relief for lone parent	Relief for childcare or education costs
IE	Spouses are usually taxed on joint income (option of being considered as singles). Here joint taxation retained.	Refundable tax credit of €1,520 for singles and €3,040 for couples. Different tax schedule according to marital status: first bracket up to €28,000 for single, €37,000 for one earner couple, €56,000 for two-earner couple	Supplementary taxable income exempted of €575 for 1st and 2nd child, and €830 for each subs. child	Lone parent refundable credit of €1,520 (added to single credit). First bracket of tax schedule at €32,000	Not for two-earner families
IT	Spouses taxed separately	Not for two-earner couples (means-tested refundable tax credit for dependent spouse)	Refundable tax credit, means-tested up to 3rd child (3 income bands, min. €285 per child, max. €516 / child), €516 / child from 4th child.	no	no
LU	Spouses taxed on joint income	Basic tax schedule applied to single income (class 1) and to halved joint income of spouses (class 2) then tax due is multiplied by two.	Refundable tax credit of €900 / child	Tax allowance of €1,920 / basic tax schedule applied to reduced income (up to €29,500)	Tax allowance for childcare costs of €3,600

NL	Tax unit is the individual but certain credits depend on joint income	no	Means-tested refundable child credit (independent of no. of children): €575 if joint Y < €27,438, €365 if joint Y <€29,108 and €41 over. Combination refundable credit if presence of children < 12: €214 if joint Y > €4,206. Wasted credit can however be reported on spouse's tax due according to a certain scheme.	Refundable tax credit of €1,348 + 4.3% of earnings (latter limited to €1,348)	no
AT	Spouses taxed separately	no	€610.8 per child but not related to income, fully refundable and paid together with child benefits, then considered as cash benefits	Lone parents are applied a different tax schedule in order to take into account the application of the general tax credit. Moreover, they are granted a tax credit of €364, fully refundable	no
PT	Spouses taxed on joint income	Refundable tax credit of €178.3 for each taxable spouse, €213.96 for each taxable single. Tax schedule is applied to halved joint income of spouses, then tax due is multiplied by two (before credits)	Refundable tax credit of €142.64 for each dependent child	Refundable tax credit of €285.28 for lone parent (instead of single person's credit)	For own and dependent education costs: refundable tax credit of 30% of costs, up to max. of 160% min. wage, raised by 30% for each dependent child in education from 3rd child. Not taken into account here since own

Table 4.A.2 (*cont.*)

	Tax unit retained	Relief for marital status	Relief for children	Relief for lone parent	Relief for childcare or education costs
					expenses are included (majority of cost influencing the limit). Moreover this credit is combined with other credits for long-term care costs and limited to €710.97.
FI	Spouses taxed separately for earned income	no	no	no	no
SE	Spouses taxed separately	no	no	no	no
UK	Tax unit is the individual but credits depend on joint income (WTC and CTC)	Means-tested non-refundable 'Working Tax Credit' (WTC) for workers, which includes couples and lone-parent element of max. €2,169. This credit is combined with the means-tested non-refundable 'Child Tax Credit' (CTC). Max amounts for CTC elements are €788 per family plus €788 if child < 1yr (family element), and €2,089 / child (child element). Max amounts of WTC + CTC are granted for joint Y < €7,317, then WTC and child element reduced at a rate of 37% for joint Y < €72,300, then family element reduced to 0 at a rate of 15%. CTC is not conditional on being in work	no	In the WTC, there is a childcare element of 70% of max €10,180 for 1c and 70% of max €15,082 for 2 children + for children < 3 cared for outside home in registered facilities or with childminders

Note: For explanation of the country abbreviations, see Table 2.1.
Source: Own calculations based on OECD (2004), Bradshaw and Finch (2002), Inland Revenue (2002) for UK, Ministère des Finances (2004) for Belgium, Administration des contributions directes (2004) for Luxembourg, Ministère des Finances (2004) for France, and Law 46/2002 of January 18 and Agencia Tributaria (2004) for Spain.

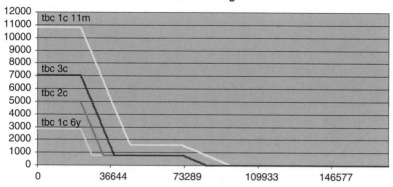

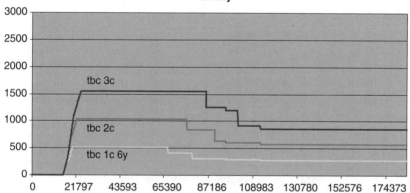

Figure 4.A.1 Tax benefits for couples, by number (and age) of children in ten countries (in euros)

Note: 4.A.1 'tbc' stands for tax benefit for couples. It is computed on annual gross earnings ranging from 0 to €100,000 (male income) plus corresponding female partner's earnings considering the average gender earnings gap. The benefit is the difference between taxes due by couples with one child (respectively, two, three and one child under one year) and childless couples. Amounts are in current euros. The first displayed value on the X-axis represents 0.5 (AME+AFE), the second, 1 (AME+AFE) and the third, 1.5 (AME+AFE). For Portugal though, the first value represents 1 (AME+AFE), the second, 2 (AME+AFE).

Source: Own calculations based on Appendix Table 4.A.2.

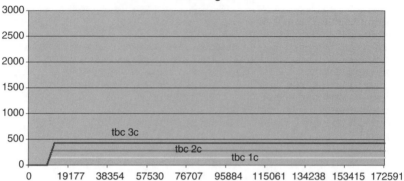

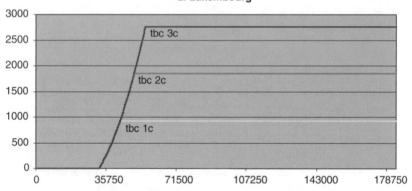

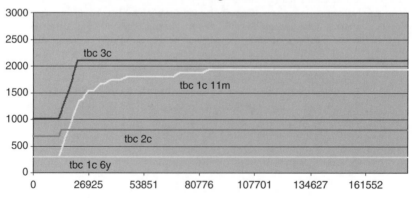

Figure 4.A.1 (cont.)

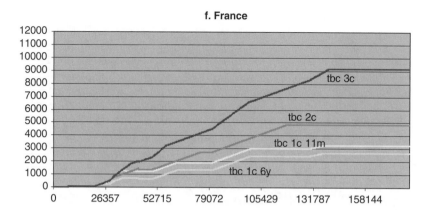

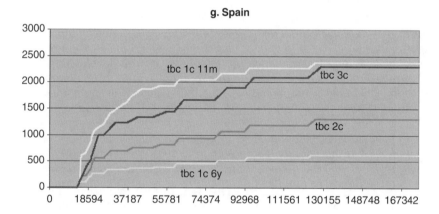

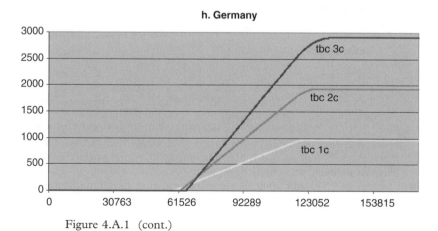

Figure 4.A.1 (cont.)

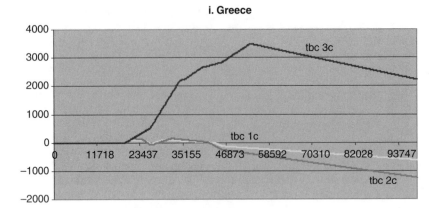

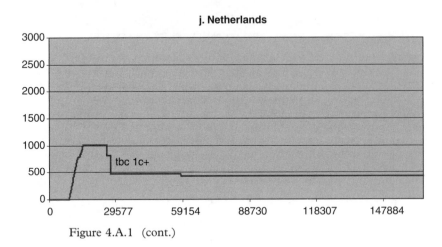

Figure 4.A.1   (cont.)

References

Administration des contributions directes 2004. *Mémento fiscal*, Luxembourg. (www.impotsdirects.public.lu/legislation/memento/memento04.pdf)

Agencia Tributaria 2004. 'Impuesto sobre la Renta de las Personas Fisicas', *Preguntas Frecuentes* (www.aeat.es/).

Atkinson, T. 1999. 'The distribution of income in the UK and OECD countries in the twentieth century', *Oxford Review of Economic Policy* 15: 56–75.

Bradbury, B., S. P. Jenkins and J. Micklewright 2000. 'Child poverty dynamics in seven nations', mimeo, June, 40 pp.

Bradshaw, J. and N. Finch 2002. 'A comparison of child benefit packages in 22 countries', *Research Report no. 174*, University of York (www.dwp.gov.uk/asd/asd5/rrep174.asp)

Del Boca, D., M. Locatelli and D. Vuri 2003. 'Childcare choices by Italian households', University of Turin and University of Florence, *CHILD Working Paper*.

Jepsen, M., D. Meulders, O. Plasman and P. Vanhuynegem 1997. *Individualisation of the Social and Fiscal Rights and the Equal Opportunities Between Women and Men*, Final report, DULBEA-ETE, Edition du DULBEA, January, LXXV, 322 pp.

Lehmann, P. and C. Wirtz 2004. 'Household formation in the EU: lone parents', *Statistics in Focus*, no. 5 /2004, Eurostat, European Communities.

Letablier, M.-T. and J.-CL. Barbier 1998. 'Etat et familles: Politiques publiques comparées en Europe', in *Collectif: L'Etat à l'épreuve du social*, Paris: Editions Syllespse, pp. 139–51.

Lewis, J. and I. Ostner 1994. 'Gender and the evolution of European social policies', Universität Bremen, Zentrum für Sozialpolitik (Centre for Social Policy Research), *ZeS-Arbeitspapier Nr. 4/94*.

Lundberg, S. J. and R. A. Pollak 1993. 'Separate spheres bargaining and the marriage market', *Journal of Political Economy* 101, 988–1010.

1996. 'Bargaining and distribution in marriage', *Journal of Economic Perspectives* 10, 139–58.

Lundberg, S. J., R. A. Pollak and T. J. Wales 1997. 'Do husbands and wives pool their resources? Evidence from U.K. child benefit', *Journal of Human Resources* 32, (3), 463–80.

Micklewright, J. 2003. 'Child poverty in English-speaking countries', *Innocenti Working Paper*, no. 24, 40 pp.

Ministère des Finances 2004a. *Mémento fiscal*, Brussels.

2004b. 'Calcul de l'impôt', *Fiche descriptive no. 1084* (www.fisc.gouv.fr/deploiement/p1/fichedescriptive_1084/fichedescriptive_1084.pdf)

MISSOC 2003. (http://europa.eu.int/comm/employment_social/missoc2003/missoc_89_fr.htm)

Naz, G. 2004. 'The impact of cash-benefit reform on parents' labour force participation', *Journal of Population Economics* 17, (2), 369–83.

OECD 2004. *Taxing Wages 2002–2003 2003 Edition*, Source OECD Taxation, 2004, no. 1, i–446.

Olier, L. 1999. 'Combien coûtent nos enfants ?', *Données sociales* INSEE: 342–32.

Phipps, S. A. and P. S. Burton 1998. 'What's mine is yours? The influence of male and female incomes on patterns of household expenditure', *Economica*, 65 (230), 599–613.

UNICEF 2000. 'A league table of child poverty in rich nations', *Innocenti Report Card*, no. 1, June, Florence.

Viitanen, T. K. 2005. 'Cost of childcare and female employment in the UK', *Labour* 19, (S1), 149–70.

Part II

5 Motherhood and participation

Daniela Del Boca and Marilena Locatelli

5.1 Introduction

Over the last few decades women's labour market participation rates have increased remarkably in the European countries, while fertility has declined and is now below the replacement rate.

Since 1970, as well as these rising participation rates (especially among married women with children), women's college attendance and graduation rates have also greatly increased relative to males. These changes are reflected in their occupations and earnings relative to those of men. They now have more years of accumulated job experience, and their return to job experience has grown as well. Given the higher investment in human capital and higher returns, women started delaying marriage and childbearing to take formal education more seriously and dedicate more time to establishing work relationships. The combination of the postponement of marriage and more divorce increased the number of years spent unmarried and made then more valuable for women's financial independence provided by stronger attachment to the labour market (Goldin 2006). The decline in fertility associated with increased labour market participation is consistent with microeconomic theory which emphasises the opportunity cost associated with women's rising level of education, stronger labour market attachment and improved earnings prospects (Becker 1991; Cigno 1991; Ermisch 2003).

Since the mid 1980s, however, cross-national studies show that the negative correlation has turned positive. Recent studies have explained this change with reference to the changes in welfare state support for working mothers which have contributed to diminishing the incompatibility between motherhood and career, by providing policies that both enhance employment flexibility (such as part-time opportunities) and reduce the opportunity costs of children (child benefits, parental leave and subsidised childcare). Empirical evidence shows that, in fact, in the Nordic countries where more generous social policies have been implemented, fertility rates and women's labour market participation

155

are both high, while in the Southern European countries where much less has been done, both fertility and participation are lower.

In this chapter, we survey important empirical evidence regarding participation and fertility, and microeconomic analyses that explore the impact of social policies on the joint decisions of labour market participation and fertility, and give some attention to the new directions of research.

5.2   The facts

The temporal relationship between fertility and female participation has changed significantly in the last decades (Figure 5.1). During the 1970s and part of the 1980s, this relationship had a strong negative sign.

The growth of women's participation in the labour market and the decline in fertility carry with them some positive and negative implications for the ability of countries and the European Union itself to meet a variety of social and economic targets. On the one hand, the increased number of workers helps to pay pensions to current retirees, while, on the other, the declining population levels make it less likely that the current form of European pension systems can be sustained.

Other important negative implications concern lower economic growth (in particular as a result of the declining working-age population), lower savings, and a greater number of people with few immediate family ties, which will increase the demand for the provision of both public and

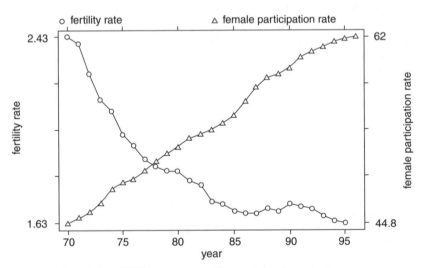

Figure 5.1 OECD average fertility and participation rates
Source: Ahn and Mira (2002).

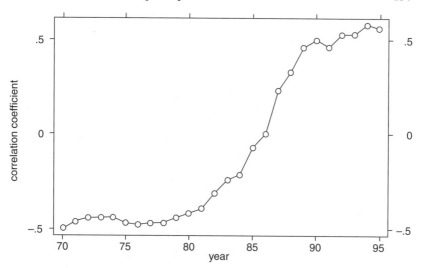

Figure 5.2 Cross-country correlation between the total fertility rate (TFR)[1] and female labour force participation rate (FPR)
Source: Ahn and Mira (2002).

private services. An understanding of this relationship is therefore relevant to policy-makers in ways which go beyond theoretical speculation.

The correlation between female participation and fertility changed sign in the late 1980s and, since then, has continued to weaken: the participation of women in the labour market continued to increase in all countries, but fertility rates started to decline at a slower rate or, in some countries, began to grow again (Figure 5.2).

This phenomenon has been attributed more often to changes in the economic constraints that women face in their choices of participation and motherhood rather than to changes in women's preferences. In fact, important changes have been implemented in Europe with the introduction of child-oriented policies such as parental paid leave and affordable childcare. These policies have contributed to reducing the costs of child-bearing and, in addition, labour market policies have increased labour market flexibility, which help to reconcile motherhood and work. Nevertheless, in spite of long-term changes in social norms, as well as new priorities centred on careers and work (at least among younger women), survey data show that in European countries preferences for number of

---

[1] The total fertility rate is computed from age-specific birth rates in a given year. Female labor force participation is the total number of women in the labour market (employed and unemployed) in a given year.

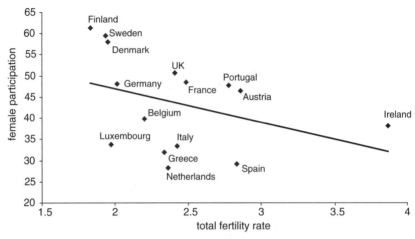

Figure 5.3 Female participation and fertility (1970)
Sources: Eurostat 1999 Demographic Statistics, OECD 2001 Employment Outlook.

children have not changed significantly: 2.2–2.4 on average, with very little variation across countries (Sleebos 2003). Comparison of desired fertility with the actual fertility rate seems to indicate important limitations in the welfare state.

However, the analysis of disaggregated data shows that the change in the sign and significance of the relationship between labour market participation and fertility reveals profound differences across countries.

The countries that currently have the lowest levels of fertility (Spain, Italy and Greece) are those with relatively low levels of female labour force participation, while the countries with higher fertility levels (Denmark and France) have relatively high female labour force participation rates. Figure 5.3 and Figure 5.4 show the cross-country relationship in the 1970s and in the 2000s. In the Southern European countries, a positive correlation is observed, as there is low participation and a low fertility rate, while in the Northern European countries there is high participation and a high fertility rate. In the high participation countries, the total fertility rate began to decline in 1970 from 2.19, eventually reaching 1.65 before turning back at the end of the 1990s to 1.79. In the low participation countries, the fertility rate was 2.72 in 1970 and declined to 1.4 (see Ahn and Mira 2002; Engelhardt and Prskawetz 2004).

These differences reflect the fact that only the Nordic countries (and France) have implemented institutional structures that enable them to balance women's work and childbearing, while in Southern Europe very little welfare state support is available to working mothers.

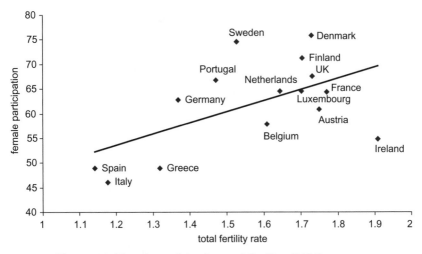

Figure 5.4 Female participation and fertility (2000)
Sources: Eurostat 1999 Demographic Statistics, OECD 2001 Employment Outlook.

The incompatibility between motherhood and career may be recon-
ciled by policies that enhance employment flexibility (such as part-time
jobs) and diminish the potential opportunity costs of children (subsidised childcare, parental leave and child benefits).

Part-time opportunities are in general widespread in the Nordic countries while this type of employment is quite rare in Southern European
countries, resulting in low employment rates of married women, particularly those with children. Where part-time opportunities are limited,
married women are forced to choose between full-time work or not working
at all, neither of which is necessarily their preferred option. Married
women who choose to work tend to have full-time work commitments that
prove incompatible with having large numbers of children (Table 5.1).

In spite of recent institutional changes, the Southern European labour
market still remains a highly regulated one, with strict regulations
concerning the hiring and firing of workers and the types of employment
arrangements permitted. The hiring system and high entry wages along
with very strict firing rules severely restrict employment opportunities
for labour market entrants. These labour market regulations have been
largely responsible for the high unemployment rates of women and
young adults. Women in Southern Europe, in fact, participate less in the
labour market and have fewer children, given that strict labour market
regulations and unemployment discourage exit from the labour market
and make re-entry a difficult enterprise. Women who decide to bear

Table 5.1 *Proportion of women working part-time and with contracts of limited duration*

	% part-time work in female employment	% employees with contracts of limited duration
Sweden	36.3	14.7
Netherlands	71.3	14.3
Denmark	31.6	9.4
UK	44.4	6.7
Germany	39.3	12.4
France	30.4	14.9
Italy	17.8	9.5
Spain	11.6	17.3
Greece	7.2	12.9

Source: Eurostat, *New Release Labour Force Survey*, 2002a.

Table 5.2 *Childcare for children under 3 and 3–6 (percentage)*

	Aged under 3	Aged 3–6
Sweden	48	80
Denmark	64	91
Netherlands	6	98
UK	34	60
Germany	10	78
Austria	4	68
Belgium	30	97
France	29	99
Italy	6	95
Spain	5	84
Greece	3	46

Source: OECD, *Employment Outlook*, 2001.

a child tend either not to withdraw from the labour market, or never re-enter after childbirth.

The empirical analyses of in-kind transfers show that the availability of childcare services significantly affects women's preferences for non-labour-market time versus time spent in paid work. Differences emerge among European countries: in Southern Europe; the childcare services are typically inadequate and characterised by extreme rigidity in the number of weekly hours available. Table 5.2 shows that in Southern

European countries the percentage of children under 3 years who are in childcare is quite low compared with Nordic countries such as Sweden and Denmark, while the proportion of children over 3 years in childcare is relatively high even compared with Nordic European countries.

Finally, longer maternity leave to alleviate the tension between the conflicting responsibilities that women may face as mothers and as workers is a topic of current policy debate. Under EU law, employed women are entitled to maternity leave of 14 weeks. This law sets minimum guaranteed levels of protection, and the Member States can therefore choose to extend these minimum requirements. The Member States are also free to decide on how to apply this protection in national law. This explains the wide discrepancy on this issue from country to country within the EU. Thus, for instance, maternity leave varies from a minimum of 14 weeks in the UK to 28 weeks in Denmark. Furthermore, pay during maternity leave varies from full pay in the Netherlands and Austria to reduced pay in other Member States. There is not always a correlation between the length of maternity leave and the benefit levels provided. Some countries offer long leave entitlements but low statutory pay, and women may not be able to afford to take extended leave (for more details on leave policies, see Part I).

The differences described above help explain the different forms of participation rates in the lifecycle of women in different countries. In

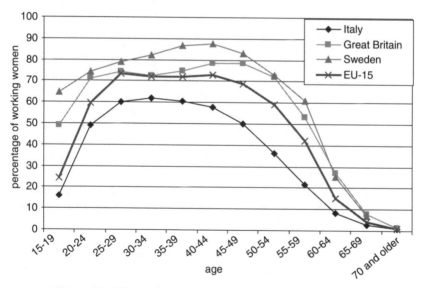

Figure 5.5 Women's participation rates, by age

Italy, for example, the participation rate of women decreases sharply during their childbearing years, while in Sweden the proportion of women working is high, and women enter the labour market in large numbers when young and stay during their childbearing years. Finally, in the UK some women leave during their childbearing years but come back after a few years (Figure 5.5). In the next section, we will review and discuss several analyses focusing on the link between participation, fertility and social policies.

5.3   Issues

In research on female labour supply behaviour, the vast majority of empirical studies found a negative effect of fertility on labour supply. However, the effect may not be causal. The negative correlation may be the result of selection effects, whereby women with stronger preferences for motherhood are also those with lower skills and motivation in the labour market. Using cross-sectional data, Mroz (1987) tested the sensitivity of the parameters of the labour supply equation of married women with respect to a number of assumptions, including the exogeneity of fertility. He concludes that, conditional on participation, fertility is exogenous to women's labour supply.

The potential endogeneity of fertility has also been addressed by adopting an instrumental variables methodology. In searching for instruments, researchers have looked at sources of unplanned births (e.g. the presence of twins (Rosenzweig and Wolpin 1980), and the availability and cost of contraceptives (Rosenzweig and Schultz 1985). Angrist and Evans (1998) suggest the use of the sibling-sex composition as an instrumental variable, given the plausible exogeneity of sibling-sex composition and the observed correlation between having two children of the same sex and further childbearing. However, this latter approach is particularly difficult to implement using European data since the number of women in Europe with at least two children is typically very small. The difficulty of finding suitable instruments and the very mixed results when testing the exogeneity of fertility hypothesis strongly suggest that fertility decisions should be examined in a more realistic manner, in which simultaneous fertility and labour market participation decisions are directly taken into account.

Several recent analyses have considered labour supply and fertility as joint decisions and have explicitly taken into account the endogeneity of fertility in the labour market participation decisions of women (Cigno 1991; Hotz and Miller 1988; Moffit 1984; Francesconi 2002; Del Boca 2002; Apps and Rees 2004; Laroque and Salanniè 2005).

In these models, fertility and labour market participation decisions are generated by the maximisation of household expected lifetime utility under budget and time constraints, in an explicit dynamic framework. Desired participation status and the desired number of children depend on the whole sequence of prices and wages and on family preferences (for a review, see Cigno 1991, Arroyo and Zhang, 1997).

The two types of decisions are simultaneous, in the sense that they are the solution to a common constrained maximisation problem. The increasing use of panel data allows researchers to take into account the dynamics involved in the relationship between childbirth and the work status of women. Moreover, it allows the inclusion of important factors such as fecundity and other individual and marriage-specific traits. These are important factors in explaining fertility decisions, but are unobservable and often omitted by the researcher. As a result of the consideration in the previous section, an understanding of the relation between fertility and labour supply is critical to a number of policy debates. We will review here what, to our knowledge, we consider the most relevant empirical results on the determinants of fertility and participation decisions. We distinguish between the empirical analyses that have considered personal characteristics (such as education and prices and income variables), and those that have also included 'environmental variables' related to labour market characteristics and social policies.

In the analysis of women's decision to both work and have children, the effects of wages have been considered among the most important variables. Table 5.3 summarises some of the results of the studies that focus mainly on the effects of wages and income. The results are quite consistent with the implications of microeconomic analysis and indicate that female wages have a negative effect on fertility and a positive effect on participation. By contrast, male wage coefficients have the opposite sign and are positive on fertility and negative on women's participation.

When only the mother's time and market goods are required for childrearing, wage increases for working women induce both income and substitution effects on fertility (as well as on labour supply). A wage increase leads to an increase in labour supply at low wages as the substitution effect dominates the income effect. At higher wages, it may even become negative. For fertility at sufficiently high levels of female wages, further wage increases could also reverse the negative sign, thus producing a positive demand for children.

A mother's time spent in childcare has a significant negative effect on the likelihood of having another birth, as well as tending to reduce the mother's labour supply, while an increase in the father's income increases the probability of another birth (Hotz and Miller 1988).

Table 5.3 *Fertility and participation: the effects of wages and income*

	Fertility		Participation	
	Female wage	Male wage	Famale wage	Male wage
Aaberge *et al.* 1998 (Italy)	–	–	0.65	−0.08
Carliner *et al.* 1980 (Canada)	−0.01~−.016	0.01~0.02	0.18	−0.05
Ermisch 1989 (UK)	−0.26~−1.01	0.18~1.18	0.69~0.87	0.24~−0.34
Colombino and Di Tommaso 1996 (Italy)	−2.3	0.2	1.34	−0.018
Di Tommaso 1999 (Italy)	$\begin{cases} -0.66 \\ -2.5 \end{cases}$	0.09 0.2	2.82 –	−0.2 –
Hotz and Miller 1988 (US)	−0.02		1.23	

Among personal characteristics, education is a very important factor in the explanation of women's participation, and some studies focus on this aspect. Differences in women's educational level affect wages, as well as wage profiles, with important effects on participation and fertility decisions and the timing of the events (see Gustafsson and Kenjo, Chapter 6 in this volume). Internationally, high levels of literacy and educational attainment by women characterise countries with the lowest rates of fertility. In contrast, high levels of illiteracy and very low levels of educational attainment by women characterise countries with the highest rates of fertility (United Nations Development Programme 2000).

While previous studies including education find a positive effect on women's labour market participation and a negative effect on fertility, more recent ones show positive links between education and fertility (Moffit 1984, for the US, Bloemen and Kalwij 2001, for the Netherlands). Del Boca and Pasqua (2005), estimating a cross-country model of participation and fertility, report that education has a positive sign in the employment equation, but also a positive effect on the probability of having a child. This effect can be interpreted in part as a permanent income effect, given that fathers' education is not included in the analysis (assortative mating). Moreover, higher education might also positively affect the preference for having more children, e.g. to provide the better socialisation of an otherwise single child. A rising fertility rate with increasing education could be explained by the prevalence of income over substitution effects at higher levels of education, especially when childcare can be purchased in the market (see, e.g., Ermisch 1989).

Most studies show that an increase in a woman's years of schooling more significantly affects the timing of births than completed fertility. Gustafsson and Wetzels (2000) have analysed the postponement of births in Germany, the UK, the Netherlands and Sweden, and have reported on the important effects of education. Postponement also leads to involuntary childlessness, as well as to increases in medical costs and health risks for both mothers and their late-born children. However, the negative consequences offset the positive ones represented by the gains in lifetime earnings (see Wetzels, Chapter 7 in this volume). Bratti (2001) explains women's participation decisions in the period surrounding a birth event, by estimating the effect of education and several economic variables on the decisions to give birth and to participate in the labour market. He found that education increases women's commitment to their work. In particular, highly educated women continue to work in the period before and after birth, and therefore education causes fertility postponement. His results imply that policies aiming at increasing women's education would have a positive effect on participation but an uncertain effect on fertility, given evidence of a U-shaped pattern of fertility with education (interpreted in terms of the prevalence of income over substitution effects due to education and by more access to private childcare for highly educated women).

In order specifically to explore the impact of social policies, some research has exploited the time or regional variation within one country. Del Boca (2002) has analysed the case of Italy and considered a simple model of labour supply and fertility in which rationing and market imperfections are taken into consideration. The analysis includes several variables reflecting levels of potential and actual family support, as well as institutional characteristics of the regional childcare system and local labour market, in order explicitly to take into account the relevant constraints that Italian households face when making their labour market and fertility decisions. Even if some of the elasticities are not large, the results seem to indicate that labour force participation and fertility decisions are both affected by similar forces. The decisions to work and to have a child are positively influenced by the available supply of public childcare as well as the availability of part-time jobs. The empirical results also indicate that the availability of family support, both in the form of transfers and in the form of time, increases both the probability of market work and the probability of having children. Similar results emerge also for Spain where a high opportunity cost is associated with childbearing because of the lack of 'social care services' and is compensated for by a strong family support network (Baizán *et al.* 2002).

Laroque and Salanié (2005) have considered a country, France, which has introduced important transfer programmes that appear to have influenced the trend of declining fertility. Taking into account the tax benefit system in great detail, they explored whether the increase in births in France since 1995 could be explained by more generous family benefits. The results that emerged from the estimation and simulation of a joint structural model of participation and fertility suggest that fertility responds to incentives in a non-negligible way. These findings are consistent with more 'indirect' estimates coming from comparative panel data of countries with similar cultural and economic characteristics, which indicate that Italian and Spanish women would substantially increase their birthrates if they had the benefit of relatively more generous French family policies (Del Boca and Sauer 2006).

Given the difficulties in isolating the effects of particular policies within one country, the most common way to test the effects of alternative policy-setting is through a comparative international analysis which can be styled as a quasi-'natural experiment' on the effects of policy variation. The problem here concerns how to compare different countries. An established method (which borrows from sociologists and political scientists) consists in grouping countries into policy 'regimes' that have a similar policy approach, even if welfare-regime classification remains a debated concept (see Part I).

Social policies oriented to reduce the incompatibility between motherhood and career can be distinguished in policies that enhance employment flexibility (such as part-time jobs), and in policies that diminish the potential opportunity costs of children (subsidised childcare, parental leave and child benefits). Comparative studies have found a high correlation between the percentage of part-time jobs and the participation rates of women, in particular married women with children. The low percentage of part-time opportunities does not seem to be consistent with self-reported preferences. A large number of women who are unemployed or who do not participate in the labour force report that they would actually prefer to work part-time: surveys at different points in time and in different areas of the country have reported similar results. Even among the employed, more people state a preference for working fewer paid hours than for working longer hours at the given hourly wage (European Economy 1995).

Bardasi and Gornick (2000) show that motherhood decreases the probability of selecting full-time work and increases the probability of both non-working and working part-time. However, the effect of the presence of young children is less in Italy (where part-time jobs are less widely available) than in other industrialised countries (the UK, the US, Canada and Germany). In some sense, it appears that the Southern European countries are stuck in a 'low female participation rate' equilibrium, in which one of the major reasons for low participation rates is the mismatch between the types of jobs sought by married women with children and the types of jobs offered (full-time).

Gutierrez-Domènech (2002), analysing the relationship between motherhood and career prospects, shows that the career transition after a first birth may be of different types: previously employed women may leave their job and the labour force, or they may experience downward occupational mobility. That is, even if a woman remains employed she may end up in an occupation that has a lower status than the one held before the birth in terms of quality, pay and responsibility. There are several potential reasons why this may occur. Mothers may be willing to supply labour that involves fewer responsibilities in exchange for being able to take care of their children. Or, employers may be reluctant to hire mothers for high profile positions since their family role may absorb their energy and interfere with their productivity. Therefore, in countries such as the UK, where a large number of part-time opportunities are available, women return to part-time jobs after childbearing. However, part-time jobs tend to be more concentrated in occupations with low qualifications and thus have a negative impact on women's career prospects. Furthermore, Gutierrez-Domenech (2002) shows that, relative to other countries, in the UK part-time jobs tend to be more concentrated in occupations with low qualifications and represent more of a temporary solution while searching for better job opportunities when women are young or during their childbearing years.

The decision to work and to have a child is also influenced by the availability of subsidised childcare. Del Boca and Pasqua (2005) comparing various policies using European Community Household Panel (ECHP) data show that the labour force participation of women and the decision to have children is affected by childcare availability. Family support, both in the form of transfers and in the form of help with the children, increases the probability of women's participation as well as their probability of having children. In countries where private childcare prevails, childcare costs are more important than its availability. The results of several studies for the US, the UK and Canada show that childcare cost is a very important variable with significant effects on the participation of mothers. By contrast, in the Northern European countries, where public childcare is readily available, the cost of childcare is less important for the mother's decision to work (for a survey on the impact of child cost across different countries see Del Boca and Vuri 2006).

Governmental measures aimed at reducing the cost of children can be expected to have a positive effect on the demand for children. Apps and Rees (2004) analysing OECD countries show that countries which support families by providing childcare facilities rather than child benefits, are likely to have both a higher female labour supply and higher fertility.

A theoretical distinction is drawn between measures aimed at reducing the direct costs of children (direct expenditures) and measures reducing the opportunity cost of children (forgone earnings). The magnitude of these effects may depend on the work status of the beneficiary. Higher cash benefits have a greater effect on unemployed women than on highly paid executives. On the other hand, higher cash benefits may lead not only to an increased demand for children but also to a demand for higher quality childcare provision. Child benefits may also be expected to have distinct effects on women with different numbers of children. If the same benefits are paid for each child regardless of birth order, benefits can have an increasing influence on the decision to have a greater number of children, since their cost would be lower with each additional child (economies of scale). Some studies suggest the existence of a timing effect: higher family benefits would encourage early entry into motherhood but not necessarily a large family size (Ermisch 1989). A cross-country comparison, which considers benefits for one-child, two-child and three-child families separately, indicated a positive but very limited effect of child benefits on fertility (Gauthier and Hatzius 1997). These results vary widely across countries and by birth order. The cross-country comparison shows that, while cash benefits do not affect fertility in Anglo-Saxon countries, they have a positive effect in Scandinavian countries, since they are likely to be correlated with other family support policies. In Southern European countries the effect is significant only for the first child, while in other countries (France and Sweden, for example) it is significant for the third child (Gauthier and Hatzius 1997). These differences reflect important differences in family support policies across countries.

The influence of child benefits on fertility has not been widely studied with individual data. The analysis of cash benefits must take into account two important factors. First, child benefit effects may be greater for lower-income households, i.e., fertility would increase in households where the average number of children is higher. The second aspect concerns the potential discouraging effects on mothers' labour supply. These effects are likely to be significant and to raise crucial policy questions. These conclusions underline the importance of estimating fertility and participation decisions simultaneously.

Another important social policy, which has an impact on balancing work and childrearing, is that of parental leave. Evidence shows that long maternity leave causes the most difficulties for employers, but for many firms an intermediate duration of maternity leave will be especially costly and may have the largest negative impact on the position of women in the labour market. Gustafsson *et al.* (1996), analysing national household panel data, found that during 1985–93 nearly 80% of the women in the UK, Germany, the Netherlands and Sweden participated in the labour market prior to having their first child. However, 24 months after giving birth to their first child, the participation rate decreased in all EU countries to under 39% except for Sweden where it decreased to 57%. The labour force participation rate around the birth of the second child and around the birth of the third child was not higher than it was before the birth and was considerably lower after the birth (less than 40%) in all countries studied except for Sweden. Gustafsson *et al.* (2002) found that at the child's fifth birthday, the labour force participation rate in these countries remains below 50%. Most of the exits occur in the child's first year. Del Boca and Pasqua (2005) considered transitions around the time of the first child's birth in several European countries and showed that only in the Netherlands, Belgium and Ireland are the transitions from full-time work to part-time work higher than transitions from in employment to out of employment.

Examining changes in the labour supply of mothers of infants in countries where maternity leave statutes were passed between 1980 and 1990, Klerman and Leibowitz (1994) show a negative relation between the employment of mothers and maternity leave legislation. Ruhm and Teague (1997), using comparative data, examine the association between leave policies and indicators of macroeconomic conditions, and found that paid leave is associated with an increased domestic GDP, increased employment and reduced unemployment. Unpaid leave is associated with increased labour force participation and employment and also with increased unemployment, presumably because unpaid leave is not sufficient to discourage mothers who want longer leave from leaving their jobs.

5.4   New research directions

In the analysis of the puzzle of the relationship between labour market participation and fertility and its differences across countries several questions remain unanswered. We summarise here some new research directions that have started to explore important issues, thanks to the availability of comparative data sets on subjective information such as religion, time use of different members of the family (the Multinational Time Use study, the European harmonised time survey (ETUS), the World Value Survey (WVS) and the International Social Survey Programme (ISSP)).

5.4.1   Heterogeneity in preferences

Most of the analyses we have discussed above have implicitly or explicitly assumed that women in different European countries have homogenous preferences but face different choice sets 'determined' by the social policies implemented in the different countries. One approach to help control for unobservable differences such as attitudes towards gender roles is to limit the set of countries to only those with 'similar' cultural characteristics (Del Boca and Sauer 2006). In this context, given the similarity of the cultural and social dimensions, the estimated differences in the patterns of work and fertility choice across countries could be attributed *ex post* to differences in the underlying institutions that govern employment and social policies.

Another approach consists of measuring the relative importance of cultural differences more 'explicitly'. Algan and Cahuc (2006) have introduced self-reported information on beliefs concerning the role of women in the labour market and the household in the analysis of the participation of European women. They use international social surveys on family values and relations (the World Value Survey and the International Social Survey Programme) which cover the main OECD countries over the last two decades. These surveys make it possible to disentangle the role played by individual characteristics and country fixed effects on family attitudes. In fact, traditional explanations which put the emphasis on labour market rigidities, and competition between demographic groups in the labour market, may explain both employment rates and family attitudes. They show that specific national family attitudes are highly correlated with the employment rates of the different demographic groups. This result is robust to the inclusion of traditional time varying labour market institutions and other country effects which could account for other cross-country differences in institutions. Fernandez's and Fogli's (2005) research started from the recognition that a significant part of the variation across time and space of fertility and participation can also be explained by beliefs such as the appropriate role of women in society. It is a difficult task to separate these effects from those of markets and institutions. They dealt with this problem by studying women born in one country but whose parents were born in another country. They have examined the work and fertility behaviour of women born in the US, but whose parents were born elsewhere. Past female labour force participation and total fertility rates from the country of ancestry are considered cultural proxies capturing beliefs held about the role of women in society. They find that these cultural proxies have a positive and a significant role in explaining work and fertility outcomes (even controlling for possible indirect effects of culture (e.g. education and spousal characteristics).

Berman *et al.* (2006) analyse the impact of religion and, in particular, special aspects of Catholicism. They report evidence that the decline of Catholic 'religiosity' is one of the major causes of subsequent fertility decline in Italy, Spain, Portugal and Ireland. In order to investigate the fertility effects of changes in social services provided by Catholic communities, they merge data on fertility and economic variables with indicators of religiosity and social service provision in Catholic communities. The cross-national nature of the data allows this effect to be distinguished from that produced by a European change in European fertility norms. Their results imply that the decline in Catholic fertility was not caused primarily by religiously induced change in *preferences* for children. Instead, institutional decline and social effects appear to be much more important, such as the loss of many child-friendly social services traditionally provided by Catholic communities, including schools, hospitals and daycare.

5.4.2 Time use and husband's role

Most studies of fertility and labour supply decisions have assumed that the primary role of the male partner consists of market work, and mainly considered his income and earnings as exogenous contributions to the household production process. With the greater labour market attachment of women, husbands' contributions to home production may be more relevant.

Only recently, data on time use have revealed some new developments. In fact, trends in parental time invested in children since the 1960s in industrialised countries using time-use survey data show that parents appear to be devoting more time to children than they did forty years ago. Mothers continue to devote more time to childcare than fathers, but the gender gap has been reduced and husbands' contribution to home production has become more relevant. Craig (2006) using ECHP data analyses the link between time allocation and women's decision to have children and finds support that birthrates are higher where male and female time allocation to paid and unpaid work is more equitable.

Apps and Rees (2005) comparing Australia, the UK and Germany argue that not only gender differences in earnings and employment can be explained by fiscal and social policy but also lifecycle variation in time use. Profiles of time use are compared over the lifecycle defined in terms of age as well as in terms of phases that represent the key transitions in the lifecycle of a typical household. They conclude that, given the decision to have children, differences in lifecycle time use and consumption decisions of households are determined significantly by public policy (e.g., on access to high-quality, affordable childcare).

De Laat and Sevilla Sanz (2006) explain the cross-country differences in fertility by attitudes in gender roles which constrain the way in which families distribute their allocation of time and, in particular, the man's contribution to household chores. Their argument is that men's contribution to household activities is not important in a world of low levels of female education, as was the case in all countries in the 1970s. Since then it has become more relevant as female education (and potential wages) increase and women find it profitable to work in the labour market. Whereas in the Northern European countries women's incorporation into the workforce was followed by an increase in men's contribution to household activities, in Southern Europe this was not the case.[2] As a consequence, Southern European women searching for ways to alleviate time pressures (facing a welfare system almost hostile to mothers working) have no choice but to reduce fertility.

Esping-Andersen *et al.* (2006) question the traditional model of family decision-making in which the husband's contribution is only monetary. Given the rapid convergence of men's and women's employment rates, it appears relevant to relax the assumptions of such models and also pay more attention to the nature of the contribution of men also in terms of time. They explore the ways couples make fertility decisions jointly, considering two very different examples of family friendly policies: Denmark and Spain. While in Denmark (with universal childcare coverage, job security and flexibility) men's contribution to household production encourages fertility, in Spain it has no significant role. Their results suggest that a decision-making logic very different from that of the traditional model is evolving in Denmark, while Spanish couples continue to adhere to the traditional model.

---

[2] Among the Southern families, adult children living with their parents much beyond the attainment of adulthood, are not expected to participate in the household production process.

5.4.3   Endogeneity of social policies

Del Boca *et al.* (2005) using ECHP data, analyse Italy, France and the UK, and show that social policies have strikingly different signs and size across countries. In fact, they are not only characterised by different levels of generosity but also have a different 'nature' (different objectives and goals), which explains the differences in the parameters across countries. These findings show that part-time work has a positive effect only in Southern European countries. In these countries, in fact, part-time jobs are characterised by higher job protection and social benefits than in the rest of Europe, and have very similar characteristics to full-time jobs (more permanent positions with higher hourly wages) than elsewhere. Social transfers, on the other hand, have a significant effect on the probability of working only in France and the UK but not in Italy. The composition of social transfers is quite different across countries: in France and the UK family benefits are a greater component of public transfers, while in Italy they consist mainly of pensions.

It is important to know whether Italian or British women would have the same fertility and labour force participation rate as the French, if they had the same incentives as the French. We do not in fact know whether they choose to have different social policies as a result of having different preferences concerning work and children. However, different institutions may themselves depend on cultural differences across countries. According to the well-known research by Heckman (1978), institutional choices may reflect preferences, and by ignoring this endogeneity one may obtain strongly biased estimates of the 'causal' effect of institutions on outcomes. The example he gave concerned the effect of state-based anti-discrimination laws on measured racial inequality in labour market outcomes. If more 'progressive' states are more likely to enact such laws, the effect of extending them to 'non-progressive' states would be expected to be considerably less. In the Northern European countries, generous social policies are likely to reflect collective preferences towards equality both across and within households. In the Southern European countries, the lack of social policies may, instead, be attributable to the persistence of a central role of the family in providing services and support with implications of unequal household allocation

For example, the low availability of childcare as well as part-time work in the Southern European countries also depends on the values that the families attach to the care of the younger children.[3] On the other hand,

---

[3] Evidence from the World Values Survey shows a high variability in attitudes regarding the use of childcare and attitudes regarding mothers' work. A larger number of parents in

the lower proportion of family-related transfers in total expenditure in social transfers across countries depends on the central role of the family that traditionally provides social and financial support to its members. The role of the extended family is very important in Southern Europe where it represents an important support in the case of both children and the elderly.[4]

Del Boca *et al.* (2006) using ECHP data have explored the reasons underlying different sets of institution and analysed the impact of social policies on women's participation and fertility using a statistical model that allows its potential endogeneity to be taken into account.

5.4.4   *Outcomes for children and social policies*

The analysis of social policies designed to increase participation rates and fertility still neglect their important effects on outcomes for children, in terms of both welfare levels and cognitive results.

Policies encouraging fertility, for example, have potential negative implications that have to do with the family 'types'. If child benefits are relatively small, only families among lower income and lower education groups will be affected by them. This may imply a negative impact on children's welfare and greater income inequality across families. Public policies directed to encourage female employment instead may also have the positive effect of reducing inequality in household income distribution and may also result in a more equitable distribution of resources and welfare within the household (Del Boca and Pasqua 2005).

Ermisch and Francesconi (2005) consider the impact of a mother's employment during childhood on the child's well-being, focusing on the trade-offs between her time spent in nurturing the child and household income. They find some empirical evidence that, while the loss of the mother's childcare time has a negative effect on the child's well-being (e.g. socio-emotional adjustment and cognitive outcomes), it is also the case that the additional income from the mother's employment has positive implications for expenditures on goods consumed by the child. These effects vary across countries and across family types, so the net impact of a mother's employment on the child's welfare can be expected to vary across national environments as well.

Southern Europe report that pre-school children are likely to suffer because their mother works. This proportion varies from 18% in Denmark to 80% in Italy and Spain.

[4] Croda and Gonzales-Chapela (2005) show that grandmothers in Southern European countries take care of the grandchildren more often than grandmothers in the North European countries.

Family policies have then to be oriented to favour *both* fertility and women's employment. So, what alternative policies positively affect fertility without discouraging labour market participation of women? Several examples concern in-kind policies (affordable childcare, after-school care, lower prices for children's goods and flexible schedules), as well as incentives to share the costs of childrearing (i.e., parental leave options for both parents). Many questions on 'what is a good policy' still remain unanswered. To evaluate what is a 'good policy' (given a specific target), a social welfare function that evaluates all costs to society (also including who pays for the policy) is needed.

5.5   Conclusion

In this chapter, we have presented important empirical evidence regarding recent trends in women's participation and fertility in European countries, and discussed and interpreted several differences across countries. We surveyed the literature that focuses on the joint decisions of labour market participation and fertility, and explores the impact of social policies. The results of most analyses indicate that social policies have a very relevant role in reducing the incompatibility between employment and child-rearing. Several open questions concerning the relevance of culture, the role of husbands' time in household production, and the effects of social policies on outcomes for children are the objectives of important ongoing research.

Table 5.A.1 *Studies on motherhood and participation: data sources and results*

Authors	Country	Data	Results
Apps and Rees (2004)	OECD countries	OECD	Countries which have individual rather than joint taxation, and which support families through childcare facilities rather than child payments, are likely to have both higher female labour supply and higher fertility
Del Boca (2002)	Italy	Bank of Italy Panel	Childcare and part-time work increase both participation and fertility
Del Boca and Sauer (2006)	Italy, Spain, France	ECHP Panel	Employment is more persistent in countries where less part-time work and childcare is available
Del Boca et al. (2005)	Italy, France, UK	ECHP Panel	Part-time work has a positive effect on participation and fertility only in Italy; social transfers have a significant effect only in France and the UK
Del Boca and Pasqua (2005)	Italy, NL, France, Spain, Denmark	ECHP Panel	Childcare has a positive effect on participation and fertility. Part-time work has a positive effect on participation. Unemployment has a negative effect on participation
Di Tommaso (1999)	Italy	SHIW (Bank of Italy)	An increase in female wages reduces the probability of having children and increases the probability of participation

Table 5.A.1 (*cont.*)

Authors	Country	Data	Results
Francesconi (2002)	US	NLS of young women (1968–91)	Work interruptions due to childbirth affect participation (differences between part-time and full-time work)
Hotz and Miller (1988)	US	PSID	Parents cannot perfectly control conception, variations in childcare costs affect lifecycle spacing of births
Laroque and Salanié (2005)	France	Labour Force Survey	Child benefits significantly affect fertility decisions
Moffit (1984)	US	NLS of young women	An increase in female wages reduces the probability of having children and increases the probability of participation

Notes: OECD = Organisation for Economic Co-operation and Development; ECHP = European Community Panel; SHIW = Survey on Household Income and Wealth; PSID = Panel Study of Income Dynamics; NLS = National Longitudinal Survey.

Table 5.A.2 *New directions: culture, time use outcomes for children*

Authors	Country	Data	Results
Apps and Rees (2005)	Germany, Italy	ABS, TUS; GSOEP	Lifecycle time use and consumption decisions of households are determined significantly by public policy (e.g. affordable childcare)
Esping-Andersen et al. (2005)	Denmark, Spain	ECHP Panel	Men's contribution to household production encourages fertility in Denmark, while in Spain it has no significant role
Ermisch and Francesconi (2005)	Britain	BHS	Women's employment negatively affects children's cognitive development but this is less so for part-time work
Del Boca et al. (2006)	15 countries	ECHP Panel	Social policies (childcare and part-time work) have an important effect on participation but do not reject endogeneity
Fernandez and Fogli (2006)	US	US Census	Female LFP and TFR in 1950 by country of ancestry are economically and statistically significant in explaining how much women work and how many children they have
De Laat and Sevilla (2006)	31 countries	ISSP94	Heterogeneity in egalitarian attitudes across all households explains fertility differences of up to 0.87 children
Berman et al. (2006)	31 countries	ISSP and WDI	Fertility is affected by the set of services provided by the religious institution
Algan and Cahuc (2006)	19 OECD countries	ISSP and WVS	Family attitudes are highly correlated with the employment rates of the different demographic groups

Notes: ABS = Australian Bureau of Statistics; TUS = Time Use Survey GSOEP = German Socio-Economic Panel; BHS = British Household Survey; ECHP = European Household Panel; ISSP = International Social Survey Programme; WDI = World Development Indicators; WVS = World Value Survey.

References

Aaberge, R., U. Colombino and S. Strom 1998. 'Evaluating alternative tax reforms in Italy with a model of joint labour supply of married couples', *Structural Change and Economic Dynamics* 9, 415–33.

Ahn, N. and P. Mira 2002. 'A note of the relationship between fertility and female employment rates in developed countries', *Journal of Population Economics* 14 (Spring), 667–82.

Algan, Y. and P. Cahuc 2006. 'The root of low employment in Europe: family culture?, Discussion paper IZA 1683.

Angrist, J. D. and W. N. Evans 1998. 'Children and their parents labor supply: evidence from exogenous variation in family size', *American Economic Review* 88(3): 450–77.

Apps, P. and A. Rees 2004. 'Fertility, taxation and family policy', *Scandinavian Journal of Economics* 106: 745–63.

  2005. 'Time use and the costs of children over the life cycle', in D. Hamermesh and G. Phann (eds.), *The Economics of Time Use*, 206–36, London: Elsevier.

Arroyo, C. R. and J. Zhang 1997. 'Dynamic microeconomic models of fertility choice: a survey', *Journal of Population Economics* 10 (Spring), 23–65.

Baizán, P., F. Billari and F. Michielin 2002. 'Political economy and the life course patterns', *Demographic Research* 6: 189–240.

Bardasi, E. and J. C. Gornick 2000. 'Women and part-time employment: worker 'choices' and wage penalties in five industrialised countries', *ISER Working Paper* 2000–11.

Becker, G. 1991. *A Treatise on the Family*, Cambridge, MA: Harvard University Press.

Berman, E., R. Iannaccone and G. Ragusa 2006. 'From empty pews to empty cradles: fertility decline among European catholics', University of San Diego, mimeo.

Bloemen, H. G. and A. Kalwij 2001. 'Female labor market transitions and the timing of births: a simultaneous analysis of the effects of schooling', *Labour Economics* 8 (5), 593–620.

Bratti, M. 2001. 'Labour force participation and marital fertility of Italian women: the role of education', *Journal of Population Economics* 16 (3), 525–54.

Carliner, G., C. Robinson and N. Tomes 1980. 'Female labour supply and fertility in Canada', *Canadian Journal of Economics* 13 (1), 46–64.

Cigno, A. 1991. *Economics of the Family*. Oxford: Oxford University Press.

Colombino, U. and M. L. Di Tommaso 1996. 'Is the preference for children so low or is the price of time so high?', *Labour* 10 (3), 475–93.

Craig, L. 2006. 'Do time use patterns influence fertility decisions? A cross-national inquiry', *International Journal of Time Use Research* 3 (1), 60–87.

Croda, E. and J. Gonzales-Chapela 2005. 'How do European older adults use their time?', in A. Borsch-Supan, *Health, Aging and Retirement in Europe*, 265–71, Manheim: Manheim Research Institute of Aging.

De Laat, J. and A. Sevilla Sanz 2006. 'Working women, men's home time and the lowest low fertility', *ISER Working Paper* 2006–23.

Del Boca, D. 2002. 'The effect of childcare and part-time work on participation and fertility of Italian women', *Journal of Population Economics* 14: 549–73.

Del Boca, D. and S. Pasqua, 2005. 'Labour supply and fertility in Europe and the U.S.', in T. Boeri, D. Del Boca and C. Pissarides (eds.), *Women at Work: An Economic Perspective*, 126–53. Oxford: Oxford University Press.

Del Boca, D. and R. Sauer 2006. 'Lifecycle employment and fertility across institutional environments', Carlo Alberto Notebooks, Collegio Carlo Alberto, Moncalieri.

Del Boca, D. and D. Vuri 2006. 'The mismatch between labor supply and childcare', *CHILD Working Paper* 6–06.

Del Boca, D., S. Pasqua and C. Pronzato 2005. 'Employment and fertility in Italy, France and the UK', *Labour* 4: 51–77.

2006. 'Motherhood and employment choices with endogenous institutions', mimeo, Collegio Carlo Alberto.

Di Tommaso, M. L. 1999. 'A trivariate model of participation, fertility and wages: the Italian case', *Journal of Cambridge Economics* 23: 623–40.

Engelhardt, H. and A. Prskawetz 2004. 'On the changing correlation between fertility and female employment over space and time', *European Journal of Population* 20: 35–62.

Ermisch, J. 1989. 'Purchased childcare, optimal family size and mother's employment: theory and econometric analysis', *Journal of Population Economics* 2: 79–102.

2003. *An Economic Analysis of the Family*: Princeton, NJ: Princeton University Press.

Ermisch, J. and M. Francesconi 2005. 'Parental work and children's welfare', in T. Boeri, D. Del Boca and C. Pissarides (eds.), *Women at Work: An Economic Perspective*, 154–93. Oxford: Oxford University Press.

Esping Andersen, G., M. Guell and S. Brodman 2006. 'When mothers work and fathers care: joint household fertility decisions in Denmark and Spain', Pompeu Fabra University, Barcelona.

European Economy 1995. 'Performance of the EU labour market: results of an *ad hoc* labour market survey', Brussels: European Commission B-1049.

Eurostat 1999. *Demographic Statistics*. Brussels.

2002a. *New Release Labour Force Survey*. Brussels.

2002b. 'Women and men reconciling work and family life', *Statistics in Focus*, Theme 3–9.

Fernandez, R. and A. Fogli 2005. 'Culture: an empirical investigation of beliefs, work, and fertility', *NBER Working Papers* 11268, National Bureau of Economic Research, Inc.

Fernandez, R., A. Fogli and C. Olivetti 2004. 'Mothers and sons: preference formation and female labor force dynamics', *Quarterly Journal of Economics* 119 (4): 1249–99.

Francesconi, M. 2002. 'A joint dynamic model of fertility and work of married women', *Journal of Labor Economics* 20 (2, part 1), 336–80.

Gauthier, A.H. and J. Hatzius 1997. 'Family policy and fertility: an econometric analysis', *Population Studies* 51: 295–306.

Goldin, C. 2006. 'The quiet revolution that transformed women's employment, education, and family', 2006 Ely Lecture, American Economic Association Meetings, Boston, MA, *American Economic Review* 96 (2): 1–21.

Gustafsson, S. and C. Wetzels 2000. 'Optimal age at first birth: Germany, UK, the Netherlands and Sweden', in S. Gustafsson and D. E. Meulders, *Gender and the Labour Market*, 188–209, London: Macmillan.

Gustafsson, S., E. Kenjoh and C. Wetzels 2002. 'Postponement of maternity and the duration of time spent at home after first birth: Panel Data Analyses comparing Germany, Great Britain, the Netherlands and Sweden', *Public Finance and Management* 2 (2).

Gustafsson, S., C. Wetzels, J. D. Vlasblom and S. Dex 1996. 'Women's labor force transition in connection with childbirth: a panel data comparison between Germany, Sweden and Great Britain', *Journal of Population Economics* 9 (3), 223–46.

Gutièrrez-Domènech, M. 2002. 'Job penalty after motherhood: a Spanish case in a European context', Family Friendly Policies Conference IZA, May, Bonn.

Heckman, J. 1978. 'Dummy endogenous variables in a simultaneous equation system', *Econometrica* 46 (4), 931–59.

Hotz, V. J. and R. A. Miller 1988. 'An empirical analysis of life cycle fertility and female labour supply', *Econometrica* 56 (1), 91–118.

Klerman, J. A. and A. Leibowitz 1994. 'Labour supply effects of state maternity leave legislation', in F. D. Blau and G. Ronald (eds.), *Gender and Family Issues in the Workplace*, 65–85, New York: Russell Sage Foundation.

Laroque, G. and B. Salanié 2005. 'Does fertility respond to financial incentives?', *C.E.P.R. Discussion Papers* 5007.

Moffit, R. 1984. 'Life cycles profile of labour supply and fertility', *Review of Economic Studies* 51: 263–78.

Mroz, T. A. 1987. 'The sensitivity of an empirical model of married women's hours of work to economic and statistical assumptions', *Econometrica* 55 (4): 765–99.

OECD 1999, 2001. *Employment Outlook*.

Rosenzweig, M. R. and T. P. Schultz 1985. 'The demand for and supply of births: fertility and its life cycle consequences', *American Economic Review* 75 (5): 992–1015.

Rosenzweig, M. and K. I. Wolpin 1980. 'Life cycle labour supply and fertility: causal inferences from household models', *Journal of Political Economy* 88 (2): 328–48.

Ruhm, C. J. and J. T. Teague 1997. 'Parental leave policies in Europe and North America', in F. D. Blau and G. Ronald, *Gender and Family Issues in the Workplace*, 133–56, New York: Russell Sage Foundation.

Sleebos, J. 2003. 'Low fertility in OECD countries', *OECD Social Employment and Migration*. OECD No. 15, Paris, OECD.

United Nations 2000. *Development Programme*, United Nations Publications, New York.

6   The timing of maternity

Siv Gustafsson and Eiko Kenjoh

6.1   Introduction

This chapter focuses on explaining the timing of maternity, trying to answer the question: When does a young woman decide to become a mother? What conditions have to be present? Del Boca and Locatelli in Chapter 5 of this volume focus on the interrelatedness of fertility and female labour force participation. For example, they ask: What is the relationship between participation and fertility decisions? What effects do childcare characteristics have on the number of children a woman has and on the probability of her remaining at work as a mother? The question 'When?' is not addressed in their work, but is instead the central question in this chapter.

Decisions about investment in human capital, how demanding a career to aspire to, how many children to have, are interdependent when considering how to spend one's time in order to achieve these various life goals. Among the pioneer models, those of the economics of fertility focused on decisions about family size. These models were static, taking the whole married life of the couple as one period (Becker 1960; Willis 1973). Later models of fertility have recognised the intrinsic dynamic character of fertility decisions. But, in spite of that, for example, the Hotz *et al.* (1997) review on fertility models spends only one and a half pages on the timing of maternity.

The facts are, as we shall see in the following section, that first-time mothers in Europe have never before been as old as they are now, and that this postponement of maternity is also causing total fertility rates to decline. The decline of European fertility rates is partly a decomposition effect and only partly due to the complete family size becoming smaller. Even if all women were to have two children, in a period when the age at maternity is increasing, we will observe falling total fertility rates.

We will try first to answer the question: Why do women and men delay family formation in Europe? This question is important for at least three reasons. First, it will contribute to the prediction of fertility trends.

Second, as ageing of maternity increases, a number of women will hit the biological limit of their reproductive capacity, leading to increasing medical costs as couples seek medical assistance in order to procreate, or individual unhappiness if such assistance fails. Third, many European governments worry about below-replacement fertility and the resulting ageing of the population and are attempting to design policies that would make it less costly for young people to form families.

In this chapter we first review the facts on birth timing in section 6.2 and then we discuss a number of issues related to birth timing in section 6.3. The issues related to the decision on when to start a family include other lifecycle events associated with having the first child. These issues include discussions on, and a review of research about, leaving the parental home, marriage markets and the decision to move in together, the length of education and its effect on the timing of maternity and the labour market conditions and individual labour market success as a determinant for the timing of maternity (Appendix Table 6.A.1 summarises the most important results of these studies). Finally, a more technically oriented section on the econometrics of birth timing is included.

6.2   The facts

The total fertility rate (TFR) is computed from age-specific birth rates in a given year. The information that one needs to compute the TFR is the number of births that take place in a given year, the age of the new mother, and the number of women in each age category in the same year. The TFR is interpreted as the average number of children that a woman would have during her life if the age-specific fertility rates prevailed during her fecund life (usually, age 15–49). The TFRs are widely available and most countries provide yearly statistics on them. Thus when fertility is discussed in the press, this is in most cases based on the TFRs. The advantage of the TFR is that it includes the most recent fertility development. In other words, the TFR makes use of the information on the fertility of women who are now in their twenties and thirties and are currently starting families. On the other hand, it does not record the fertility of actually completed family size.

The completed or cohort fertility rate (CFR) is a different measure which records the actual life-time fertility of women who are old enough not to have any more children. The CFR records birth events that have already taken place. Therefore, it does not have to project that women who are now 20 years old will have a similar birth behaviour in ten years' time as women who are now 30 years old. The main disadvantage in working with CFRs is that one cannot use data on women who are

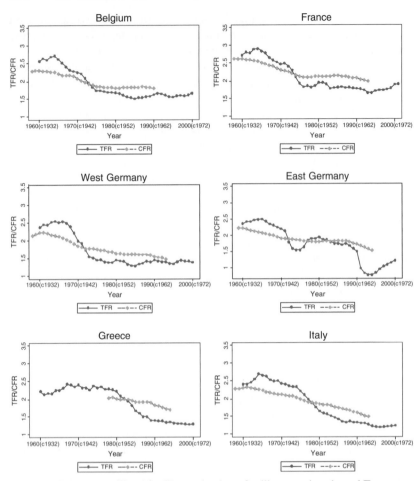

Figure 6.1a Total fertility and cohort fertility rates in selected European countries
Source: Council of Europe (2002), *Recent Demographic Developments in Europe.*

still in their fecund years. One must wait until the women become 45–50 years old.

Figures 6.1a and 6.1b depict the TFRs and CFRs in selected European countries. Each graph presents both the TFRs from 1960 onwards and the CFRs for female birth cohorts from 1930 onwards for each country. The years for the CFR curves are shown within parentheses. They correspond to the years for the TFR when the birth cohort turns age 28: for example, year 1960 for the TFR indicates birth cohort

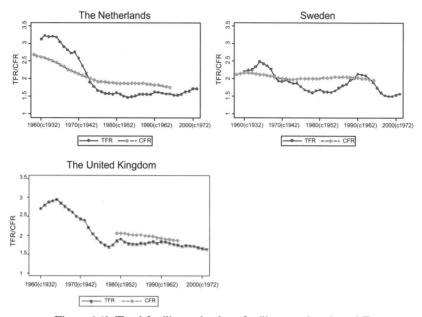

Figure 6.1b Total fertility and cohort fertility rates in selected European countries
Source: Council of Europe (2002), *Recent Demographic Developments in Europe.*

1932 for the CFR. The CFR for birth cohorts of women who are still at their reproductive age in the last year observed are estimated by the Council of Europe based on the most recent fertility data available. We use age 35 instead of the more correct age 45 as the age at which we consider fertility to be completed. This is done because we want to show more younger cohorts.

As we can see in the graphs, both the TFRs and CFRs have decreased during these forty years. We can also find that the TFRs are more variable than the CFRs. In the 1960s the TFRs in most of the countries in the graphs recorded around 2.5 children per woman, whereas in 2000 the lowest TFR was 1.24 in Italy followed by 1.29 in Greece. Compared with this sharp drop in the TFRs, the CFRs declined more gradually. In Italy, for example, the CFR decreased from 2.28 for women born in 1935 to 1.49 for women born in 1965. Among the countries we study here, France and Sweden had the highest CFRs in 2000. The CFR curves are around two children per woman for all the birth cohorts in the graphs in these countries. While the Swedish CFR curve shows a rather stable movement, the TFR curve strongly fluctuates. More particularly, the TFRs in 1965 and in 1990 are much higher than those in adjacent years. This suggests that there may have been period-specific effects that influenced fertility decisions (for related discussions, see, e.g. Kohler 1999).

When the CFR curve is at a higher level than the TFR curve, in general younger cohorts of women are having their children at a later age than older cohorts of women did. The decline in the TFRs can be decomposed between the tempo effects or postponement of mother-hood and the quantum effects or the decreases in family size. Removing the tempo effects from the TFRs, the tempo-adjusted period fertility rates, or estimates of the completed cohort fertility associated with currently observed TFR levels, are calculated (Bongaarts and Feeney 1998; Bongaarts 1999; Kohler and Philipov 2001; Kohler *et al.* 2002 Lesthaege and Willems 2002). For instance, Kohler *et al.* estimate the tempo-adjusted fertility rates for several countries in two three-year periods in the early to mid 1980s and mid-to-late 1990s.

Their rates show, for example, for Italy (1994–96) and Spain (1996–98), that the TFRs averaged 1.19 and 1.15 children per woman, respectively, whereas the tempo-adjusted fertility rate was 1.43 and 1.67, respectively. The tempo-adjusted fertility rates were higher than the observed TFRs. In other words, postponement of motherhood is an important factor in the recent low fertility, especially in 'the lowest-low fertility' countries with fertility rates below 1.3.

In Figures 6.2a and 6.2b the mean age of the mother when she gives birth to her first child is shown year by year from 1960 to 2000 for selected European countries. From around 1970 or 1975 there is a steady increase. First-time mothers were on average 24–25 years old in 1970, whereas they were 27–29 years old in 2000. This means that younger cohorts have postponed motherhood in comparison to older cohorts.

In Table 6.1 we have computed the proportion of women who are still childless, for some European countries. This table gives us additional information on the timing of motherhood: (1) fertility patterns of all women including not only women who have had children but also women who do not yet have children; (2) the age distribution of the timing of motherhood; and (3) an indication of ultimate childlessness. The table shows the proportion for two cohorts of women: an older cohort born in 1940–54 and a younger cohort born in 1955–69.

Table 6.1 shows that there is postponement of the first birth between the younger and the older cohort except for East Germany. In the UK, for example, by age 24, 50% of the women in the older cohort had given

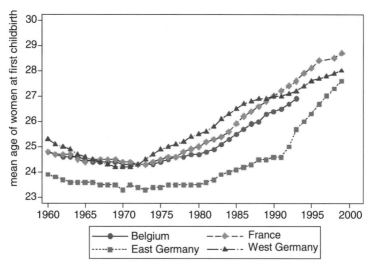

Figure 6.2a Mean age of women at birth of the first child
Source: Council of Europe (2002), *Recent Demographic Developments in Europe.*

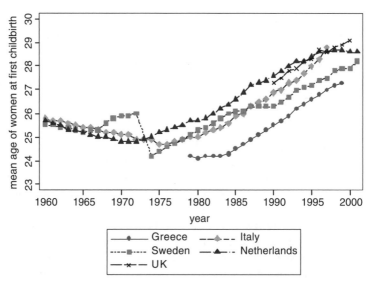

Figure 6.2b Mean age of women at birth of the first child in selected European countries
Source: Council of Europe (2002), *Recent Demographic Developments in Europe.*

Table 6.1 *Percentage of childless women for selected European countries according to age*

	UK	West Germany	East Germany	Netherlands	Sweden
Women born in 1940–54					
20	82	83	74	90	81
24	50	50	34	59	48
28	28	30	18	23	24
32	18	20	12	11	15
36	14	16	10	8	11
Women born in 1955–69					
20	84	90	73	94	88
24	60	70	29	71	61
28	41	44	13	42	38
32	28	29	8	24	21
36	22	22	8	18	12

Note: Figures in the table indicate the Kaplan-Meier estimates of not giving birth to the first child at women's ages 20, 24, 28, 32 and 36.
Source: Own computations, based on Kenjoh (2004: Fig. 5.1).
Primary source: BHPS 1991–98 for the UK; Sample A of GSOEP 1984–96 for West Germany; Sample C of GSOEP 1984–96 for East Germany; OSA 1985–96 for the Netherlands and HUS 1984–98 for Sweden.

birth to their first child, whereas 60% of those in the younger cohort were still childless. Since we know that very few women become first-time mothers after the age of 36 (although in recent years the proportion of first-time mothers aged 37 and older has increased, the proportion of childless women at age 36 could be interpreted as an indication of the proportion of women who are likely to remain childless). Table 6.1 shows that in the UK at age 36 among the older cohort of women only 14% of the women did not have a child, while for the younger cohort this proportion had increased to 22%. Similar increases in the proportion of women childless at age 36 occurred in West Germany and the Netherlands, whereas in Sweden and East Germany there was hardly any change between the two cohorts in the proportion of childless women at age 36.

Because the TFR is computed on the basis of age-specific fertility rates, the postponement of maternity results in decreases in the TFR even if the CFR were to remain constant. In Figure 6.3 we show the correlation between the increase in the mother's age at first birth during the period 1990–2000 and the TFR in 2000. There is a negative correlation between the two variables: correlation coefficient $= -0.5833$, p-value $= 0.0055$, for twenty-one countries. This indicates that those countries that had the

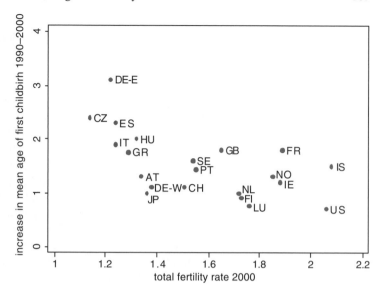

Figure 6.3 Correlation between increase in mean age at first birth and total fertility rate

Note: The abbreviations indicate the following countries. AT: Austria, CH: Switzerland, CZ: Czech Republic, DE-E: Former GDR, DE-W: FRG before unification, ES: Spain, FI: Finland, FR: France, GB: The United Kingdom, GR: Greece, HU: Hungary, IE: Ireland, IS: Iceland, IT: Italy, JP: Japan, LU: Luxembourg, NL: The Netherlands, NO: Norway, PT: Portugal, SE: Sweden, US: The United States.

Source: Own computations based on the following data. Council of Europe (2002), Recent Demographic Developments in Europe. Japan's Ministry of Health, Labour and Welfare (2002), Vital Statistics. United States' Bureau of Census: www.census.gov/ipc/www/idbconf.html and United States' National Center for Health Statistics (2002), 'Mean Age of Mother, 1970–2000,' National Vital Statistics Reports, 51(1), www.cdc.gov/nchs/births.htm.

largest increase in the mother's age at first birth were also those with the lowest TFRs.

East Germany, after being reunited with West Germany in 1990, has shown a rapid increase in age of the mother when having her first child, while the TFR has decreased. A similar development has taken place in other Central and East European countries after the fall of the Soviet Union. Of these countries, the Czech Republic and Hungary are included in Figure 6.3. Moreover, the South European countries of Spain, Italy and Greece are among the countries with the largest increases in the mother's age at first birth and the lowest TFRs. In the lower-right-hand corner of Figure 6.3, of the countries with a small increase in the mother's age at first birth during the 1990s and a relatively high TFR, we find the US, Norway, Iceland and Ireland.

6.3   Issues

The decrease in fertility rates, and the increasing age of women at maternity are the results of individual decisions on when to make the transition from the state of being childless to the state of being the mother of one child. An individual goes through many such demographic transitions during his or her lifecycle. For example, a young person must make a decision on when to leave the parental home, when to leave full-time education to enter the labour market, when to marry or cohabit and with whom, when to have the first child and possible successive children. More lifecycle events come later, such as decisions on whether to stay married or get divorced, whether to work until age 65 or retire early. However, in this chapter we will not look at events that most likely occur after a woman is a first-time mother.

The economic approach to explaining the timing of lifecycle events is to view them as the outcome of a constrained utility maximisation problem. If a young adult receives higher utility from living apart from his/her parents, he/she will move out of the parental home. The individual makes every period a cost-benefit analysis. If the benefits exceed the costs of living apart, the young person will move out of the parental home. Benefits are thought of as including psychic benefits, and the financial benefits can be negative if the psychic benefits are large enough. The psychic benefits of marrying include love, companionship and sex, in addition to the opportunity to start a family.

There are always opportunity costs to consider. For example, a young adult living in his/her parental home may have more money to spend on ski vacations and travelling. A childless couple can spend their time differently than they could as a family with children. Eating out and going to concerts are less compatible with caring for young children. Children cost childcare time. Parents cut back on their career ambitions and pay for childminders, childcare centre or nursery school fees. The opportunity costs of having a child include earnings forgone and investments in human capital not carried out. The opportunity costs can be lower by choosing a point in the lifecycle when, for example, intended full-time education has been completed and a good job has been secured which includes the opportunity of parental leave with a job-protected leave period which is perhaps paid. In addition to the intertemporal budget constraint, there is also a biological constraint because the fecund period of a woman is limited. Very few first children are born to women after the age of 35. In the following, we will review some of the issues which can be raised in the study of the timing of maternity.

6.3.1   Leaving the parental home

If young adults begin living independently from their parents at a later age, they may also be older when they have their first child. According to economic theory, young adults will leave their parental home when the utility of living apart exceeds the utility of living with their parents. A recent textbook (Ermisch 2003) compares a model of selfish parents to a model of altruistic parents. The adult child can be asked to contribute to housing costs or can receive a transfer from the parents. The parents can dictate the choice of moving out by manipulating the size of the transfer. How large this transfer will be depends on the utility function of the parents and how rich they are relative to their adult child. A transfer to the child is likely to be made if the parents have an altruistic utility function and are sufficiently rich. Depending on housing prices, other things being equal, and the adult child's own utility from each living arrangement, such a transfer may be large enough for the child to move out of the parental home. Parents may also only make a transfer to their child if the child lives apart. When the child's own income increases relative to that of his parents, he can be asked to contribute more to the parent and child joint housing costs, or he can move out.

There is a relatively large demographic literature on leaving the parental home, which is reviewed by Billari *et al.* (2001). Among the explanations that demographers have promoted are the cross-country unequal paths to individualisation, institutional characteristics, religion and family culture, in addition to economic resources.

Billari *et al.* (2001) have computed the median age at leaving the parental home, using Fertility and Family Surveys (FFS) carried out in the early 1990s in various countries. They focus on cohorts born around 1960. Their results, based on Kaplan–Meier estimates from the country-specific FFS data, are presented in Table 6.2.

In Italy, the median age of young males is 26.7 years when they move out. At the other extreme, Swedish males move out when they are 20.2 years old. Also among women, Italy has the oldest parental home leavers and Sweden has the youngest ones. Leaving the parental home is often a joint decision, which coincides with either starting higher education or moving in together as a couple into consensual cohabitation or marrying.

Billari *et al.* (2001) compute the proportion of young adults who leave their parental home before they have completed their full-time

Table 6.2 *Median age at leaving home in selected European countries (cohorts born around 1960)*

	Women	Men
Austria	19.9	21.8
Belgium	21.5	23.3
Czech Republic	21.2	23.8
East Germany	20.6	22.4
Finland	19.8	21.7
France	19.8	21.5
Hungary	21.3	24.8
Italy	23.6	26.7
Latvia	21.3	24.1
Lithuania	19.8	20.3
Netherlands	20.5	22.5
Norway	19.8	21.4
Poland	22.5	25.8
Portugal	21.8	24.3
Slovenia	20.5	20.9
Spain	22.9	25.7
Sweden	18.6	20.2
Switzerland	19.2	21.5
United Kingdom	20.3	22.4
West Germany	20.8	22.4

Note: Data represent exact ages (with decimal points).
Source: Adapted from Billari *et al.* (2001).
Primary data: Computations by Billari *et al.* based on Fertility and Family Surveys carried out during the early 1990s in the various countries.

education. Because the data are retrospective lifecycle data, one can compute the sequence of the timing of the events. Indeed, in those countries where leaving the parental home occurs at a younger age, this transition to a greater extent takes place before finishing education. In Finland 67% of young women and in Sweden 72% leave their parental home before they finish formal education. The corresponding proportions for Spain and Italy are 16% and 15%, respectively. In Spain and Italy, it is very common to leave the parental home when marrying, while Swedish and Finnish young people move out long before they marry. Again, there are huge country differences. In Spain 73% and in Italy 72% of young women leave their parental home at first marriage, whereas this is the case for only 3% of Swedish and 5% of Finnish women. However, when including unmarried cohabitation, the differences narrow somewhat to 31% of Swedish and 40% of Finnish women. The majority of the Swedish and Finnish women and men move out as

Table 6.3 *Pathways to the first child*

	Women born before 1960	Women born in 1960 and later
Netherlands		
HMK	56.0	28.7
HCMK	6.9	27.3
HCK	1.1	6.2
HCACMK	0.6	2.4
HAMK	14.2	5.0
HACMK	11.4	14.7
HACK	1.0	4.0
Other pathways	8.8	11.7
Total	100.0	100.0
Japan		
NPEMK	90.8	90.8
Other pathways	9.2	9.2
Total	100.0	100.0

Note: H = living at parental home; A = living alone; C = cohabiting; M = married; K = birth of first child; N = no partner; P = has met a partner; E = engaged.
Source: Adapted from Matsuo (2003).
Primary sources: Computations by Matsuo based on the 1998 Netherlands Fertility and Family Survey and the 1992 Japanese National Fertility Survey.

singles, and spend some portion of their young adult life living alone. One of the reasons for the large differences between countries is due to the way higher education is organised. If higher education is available geographically across a country, it is easier for students to continue living with their parents.

Matsuo (2003) using the Dutch Fertility and Family Survey, and a similar data set for Japan, computes the sequencing of pathways to the first child. Her main results are shown in Table 6.3. In the Netherlands, the younger cohort leave the parental home to start unmarried cohabitation rather than marriage to a much greater extent than the older cohort. In Matsuo's study, living in the parental home, 'H', is followed by cohabiting, 'C', more often for the younger cohort in Table 6.3, but marriage precedes the birth of the first child for an overwhelming majority of the women of the younger cohort: namely, married, 'M', precedes the birth of the first child, 'K'.

In Japan the traditional pattern of engagement and marriage before having a child is followed by 90.8% of Japanese women of both the younger and the older cohort. Unmarried cohabitation hardly occurs in Japan, at least there is no increase when comparing the younger cohort to the older cohort. The Japanese data do not inform us whether there was a period of living alone as a single person preceding engagement and marriage.

It seems likely that a person who waits a long time to leave the parental home will also be older when starting a family. However, there is no direct correlation, since one can leave the parental home at an early age to live alone or in a childless cohabitation relationship for an extended period. A woman's decision to leave the parental home, finish education, move in together with the potential father of her child and the actual timing of motherhood can occur widely apart. Although Matsuo's research gives interesting results on the sequencing of life events, it does not provide information either on the timing of the included life events or on the causes for different timing across individuals in a country and across countries.

6.3.2   *Marriage markets and assortative mating: who marries whom?*

Economists have theorised on spouse selection, on who remains single and on search in the marriage market. The pioneering work by Gary Becker (1973) and Becker *et al.* (1977) already contained the main elements. Formal textbook presentations are given in Cigno (1991) and Ermisch (2003), whereas the papers collected in Grossbard-Shechtman (2003) give reviews of recent empirical and theoretical results on marriage and the economy. Every woman who wants a child will try to find a man who is good enough to live with and good enough to be the father of her child. Therefore, search in the marriage market precedes having the first child, and late marriages will then most likely lead to late first births. Unmarried cohabitation has become common, and in many cases it is like a test marriage, while in other cases it is an alternative to marriage. In this section unmarried cohabitation and marriage are treated as synonyms and the decision under study is the decision by a woman to move in together with a man. The basic idea is that there is search on the marriage market, an idea adopted from theories of search on the labour market. A woman will accept a marriage offer rather than continue searching if her expected utility of marrying that particular man is larger than her expected utility of continuing to search and perhaps find a more attractive man. This search process includes a perception of what is a good match.

Becker (1973) theorised that, by marrying, a man and woman together produce a marital output, which is not available to them as singles. This marital output contains love, affection, sex and the opportunity to start a family. When a woman, searching in the marriage market, thinks about what characteristics she would wish to find in her future husband, these characteristics will be either complementary to her own or will substitute for characteristics that she lacks. Complementary characteristics will lead to positive assortative mating, that is, the more the woman has of that characteristic, the more she will want the man to have the same characteristic. The result is that 'likes marry like', for example, highly educated women marry highly educated men. There is strong evidence of positive assortative mating on education. Mare (1991) finds that there have been five decades of educational assortative mating in the United States.

Blossfeld and Timm (2003) have collected papers from studies of thirteen countries on the question 'Who marries whom?' Table 6.4, compiled from the various chapters, shows the proportion of newly married women who had equal education levels to their husbands, and the proportion whose education was lower. The category left out is the brides who have a higher education than their grooms. There is a wide variation between the countries included. The country-specific educational categorisation used by the researchers differs in terms of the number of education levels that are distinguished. The probability of being at an equal education level is larger, other things being equal, the fewer the categories that are distinguished.

The number of categories distinguished varies between three and five over the countries. In six of the eleven countries included in Table 6.4, more than 50% of the couples born around 1960 and thus marrying in the 1980s and 1990s have an equal level of education: namely, Hungary, West Germany, Italy, Netherlands, Spain and the USA. Most of the brides, who are not as well educated as their husbands, have lower education and thus marry upwards. However, this is not the case in France and Flemish Belgium where the left-out category is larger, so that brides having higher education than grooms is more common than the reverse. Looking over time at the development of the proportion of educationally homogenous marriages, some countries show a decreasing trend: Hungary, Italy, Spain and the UK, while Sweden has a U-shaped development, and Germany an increasing trend. The strongly increasing proportion of homogenous marriages in Germany is due to the fact that women used to have significantly lower education than men but are catching up with men in the younger cohorts.

When, among older cohorts, the majority of both men and women are less educated and the educational expansion initially benefits men more than women there will be decreasing proportions of homogenous marriages. When women catch up with men later the proportion of marriages with equally educated couples increases again. In Table 6.4, men in

Table 6.4 *Education level of brides compared with that of grooms (percentage)*

	Equal			Lower		
	Cohorts born around:			Cohorts born around:		
	1920	1940	1960	1920	1940	1960
France		47.7	38.2		13.4	28.3
Flemish Belgium		37.0	38.0		40.0	23
Hungary	73.4	65.5	61.5	17.1	13.1	13.9
West Germany	43.9	58.1	70.0	52.1	36.1	21.6
Italy	71.2	59.7	58.2	4.0	16.4	20.3
Netherlands		43.0	55.0		31.0	23.0
Slovenia	45.9	50.0	48.8	44.3	33.3	30.0
Spain	93.2	82.5	66.8	6.0	13.6	17.0
Sweden	55.5	41.3	44.7	28.5	30.8	32.0
UK	43.7	42.0	37.2	36.8	37.0	39.4
US	60.8	47.2	51.4	26.5	38.0	27.4

Note: Number of education levels: 5: Slovenia, Flemish Belgium, 4. UK, Sweden, US, Netherlands, France; 3: Spain, Italy, Germany.
Cohorts: Birth year of the bride (unless specified otherwise below). France: 1939–43 and 1959–63; Flemish Belgium: 1940–49 and 1960–69 cohort refers to the groom's birth year; Hungary: first married in years 1950–59, 1970–79 and 1980–92; West-Germany: 1919–23, 1939–43 and 1959–63; Italy: 1918–27, 1938–47 and 1958–67; The Netherlands: 1940–47 and 1956–63; Slovenia: 1920–29, 1940–49 and 1960– and later; Spain: 1920–24, 1940–44 and 1960–64; Sweden: first partnerships cohorts born 1915–39, 1940–54 and 1955–73. UK: 1924–33, 1944–53 and 1954–63; US: 1921–25, 1941–45 and 1961–65.
Source: Compiled by the authors from Blossfeld and Timm (eds.), (2003), various chapters.

Italy and Spain are in the process of gaining increased access to higher education while catching up by women is not yet visible. For Sweden, Table 6.4 shows men's advantage between cohorts born in 1920 and 1940 and women catching up in the cohorts born in 1940 and 1960, while for West Germany over the whole period this table shows women catching up.

Gustafsson and Worku (2006) have studied the education composition of couples in Sweden and the UK based on the British Household Panel Study (BHPS) and the Swedish Household Market and Non-Market Activities data (HUS, from Hushållens ekonomiska levnadsförhållanden). In this study, 'medium' education is determined as corresponding to US high school and is equal to A-level education in the UK and 'studentexamen' in Sweden. This education takes twelve to fourteen years from starting school. A shorter period of education is

Table 6.5 *Percentage of never-married women and men by education and age in West Germany*

	Women			Men		
	High[a]	Medium[b]	Low[c]	High[a]	Medium[b]	Low[c]
20	97	76	73	98	94	96
24	69	35	34	80	57	57
28	40	19	15	48	28	35
32	27	11	10	28	16	24
36	20	8	6	16	10	19

Notes:
[a] Professional college qualification (Fachhochschule) and university degree.
[b] Lower secondary school qualification (Hauptschule) with vocational training; middle school qualification (Mittlere Reife) with vocational training; higher secondary qualification (Abitur) without vocational training; and higher secondary school qualification (Abitur) with vocational training.
[c] Lower secondary school qualification (Hauptschule) without vocational training; and middle school qualification (Mittlere Reife) without vocational training.
Source: Adapted from Blossfeld and Timm (2004).
Primary source: German Socio-Economic Panel, Waves 1984–94.

labelled 'low education' and a longer period 'high'. Gustafsson and Worku found that 59% of couples who were living together and had at least one child together were educationally homogenous.

Even if everyone regards education of the spouse as a complementary attribute that increases marital output for a given level of education of oneself, perfect assortative mating (i.e., everyone marrying someone with the same education), will only result if there are equal numbers of men and women on the marriage market (Becker 1981: ch. 4; Cigno 1991; ch. 1). If there is positive assortative mating and unequal numbers on the marriage market the 'lowest' quality of the redundant sex remain single (Becker 1981: 78).

Table 6.5, adapted from Blossfeld and Timm (2003), shows the number of women and men according to educational level who remain single in West Germany. The last column of this table shows that at age 36 women with high education and men with low education are most likely to remain single. The results of Table 6.5 seem to run counter to Gary Becker's prediction, but there is more to his theory of marriage. The marital output, which is the total improvement for the two spouses in comparison to their premarital status, can be divided in any arbitrary way between the spouses. Then, if a woman of lesser 'quality' is willing to give a larger share of the marital output to her husband than a higher 'quality' woman would do, the lower-'quality' woman wins the competition. This will be the case if the high-education woman has a good quality of life already while single. She will not enter a marriage where her personal benefit will be lower as a married woman than her benefit while single. The highly educated women are according to this theory not willing to give enough of the marital output in order to get married. Another interpretation of this result is that men prefer to marry women with less education than themselves in order to keep control of power in the relationship more easily. The data in Table 6.5 also show that men are older at marriage than women, which may also be interpreted as a reason for men wishing to control power, but it can also be the result for greater pressure on men than on women to have a high enough income before marriage.

For the level of wages, Becker (1981) predicts negative assortative mating because a high-earning man would prefer a woman who takes care of the household, a role for which a high-earning woman would not be a candidate. This prediction receives little empirical support, the case is rather that high-wage men marry high-wage women. The reason for negative assortative mating with respect to wages, according to Becker (1973), is that a woman who spends much of her life in paid work earns a higher wage because of on-the-job investment in human capital, but this time use limits her use in household production and investment in household human capital. Therefore, high-wage women are poor homemakers and high-wage men want good homemakers but care less about their wife's market earnings.

Lam (1988) introduces utility from a household public good as well as the production of the household public good into his model. A household public good is defined as giving utility to the husband without decreasing its utility to the wife. Examples are the welfare of the joint children, a comfortable and beautiful home, pleasant vacations, and enjoying good meals together. Lam (1988) shows that while the production of the public good tends to lead to negative mating with respect to wages the utility from the public good tends to lead to positive assortative mating with respect to wages because persons with similar incomes share similar preferences in consumption. In this way, there are two opposing effects and if the consumption outweighs the returns to division of work, there will be positive assortative mating on wages. Gains to division of work decrease if good market substitutes, such as buying home cleaning services, catering and restaurant meals, and childcare, can be found.

Public policies such as Swedish childcare subsidies, paid and job-protected parental leave, and tax systems that benefit the dual-earner family decrease gains to division of work (Gustafsson 1992; Gustafsson and Stafford 1992).

6.3.3   Marriage markets and the proportion of single people

The tendency for men to be two or three years older than their brides has been taken as indicating men's preference to be the older partner (Bergstrom 1997), perhaps because it will give them a bargaining advantage within marriage, or perhaps because they have an educational plan which is longer than the educational plan of women or perhaps because the social pressure on men to be able to provide financially for a family is greater, so they have to wait until that is achieved. If men want to be two years older than women, fluctuations in the fertility rate cause fluctuations in the sex ratio defined as M_t/F_{t+2}, where M_t is the number of men born in year t, and F_{t+2} is the number of women born two years later. Bergstrom and Lam (1989) exploit variations in the Swedish fertility rate to predict the number of marriages in any given year. Marriage markets can be constructed by region (Ono 2002), by race, as is done in several US studies cited by Brien and Sheran (2003), or by education, as in the studies collected in Blossfeld and Timm (2003). The literature on the marriage market has focused on the availability of marriageable men.

Table 6.6 shows age at marriage and the percentages of births out of wedlock. In general, the proportion of births out of wedlock is highest in the Nordic countries: Denmark, Norway, Sweden and Iceland. These countries also have a higher age at marriage in general. Note that, because most of the countries report age at marriage rather than age at first marriage, countries with a high frequency of remarriages will also report a higher age at marriage.

Actually, age at first birth is lower in Sweden than age at marriage. The wedding party no longer marks the young woman's transfer from the parental home to her adult life. Young couples may wait to marry and give the wedding party only when they can afford to give a big one. Legislation has changed accordingly. The default case is that both biological parents have joint custody of their child. Children out of wedlock inherit from both their parents on equal grounds with children in a marriage. There are no tax or other advantages for a couple to choose married cohabitation rather than unmarried cohabitation.

In a recent paper, Angrist (2002) uses variation in immigrant flows into the USA from the censuses of 1910, 1920 and 1940 to create sex ratios of different ethnic groups. The motivation is that more than half of all

Table 6.6 *Age at marriage and out-of-wedlock childbearing in developed countries*

	Average age at marriage, 1991–97		% births out of wedlock, 1994–98
	Women	Men	
Australia	27	29	23
Austria	26	29	30
Belgium	25	28	18
Canada	26	29	37
Denmark	30[a]	32[a]	45
Finland	29	32	37
France	28	30	40
Germany	28	30	19
Greece	25	29	4
Iceland	30	32	64
Ireland	28	29	30
Italy	27[a]	30[a]	9
Netherlands	28	31	21
New Zealand	27	29	41
Norway	29	31	49
Spain	26	28	12
Sweden	31	33	55
Switzerland	27	30	9
United Kingdom	26	28	38
United States	25[a]	26[a]	32

Note: [a] *Average age at first marriage.*
Source: Brien and Sheran (2003).
Primary source: The World's Women 2000: Trends and Statistics.

marriages take place within the ethnic group, i.e. ethnically homogamous marriages. Because new immigrants were predominantly men, the sex ratio, defined as the number of men aged 20–35 divided by the number of women aged 18–33 in the same ethnic group, was on average 1.29 in 1910, 1.22 in 1920 and 1.15 in 1940. He then studies the effects on the second generation (p. 25):

Estimates using variation among immigrant groups provide strong evidence for a reduced form of relationship between sex ratios and a range of characteristics related to second generation family structure and economic circumstances. Higher sex ratios are associated with higher marriage rates for both men and women, lower female labor force participation, and higher spouse and couple income. The effects on women are much larger than those for men, though the results for men are consistent with the view that higher sex ratios cause men to marry sooner and try to become more attractive to potential mates.

A marriage of a woman from a high sex ratio group also produces more children (Angrist 2002: Table 5). The Angrist (2002) study does not try to explain the timing of marriage and motherhood, but uses a static model to explain the frequency of marriage and motherhood.

6.3.4   Education and the timing of maternity

The decision on how long to study and what to study is a decision about investment in human capital. An individual will continue studying as long as the benefits of future increased earnings exceed the costs of another period of study. The most important costs are earnings forgone by being in education rather than in work. The founding fathers of human capital theory, Becker (1964) and Mincer (1962, 1974), hypothesised that women would invest less than men in labour-market-related human capital because they expect to have children. However, recently, younger cohorts of women have been studying for at least as long as men. Freeman (2000) shows that the female to male ratio of receiving Bachelors' and Masters' degrees was 1.2 in 1995 in the USA. In France, in 1993 the female to male ratio of receiving a post-Baccalauréat degree was 1.2 (Goux and Maurin 2003: Table 4.3). In the UK, on the other hand, in 1993, among cohorts born in 1964–73 the proportion of men who had a university education exceeded the proportion of women (Chan and Halpin 2003: Table 8.11).

UNESCO (2002) presents estimates on expected duration of education for males and females currently in education for a number of countries and a number of years.[1] These numbers show an increased duration of formal schooling for both men and women for all included countries during the period 1970 to 1995. The Gustafsson, Kenjoh and Wetzels (2002) study, based on household panel data, show increasing age at leaving full-time education for younger cohorts in the UK, Germany, the Netherlands and Sweden. Over thirty years, comparing women born in 1930–39 with those born in 1960–69, the time that women spend in school increased by between 1.2 and 2.8 years in these countries.

This overwhelming evidence of increasingly well-educated women, together with the observation that, across countries, the correlation between female labour force participation and fertility has turned from

---

[1] This statistic is computed as follows: $E(S)_t = \sum_{i=a}^{n} (S)_{it}$, where $E(S)_t$ school life expectancy in year t is the sum of age-specific enrollment ratios S_i at all levels of education for the years t that countries have delivered workable data. Countries have to report data by single year of age and by gender for both the population in school and the population of school age not in school in order to make it possible to compute this statistic. For more explanations and the data, see Gustafsson (2006).

Table 6.7 *Mean age at first childbirth of 1990s mothers, according to education in selected European countries*

	High education	Medium education	Low education
UK[a]	29.2	25.5	24.2
West Germany[b]	29.8	29.2	26.4
East Germany[b]	26.0	23.8	23.3
Netherlands[b]	30.7	28.0	26.6
Sweden[a]	29.8	26.1	25.5

Note: [a] 1990–98; [b] 1990–96.
'High education' means that the highest educational level attained by each of the women normally requires longer than 14 years of schooling. Similarly, 'medium education' requires between 12 and 14 years of education; and 'low education' requires less than 12 years of education.
Source: Table 5.3 of Kenjoh (2004).
Primary source: Computations by Kenjoh based on BHPS 1991–98 for the UK; Sample A of GSOEP 1984–96 for West Germany; Sample C of GSOEP 1984–96 for East Germany; OSA 1985–96 for the Netherlands and HUS 1984–98 for Sweden.

negative into positive (Del Boca and Locatelli: Figure 5.1 in this volume) calls for a reconsideration of the economic theory of fertility. In our view, women want both children and a career just like men, rather than trading off a wish for a child in favour of a job-market career.

We noted in Section 6.2 above that total fertility rates are decreasing as age at maternity is increasing, and that completed or cohort fertility decreases much less than one would think looking at the period total fertility rates. For example, in Sweden (see Figure 6.1b above), there is no tendency for completed fertility to deviate much from two children per woman. However, the question is whether the younger cohorts who delayed parenthood in European countries will catch up in order for replacement fertility of two children per woman to be achieved.

Table 6.7 shows that the average age of maternity is higher the higher the education of the mother. This is in line with the idea that a woman chooses the timing of motherhood to minimise life-time earnings loss. Wetzels (2001: ch. 7) exploits this idea and calculates life-time incomes from Dutch data for different birth timing decisions by making use of the fact that later birth timing because of the convex age-earnings curve entails less human capital investment forgone. On the other hand, later birth timing means a higher current wage forgone. The results are that it is economically always better to wait. Gustafsson and Wetzels (2000) also supply similar calculations for Germany, the UK and Sweden. A woman with a less ambitious job market career plan has less to gain by a careful timing decision because her prospective age-earnings curve will be less steep.

There are three main reasons why highly educated women are most likely to postpone motherhood. First, being in school may be less compatible with having children because of lack of adequate income to pay for childcare and other costs, or because the student lifestyle does not fit with family responsibilities. It follows that, since highly educated women stay longer in school, they will have children later.

Second, after finishing school, high-education women may spend more time seeking employment and engaging in career planning. Age-earnings curves of more highly educated people rise more quickly than age-earnings curves of less-educated people, and for all educational groups the first years after finishing education show more steeply rising wages than later on in life. This has been shown for many countries since the pioneering work of Mincer (1974), who interprets the steepness of the age-earnings curve as effects of investments in on-the-job training that, in addition to schooling, increase a person's human capital. In general, there is a positive correlation between schooling and job investments, which results in the steeply rising wages of highly educated people. It is therefore costly to leave a job and spend time caring for a child, not only in the short run because of income loss but also in the long run because of forgone investments in job training (see also Wetzels, Chapter 7, this volume).

The third reason why highly educated women postpone maternity longer is that they may have a different attitude. A woman who discontinues education at an early age may make a family plan and fit in labour market work only if there is time left after the needs of the children. By contrast, a highly educated woman is more likely to make a career plan and think carefully about when her career would suffer least from a career break or part-time employment. There is reason to believe that the proportion of 'career-aware' women increases in relation to education.

Table 6.8 presents the timing of the first birth according to education by focusing on the proportion of childless women at a given age. Such figures were computed in Table 6.1 separately for older and younger cohorts, while this table provides the information according to educational levels for the recent cohort. The last line which shows childless women at age 36 gives an indication of ultimate childlessness as explained earlier. The numbers show that childlessness at age 36 is much more frequent among high-education women than among lower-education women. For instance, in the UK, West Germany and the Netherlands, the proportion of childless among highly educated women is 38%, 27% and 26%, respectively, whereas the corresponding figures

Table 6.8 *Proportion of childless among women born 1955–69 at a given age in selected European countries (in percentages)*

	UK	West Germany	East Germany	Netherlands	Sweden
High education					
20	96	98	95	100	96
24	86	88	49	93	85
28	70	72	22	73	61
32	52	38	6	40	30
36	38	27	6	26	15
Medium education					
20	93	98	83	97	93
24	73	89	28	78	69
28	47	57	11	47	42
32	31	35	7	26	26
36	29	28	7	20	18
Low education					
20	76	87	63	88	81
24	47	64	24	55	45
28	28	36	11	26	22
32	18	27	8	15	14
36	14	21	8	12	9

Note: Figures in the table indicate the Kaplan-Meier estimates of not giving birth to the first child at women's age 20, 24, 28, 32 and 36. High education means that the highest educational level attained by each of the women normally requires longer than 14 years of schooling. Similarly, medium education requires between 12 and 14 years of education and low education; requires less than 12 years of education.
Source: Own computations based Kenjoh (2004: Figs. 5.1–5.5).
Primary source: BHPS 1991–98 for the UK; Sample A of GSOEP 1984–96 for West Germany; Sample C of GSOEP 1984–96 for East Germany; OSA 1985–96 for the Netherlands; and HUS 1984–98 for Sweden.

among low-educated women is considerably lower: namely, 14%, 21% and 12%, respectively. In Sweden and East Germany, on the other hand, there are hardly any differences according to education in the proportion of women who do not have a child at age 36.

In all countries there are educational differences in the proportion of childless women at age 28 and age 32, implying that highly educated women are older when they have their first child. In addition, the age at which highly educated women become mothers is rather early in East Germany. However, since reunification in 1990 fertility rates in East Germany have fallen dramatically and it now has a similar education fertility pattern to that of West Germany (Kreyenfeld 2004).

Blossfeld and Huinink (1991) study the timing of the first birth by separating the effect of being in school by means of a time varying explanatory variable in addition to level of education. Gustafsson, Kenjoh and Wetzels (2002) extend this approach to a cross-country comparative study using welfare state theories to explain country differences. Using household panel data from the UK, Germany, the Netherlands and Sweden, Gustafsson, Kenjoh and Wetzels estimate two Cox proportional hazard models: on the duration since age 15 until giving birth to the first child and the other on the duration since leaving education. The results of the former duration model show that having higher levels of education implies that maternity comes later. The effects are strongest in the UK and the Netherlands, whereas no significant effect of education is detected in East Germany. The second duration model of time since full-time education has finished shows no differences according to education. This suggests that time spent in education is very important. The results differ in size by country. Among the four European countries, the former East Germany and Sweden, where family policy helps to make work and family more compatible, show smaller educational differences in maternity timing and ultimate childlessness. By contrast, in the Netherlands, West Germany and the UK, strong educational differences are detected with respect to these variables. In these countries, approximately a quarter of highly educated women born between the 1930s and the 1970s are childless at age 36.

Kreyenfeld (2006) and Kantorová (2006) examine the effects of education on fertility timing in Germany and the Czech Republic, respectively. Institutions before unification in East Germany and during the state-socialist period in the Czech Republic were characterised by policies that assumed that mothers were full-time workers, therefore they had paid maternity and parental leave and access to subsidised childcare. However, after 1990 the policies in these countries have become less focused on helping mothers to combine family life with labour market demands and full-time jobs. Kreyenfeld analyses recent German data and compares the West German sample with the East German sample by a piecewise constant event history model. She splits the samples into births that took place before unification and births after unification. She finds that before unification there were no educational differences in the probability of entry into maternity between East Germany and West Germany, where university-trained women enter maternity much later. Kreyenfeld, like Blossfeld and Huinink (1991) and Gustafsson, Kenjoh and Wetzels (2002), uses a time-varying being-in-school variable and finds, like the previous studies, that both in East and West Germany women are very unlikely to become mothers before they have finished their studies. After unification, similar educational differences in maternity timing appear in both East Germany and West Germany.

Kantorová (2006) notes that, after 1990, women who had university education would be confronted with similar opportunity costs of having children, as in western market economies. As shown in Figure 6.3 above, the Czech Republic in 2000 had the lowest fertility rate among the countries considered and the increase in the mother's age at the first birth has been very rapid since 1990. Kantorová presents two possible explanations of the sharp decline in fertility and long postponement of maternity in the 1990s in the Czech Republic. First, the opportunity costs of having children increased, which would mostly affect women with higher education, second, the transition period has been characterised by economic hardship, which would mostly affect the less-educated people. She concludes that there is little support for the hardship hypothesis. Those who changed their fertility patterns the most were the highly educated women. These women postponed their first birth not only until they had finished their education, but also until several years later, allowing for a period of post-school investment. The less-educated women postponed their first births the least in comparison with similarly educated women in the state-socialist period. Fertility dynamics in the Czech Republic are therefore becoming more like those of Western European countries.

With reference to Greece, Symeonidou and Mitsopoulpos (2003) analyse the duration from age 15 to first childbirth, from first to second childbirth, and from second to third childbirth. They find that women's highest level of education has a negative effect which is strongest for the first birth, then smaller for the second birth, and negligible for the third birth. They also include the husband's education level in their estimation, and also find a negative effect on the first birth, that is, the longer the duration of the husband's education the older is his wife when having their first child.

Bratti (2006) analyses female labour force participation and marital fertility in Italy. He finds that increasing education up to the upper secondary level has a positive effect on marital fertility and that highly educated women both postpone fertility and have a higher labour market attachment around childbirth. Note that only marital fertility is selected, so that marital fertility is analysed. This leaves out the possible effects of education on the births that take place among unmarried cohabiting couples. These are, however, not as many in Italy as in the Nordic countries (Table 6.6 above). In addition, Bratti finds that increasing the husband's income has a negligible effect on the woman's labour force participation and fertility.

Naz *et al.* (2006) study the effect of education on completed fertility in Norway for women born in 1955, estimating one variant of a count data method. They find that in an analysis where the wife's education is included as an explanatory variable but the husband's education is not, highly educated women have more children than less-educated women. This result is at odds with results from other earlier studies that show highly educated women have fewer children than less-educated women. Such studies have often included all women with a particular type of education rather than only married women. If highly educated women are more likely to remain single (or choose cohabitation without legal marriage), the finding that married highly educated women have more rather than fewer children may not be in contrast to these earlier results. The interesting result in the Naz *et al.* study now appears to be that when entering the husband's education in addition to the wife's education, wife's education ceases to be a significant explanatory variable and, instead, the husband's education explains the number of children that a Norwegian married couple has at the time when the woman is 40 years old. Another way of expressing this result is to say that comparing two women with the same education, the one whose husband has higher education will have more children. This looks like an income effect: because highly educated men earn more, they have more children.

6.3.5   *The labour market and the timing of maternity*

A given investment in human capital will give less expected returns in a severe labour market situation with high unemployment rates than in a situation where it is easy to find a job. When deciding about the timing of parenthood, a young couple will consider the probability of having a job and the income likely to be earned in the years to come. Del Boca and Locatelli (Chapter 5, this volume) show that the correlation between female labour force participation and fertility across countries has changed from negative to become positive. Furthermore, they point out that fertility is lower in countries where unemployment is higher. Adsera (2004) finds that youth unemployment rates, other things being equal, lower fertility rates.

Having access to panel data makes it possible to analyse the timing sequence of the correlation between fertility and labour force participation because the same individuals are interviewed a number of times. We can decompose the correlation into studying, first, the effect of labour force participation in a given year on the probability of having a child in the next year and, second, the effect of having a child in a given year on labour force participation next year. Ahn and Mira (2001) find that the most important variable to determine marriage among Spanish men is that they had a job the previous year. Once they marry, fatherhood follows very quickly. De la Rica and Iza (2006) find that the widespread use of fixed-term employment contracts is one of the explanations for the low fertility rate in Spain. A man who did not work in a given year is less likely to marry in the next year, and also a man who has a fixed-term job contract is less likely to marry than a man who has an open-ended job contract. They also find that married women are less likely to have a child in the next year if they have a fixed-term job contract than if they have a regular open-ended job contract. Becoming a mother in a given year may lower labour force participation in the next year. The mothers' labour force behaviour around the first childbirth is the topic analysed by Gustafsson *et al.* (1996), Wetzels (2001), Kenjoh (2004, 2005) and Bratti *et al.* (2003).

In Figure 6.4 the proportion of women at work by month is shown from 12 months before the first birth until 60 months later when the child is 5 years old. The data of Figure 6.4 includes the same woman at different points in time. Women are selected for the sample because they have a first birth during the panel period, which differs between the household panel studies across the countries included (see Figure 6.4, note). Because we have panel data, we can create this graph by looking at the same woman's labour force status from 12 months before delivery (month 0) to her child's 5th birthday (month 60). In all five countries, a majority of the women were in paid employment one year before they had their child. The countries included differ in the length of maternity and parental leave allowed and the generosity of compensation during leave. Germany, followed by Sweden, has the most mothers at home when the child is 1 year old. Sweden, followed by the Netherlands, has the most mothers at work when the child is 5 years old. The Dutch and Japanese data do not supply information to separate between being at work and being employed so that the sharp drop at month 0 observed in Sweden and West Germany when new mothers take maternity and parental leave is absent in the curve representing the Netherlands and Japan.

Labour force behaviour around childbirth differs according to the education level of the mother. In Table 6.9 the predicted probability that the mother does not work when the child is 36 months old is shown using table 3.7 from Kenjoh (2004). Not working when the child is 3 years old is substantially more common among less-educated women than among highly educated women in the UK, West Germany and the Netherlands. In Sweden and Japan there are hardly any educational differences but the proportion of women not working is substantially larger in Japan than in Sweden.

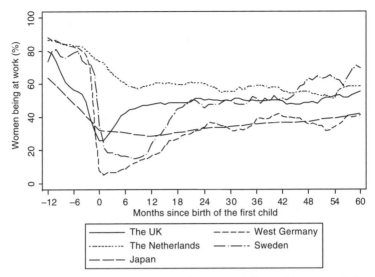

Figure 6.4 Proportion of women who are actually working around the birth of their first child (for births occurring in the 1990s)

Note: The data for, West Germany, the Netherlands, and Sweden are based on information on monthly employment status. For Japan, the data present respondents' main employment status on a yearly basis. Thus, for that country, '−12' indicates 1 year before first childbirth and '0' indicates year of the childbirth, and '12' indicates 1 year after childbirth etc. The Dutch and Japanese data also include women who are on leave.

Source: Own computations based on Kenjoh 2005: Figures 1.1–5.2.

Primary source: BHPS 1991–98 for the UK; Sample A of GSOEP 1984–98 for West Germany; OSA 1985–98 for the Netherlands; HUS 1984–98 for Sweden; and JPSC 1993–97 for Japan.

Although we do not have similar data for the Southern European countries, there is some evidence that the problem is different in Italy and Greece. Symeonidou and Mitsopoulpos (2003) conclude that Greek women either have to continue working through childbearing, pregnancy and care for their very young child or leave the job permanently. The proportion leaving their job after giving birth is 67% among first-child mothers and 77% among second-child mothers. The data come from the Greek Fertility and Family Survey of 1999 of women 18–49 years, and the average number of children is close to two for the cohorts included, although decreasing: 2.2 for women aged 45–49, and 2.0 and 1.9 for women aged 40–44 and 35–39, respectively.

Del Boca (2002) and Del Boca *et al.* (2003) study the effects of access to childcare on mother's employment in Italy. Bratti, Del Bono and Vuri (2005) study labour force status after first childbirth in Italy. They show

Table 6.9 *Predicted probability that the mother does not work when her first child is 3 years old.*

	High education	Medium education	Low education
UK[a]	0.30	0.34	0.45
West Germany[a]	0.46	0.60	0.57
Netherlands[b]	0.22	0.39	0.54
Sweden[a]	0.35	0.38	0.34
Japan[b]	0.62	0.60	0.62

Note: [a] not at work; [b] not employed.
Based on multinomial logits of household panel data for each country (BHPS, GSOEP, OSA, HUS, JPSC) last wave included 1998, 1997 for Japan. Prediction assumptions: Births in the 1990s, no second child, mothers are aged 28 at their first childbirth, unemployment rate average over the observation period stated in Kenjoh (2004) for each country, no grandparents living in the household for Japan.
Source: Kenjoh (2004: Table 3.7).
Primary source: Computations by Kenjoh based on BHPS 1991–98 for the UK; Sample A of GSOEP 1984–98 for West Germany; OSA 1985–98 for the Netherlands; HUS 1984–98 for Sweden; and JPSC 1993–97 for Japan.

that the mothers' labour force participation rate is almost the same, when the child is 12, 24 and 36 months old given that a woman had at least one spell of labour force participation before childbirth the sequence is 68%, 67% and 66%, respectively. The dependent variable is being in the labour force rather than being at work. Bratti *et al.* find a high correlation between women's pre-marital employment and motherhood employment in Italy. Having a regular job contract before marriage has positive effects on mothers' employment at 12, 24 and 36 months after childbirth. Women's education, pre-marital work experience and work in the public sector increase the probability that women will continue to work after having children.

All in all, there is substantial evidence from many studies that women decrease their work for pay when they become mothers, and couples with children therefore have less income. This decrease in income has given rise to the family wage gap literature reviewed by Wetzels (in Chapter 7, this volume). Kalwij (2006) analyses how much income is lost in the transition from being a childless two-person household into becoming a three-person household when a child is born. Using the Dutch socio-economic panel, he is able to follow income, savings and consumption from year to year. It turns out that the childless couple foresees to some extent that their household income will decrease. Hence, they save more before having a child, but by no means enough to keep the same consumption standard as before they had the child. The three-person household consumes less than they did when they were a two-person household. Given that there is an income loss due to labour force withdrawal to care for a young child, it is no wonder that young people today try to minimize that income loss by starting their family at a point in time when the loss would be smaller. Most women draw the conclusion that postponing maternity until the most important human capital investments have been made in education, as well as on the job market, will make them better off. Amuedo-Dorantes and Kimmel (2006) ask whether it pays to postpone maternity. They find that college-educated women in the USA who had their first child after they turned 30 earn more than similarly educated women who had their first child before they were 30.

6.4   The econometrics of the timing of maternity

There are two basic approaches to dynamic fertility modelling: the hazard model approach (Heckman and Walker 1990), and the dynamic stochastic discrete choice models (Wolpin 1984). Gustafsson and Kalwij (2006) discuss the advantages and disadvantages of these two approaches. Both methods aspire to model lifecycle fertility. Both methods put large demands on the data. Data have to cover the whole fecund life of a woman and her husband and there has to be information on the history of education, labour market behaviour and wages, in addition to birth and marital histories. Both methods require programming skills from the researcher and cannot be estimated using standard statistical packages. Both methods have only had a handful of followers.

The Wolpin (1984) method runs by backwards recursion and maximises a utility function for each period. The analyst knows what decision the woman will take in period $t+1$ because he has data on the whole lifecycle fertility. The values of the explanatory variables in period t are also known from the data. Therefore, we can estimate the parameters of a utility function for period t. This makes the Wolpin method *a structural model* because the parameters of the constrained utility maximisation problem are estimated. On the other hand, the Heckman and Walker (1990) method is *reduced form* because it estimates the effects on fertility decisions from exogenous variables without specifying a utility function. The estimated parameters for values of the explanatory variables in period t cannot be interpreted as increases in the utility of having a child in time period $t+1$.

The structural character of the Wolpin method is one of its weaknesses because one has to assume a specific form of the utility function, for which there is no guidance in economic theory. Furthermore, this form has to be simple because of computational tractability. The computations are already very complicated with a simple utility function. Another problem with the Wolpin method is that data on recent cohorts of women who are currently in their childbearing period cannot be used, since one needs to know the full fecund period, and the included women must therefore be about 45 years old. When there are big changes between generations in childbearing behaviour, the behaviour of 45-year-old women when they were 25 may not tell us very much about the behaviour of women who are currently 25 years old. This problem is not present in the Heckman and Walker method because they can also use incomplete lifecycles in their system of hazards analysis.

Another problem with these types of ambitious models is that it is extremely difficult to find exogenous variables. An ideal econometric model on the timing of parenthood should use exogenous variation in all past, current and expected future prices that have an impact on the choice of when to have a child. Hotz *et al.* (1997) summarise their review on the econometrics of fertility:

As is true of much applied economics, the theory and econometric methods are much better developed than the empirical literature. The crucial challenge is to find plausibly exogenous variation in proxies for the price and income concepts appearing in the theories.

Of course, a woman who thinks about how much she will work in the next year must take her two children as exogenous to her labour supply decision, because the children are already there. The analyst aspires to explain why she has two children rather than one, or why she had them at ages 22 and 26 rather than at ages 32 and 36. Her labour supply can not be taken as exogenous to that decision. The econometrician distinguishes between predetermined variables and exogenous variables. In explaining the lifecycle labour force participation of a woman, her two children, which she has at time period t, are predetermined to her labour supply at time period $t + 1$, but they are not exogenous to her full lifecycle labour supply.

Some econometricians think that the truly exogenous variable is unobserved by the econometrician, but not by the woman. This unobserved variable is the woman's 'child mindedness'. A woman with a high degree of 'child mindedness' will be willing to forsake more of her job market career. On the other hand, having an ambitious job market career will make it profitable for a woman to delay motherhood until she has finished her education and established herself on the labour market (Gustafsson, 2001).

Recently, econometricians have increased their ambitions about being able to draw causal conclusions from their estimations. In the 1970s, causality was seen in the following way: by statistical methods one can estimate the correlation between two variables, but one cannot say anything about causality. There could be a correlation between the rainfall in a Swedish summer and the number of lions in a South African national park, but because there is no theory there is no causality. If, on the other hand, we find a correlation between education and earnings, because the human capital theory predicts that education is producing earnings capacity, we would be allowed to draw the conclusion that education causes higher income.

Today, econometricians think that if they estimate a structural model, that is a model which is derived from economic theory, and find truly exogenous variation in the explanatory variables, they have estimated a causal relation. However, for this to be the case, the sample must not be selected with respect to the endogenous variable, such as using only women who have at least one child for the estimation of lifecycle fertility. In such an estimation the estimated coefficients will suffer from *endogeneity bias*.

Also, one must have access to all relevant variables, such as the husband's earnings, otherwise there will be an *omitted variables bias*. But if one selects only married or cohabiting couples in order to get the husband's earnings, the estimated coefficients will suffer from *selection bias*.

It is very likely that any econometric work on lifecycle fertility will err on some of these requirements, and the econometrician will have to trade off endogeneity bias, sample selection and omitted variables bias against each other and the information available in the data.

Much econometric research energy has been spent on developing techniques to correct for sample selection and endogeneity bias. To correct for sample selection bias, one should in principle first estimate the probability of being in the selected sample, as suggested by Heckman (1979) for estimating female labour supply in a cross-section. To correct for endogeneity, one should try to find exogenous variables that are correlated with the explanatory variable but not with the dependent variable. Such exogenous variables are known as 'instrumental variables'. A stringent econometric analysis is very often poor in information about the problem analysed and the fear of using explanatory variables which are likely to cause some kind of bias results in underutilisation of the information which is actually available.

A different way of thinking about causality is to use only predetermined explanatory variables (Blossfeld and Huinink 1990; Blossfeld and

Timm 2003). The idea is that an event that occurs before another event can be said to cause the second event, but the reverse can never be true. This kind of causality thinking is related to Granger causality (Granger 1969, 2005). Another solution to the problem is to use situations that can be referred to as 'social experiments' for the estimations. Examples are increases in the number of years of compulsory school at a given point of time, the fall of the Soviet system, the adoption of a child by a couple who are not its biological parents and therefore have no genetic influence on the child's outcomes whereas their socio-economic and socialisation behaviour may have a large impact. Many researchers accept a less stringent causality concept such as the one that the early econometricians used. The reason for that is to be able to theorise about the likely effects of institutional changes on a particular correlation and be able to use information on institutional changes in the discussion of research results.

6.5   Conclusion

In this chapter we have reviewed research about the timing of maternity and other life events that precede this life event. What conclusions can we draw that will guide a government worried about the ageing of the population that follows from the low fertility rates? To a great extent, the decrease in fertility rates in European countries is caused by young adults delaying family formation in comparison with older cohorts. The observed decrease in total fertility rates therefore exaggerates the decrease in expected completed fertility. However, as our graphs on completed or cohort fertility rates show, family size has decreased for women who are now 35 years old compared with women who were 35 years old thirty years ago. There is an unknown possibility that fertility rates will increase so much at ages over 35 that completed fertility rates at age 45 are now less different between generations. However, many women will become infertile before they and their husbands are ready to start a family.

Young couples need to have enough resources before they can start a family. In Spain, for example, housing markets and labour markets make it more difficult for young people to afford their own housing. The most important determinant for a man to marry in year t is if he had a job at year t-1. But this is not enough. The use of fixed-term labour contracts rather than regular open-ended contracts creates insecurity about future earnings and delays family formation until an open-ended labour contract has been secured. It is costly to start a family. A three-person family after a child has been born to a couple consumes less than they did when they were a two-person household without a child. The main reason is that the woman's market earnings decrease. But this is not what the couple plans for.

These days, women are more ambitious and want to have their own income and a fulfilling labour market career. Today, many marriages are not lifelong. In the face of increasing divorce rates, women are wise to invest in more human capital for themselves in order to increase their earning capacity. There are hardly any children born to studying parents, in spite of the fact that the labour market nowadays increasingly demands lifelong education. The family with small children in European countries is under severe pressure and needs an infrastructure where quality childcare to complement the parents' own care is easily available. Families must have sufficient income to purchase quality care and good quality food instead of the bad quality fast food that young families with low incomes tend to buy. There is also a need for household cleaning services and help to bring up the children.

It is a political challenge to turn all negative experiences that families with children have today into the joyful time that family life should be. This change must come, keeping in mind that women have equal rights with men. A return to the old times when women were tied to their home over many years is not a feasible situation, because it will not be accepted by women, and it will not increase fertility rates to alleviate the burden of ageing populations.

Table 6.A.1 *Review of recent studies on the timing of maternity*

Author(s)	Year	Country of study	Methodology	Findings
N. Ahn and P. Mira	2001	Spain	Proportional hazard on marriage and first birth conditional on marriage for men	• Spells of non-employment have a strong negative effect on the hazard of marriage. Part-time or temporary employment has a negative effect on the hazard of marriage. • Non-employment has an indirect effect on births through the delay of marriage.
C. Amuedo-Dorantes, and J. Kimmel	2006	USA	Hourly wage estimations by pooled OLS or fixed effects, controlling for selection into employment	• College educated mothers do not experience a motherhood wage penalty. Women who delayed motherhood in comparison with equally educated mothers who had children earlier in life earn substantially higher wages. Thus it is worth postponing having a child.
M. Bratti	2003	Italy	Multinomial logit on fertility and labour force participation	• Married women with higher education tend to combine work and have children to a greater extent than less-educated women. They also postpone motherhood more.
S. De la Rica and A. Iza	2006	Spain	Logit and hazard on marriage and first birth	• Having a fixed-term rather than an indefinite labour contract delays entry into marriage for men, but not for women, but a fixed-term contract held by a woman makes her delay motherhood.

Author	Year	Country	Method	Findings
S. Gustafsson et al.	2002	UK, Germany, Sweden, Netherlands	Cox proportional hazard on first birth	• Highly educated women become mothers later in their life in all four countries, especially in the UK and the Netherlands. • Small educational differences in the timing of maternity, and also find ultimate childlessness in Sweden and former East Germany.
S. Gustafsson and C. Wetzels	2000	West Germany, UK, Netherlands, Sweden	OLS on timing of first birth and simulations of present value of lifetime earnings loss of having the first child	• First births occur later the higher the mother's and father's respective levels of education. However, there is no evidence that having husbands with high incomes encourages earlier birth. A woman with higher education gains more than a woman with lower education by a careful timing decision.
S. Gustafsson and S. Worku	2006	UK, Sweden	Weibull hazard with individual unobserved heterogeneity	• Compared with Swedish women, British women are on average younger at finishing education, younger at entering a marriage or cohabitation. Once the couple is formed, however, British women are slower to have their first child.
A. S. Kalwij	2006	Netherlands	Conditional Euler equations on income growth and consumption growth	• Couples save more before having a child than after, which is in line with a consumption smoothing hypothesis. Couples with children consume less, not more than childless couples.
V. Kantorová	2006	Czech Republic	Event-history (generalised Gompertz) on first birth	• In the 1990s, the period between the completion of studies and entry into motherhood is prolonged, especially for university graduates. Greater education differentiation of labour market opportunities and constraints have brought about greater education differentiation in the timing of entry into motherhood.

Table 6.A.1 (*cont.*)

Author(s)	Year	Country of study	Methodology	Findings
E. Kenjoh	2004	Japan	Random effects model on hourly wage controlling for selection into employment and Cox proportional hazard on first birth	• Mother's hourly wage on average drops by 23–26 % at re-entry compared to continuous employment. A woman who holds an occupational certificate avoids one third of this wage drop. For high-educated women, those with an occupational certificate have higher conditional probability of having children than those without.
M. Kreyenfeld	2006	Germany	Piecewise constant-event history on first birth	• Compared with the situation before reunification, parenthood and educational participation is less compatible in present-day East Germany. The variation in the timing of the first birth caused by woman's education attainment has substantially increased after reunification in East Germany.
G. Naz *et al.*	2006	Norway	Restricted generalised Poisson regression	• Higher-educated married couples have more children than less-educated couples. This effect is primarily driven by the husband's education rather than the wife's education. For unmarried women, the relationship between education and fertility is negative, suggesting that these women suffer a more detrimental impact of motherhood on their careers than do married women.

C. O'Donoghue and E. O'Shea	2006	Ireland	Logit and decomposition of percentage age change in female fertility propensity	• The propensity of first births in 1994 in comparison to 1970 decreased mainly because female wages had increased and the proportion of time women spent in the labour market had increased but also because couples waited longer after marriage.
V. Skirbekk *et al.*	2006	Sweden	Regression on age at first birth with birth month dummies	• School leaving age has a strong effect on the timing of the first and second childbirths. For example, women born in December enter and leave compulsory school when they are 11 months younger than women born in January of the next calendar year. However, the former women have their first birth at an age which is 4.9 months younger than the latter women.
H. Symeonidou and G. P. Mitsopoulos	2003	Greece	Piecewise constant event history on first birth, first to second birth, and second to third birth.	• Greek women either stick to a job or leave work permanently. Women with stronger labour force attachment are less likely to make the transition to have (more) children. Younger cohorts postpone childbearing in comparison with older cohorts.
C. Wetzels	2001	Netherlands	Simulations of present value of lifetime earnings loss of having the first child	• Women with higher education postpone first birth more than women with lower education. The total lifetime earnings loss always decreases for later births in comparison with earlier births.

References

Adsera, A. 2004. 'The changing fertility rates in developed countries: the impact of labor market institutions', *Journal of Population Economics* 17: 17–43.

Ahn, N. and P. Mira 2001. 'Job bust, baby bust?: evidence from Spain', *Journal of Population Economics* 14: 505–21.

Amuedo-Dorantes, C. and J. Kimmel 2006. 'The family earnings gap and postponement of maternity in the United States?', in S. Gustafsson and A. Kalwij (eds.), *Education and Postponement of Maternity: Economic Analysis of Industrialized Countries*, Dordrecht: Springer, 175–224.

Angrist, J. 2002. 'How do sex ratios affect marriage and labor markets? Evidence from America's second generation', *Quarterly Journal of Economics* August: 997–1038.

Angrist, J. D. and W. N. Evans 1996. 'Children and their parents' labor supply: evidence from exogenous variation in family size', *American Economic Review* 88 (3), 450–77.

Becker, G.S. 1960. 'An economic analysis of fertility': demographic and economic change in developed countries, *Universities-National Bureau of Economic Research Conferences Series* 11. pp. 209–31, Princeton, NJ: NBER.

  1964. *Human Capital*, Cambridge, MA: Harvard University Press.

  1965. 'A theory of the allocation of time', *Economic Journal* 75: 493–517.

  1973. 'A theory of marriage: Part I', *Journal of Political Economy* 81 (4), 813–46.

  1981. *A Treatise on the Family*, Cambridge, MA: Harvard University Press, 2nd edn 1991.

Becker, G. S., E. Landes and R. Michael 1977a. *Economics of Divorce*.

  1977b. 'An economic analysis of marital instability', *Journal of Political Economy* 85 (6), 1141–87.

Bergstrom, T. C. 1997. 'A survey of theories of the family', in M. R. Rosenzweig and O. Stark (eds.), *Handbook of Population and Family Economics*, Amsterdam: Elsevier.

Bergstrom, T. and D. Lam 1989. 'The effects of cohort size on marriage markets in twentieth century Sweden', in Tommy Bengtson *The Family, the Market and the State in Industrialized Countries*, Oxford: Oxford University Press.

Billari, F. C, D. Philipov and P. Baizan 2001. 'Leaving home in Europe: the experience of cohorts born around 1960', *International Journal of Population Geography* 7: 339–56.

Blossfeld, H. P. and J. Huinink 1991. 'Human capital investments or norms of role transition? How women's schooling and career affect the process of family formation', *American Journal of Sociology* 97 (1), 143–68.

Blossfeld, H. P. and A. Timm (eds.) 2003. *Who Marries Whom? Educational Systems as Marriage Markets in Modern Societies*, Dordrecht: Kluwer Academic Publishers.

Bongaarts, J. 1999. 'Fertility in the developed world: where will it end?', *American Economic Review*. Papers and Proceedings, May, 256–60.

Bongaarts, J. and G. Feeney 1998. 'On the quantum and tempo of fertility', *Population and Development Review* 24 (2), 271–91.

Bratti, M. 2006. 'Labour force participation and marital fertility in Italy', in S. Gustafsson and A. Kalwij (eds.), *Education and Postponement of Maternity: Economic Analysis of Industrialized Countries*, 113–45, Dordrecht: Springer.

Bratti, M., E. Del Bono and D. Vuri 2005. 'New mothers: labour force participation in Italy: the role of job characteristics, *Labour* 19: 79–121.

Brien, M. J. and M. E. Sheran 2003. 'The economics of marriage and household formation', in Shoshana A. Grossbard-Shechtman (ed.), *Marriage and the Economy: Theory and Evidence from Advanced Industrial Societies*, Cambridge: Cambridge University Press.

Chan and Halpin 2003. 'Britain', in H. P. Blossfeld and A. Timm (eds.), *Educational Systems as Marriage Markets in Modern Societies*, Dordrecht: Kluwer Academic Publishers.

Cigno, A. 1991. *Economics of the Family*. Oxford: Clarendon Press.

Council of Europe 2002. *Recent Demographic Developments in Europe*.

Del Boca, D. 2002. 'The effect of childcare and part-time opportunities on participation and fertility decisions in Italy', *Journal of Population Economics* 15: 549–73.

Del Boca, D. and S. Pasqua, 2005. 'Labour supply and fertility in Europe and the US', in T. Boeri, D. Del Boca and C. Pissarides, (eds), *Women at Work: An Economic Perspective*, Oxford: Oxford University Press.

Del Boca, D., M. Locatelli and D. Vuri 2003. 'Childcare choices by Italian households', working paper, University of Turin and University of Florence.

De la Rica S. and A. Iza 2006. 'Career planning in Spain: do fixed-term contracts delay marriage and parenthood?', in S. Gustafsson and A. Kalwij (eds.), *Education and Postponement of Maternity: Economic Analysis of Industrialized Countries*, 147–74, Dordrecht: Springer.

Ermisch, J. 2003. *An Economic Analysis of the Family*, Princeton, NJ: Princeton University Press.

Freeman, R. 2000. 'Feminization of work', in S. Gustafsson and D. Meulders (eds.), *Gender and the Labour Market: Econometric Evidence of Obstacles to Achieving Gender Equality*, London: Macmillan.

Goux and Maurin 2003. 'France', in H.-P. Blossfeld and A. Timm (eds.), *Who Marries Whom? Educational Systems as Marriage Markets in Modern Societies*, Dordrecht: Kluwer Academic Publishers.

Granger, C. W. J. 1969. 'Testing for causality and feedback', *Econometrica* 37: 424–38.

   2005. 'Granger causality', entry in *Encyclopedia of Economic Methodology*, Edward Elgar Publishers.

Grossbard-Shechtman, S. A. (ed.) 2003. *Marriage and the Economy: Theory and Evidence from Advanced Industrial Societies*. New York and Cambridge: Cambridge University Press.

Gustafsson, S. 1992. 'Separate taxation and married women's labor supply: a comparison between West Germany and Sweden', *Journal of Population Economics* 5: 61–85.

2001. 'Optimal age at motherhood: theoretical and empirical considerations on postponement of maternity in Europe', *Journal of Population Economics* 14 (2), 225–47.

2006. 'Introduction' and contributions of this volume in S. Gustafsson and A. Kalwij (eds.), *Education and Postponement of Maternity: Economic Analysis of Industrialized Countries*, 1–30, Dordrecht: Springer.

Gustafsson, S. and F. Stafford 1992. 'Daycare subsidies and labor supply in Sweden', *Journal of Human Resources* 27(1): 204–30.

Gustafsson, S. and C. Wetzels 2000. 'Optimal age for first birth: Germany, Great Britain, the Netherlands and Sweden', in S. Gustafsson and D. Meulders (eds.), *Gender and the Labour Market: Econometric Evidence of Obstacles to Achieving Gender Equality*, 188–209. London: Macmillan.

Gustafsson, S., E. Kenjoh and C. Wetzels 2002. 'The role of education in postponement of maternity in Britain, Germany, the Netherlands and Sweden', in E. Ruspini and A. Dale (eds.), *The Gender Dimension of Social Change: The Contribution of Dynamic Research to the Study of Women's Life Courses*, 55–79. Bristol: The Policy Press.

Gustafsson S. and S. Worku 2006. 'Assortative mating by education and postponement of couple formation and first birth in Britain and Sweden', in S. Gustafsson and A. Kalwij (eds.), *Education and Postponement of Maternity: Economic Analysis of Industrialized Countries*, 259–83, Dordrecht: Springer.

Gustafsson, S., C. Wetzels, J. Vlasblom and S. Dex 1996. 'Women's labor force transitions in connection with childbirth: A panel data comparison between Germany, Sweden and Great Britain', *Journal of Population Economics* 9 (3), 221–46.

Gustafsson, S. and A. Kalwij 2004. 'Economic theory of fertility, methods and empirical approaches', in S. Gustafsson and A. Kalwij (eds.), *Education and Postponement of Maternity: Economic Analysis of Industrialized Countries*, 31–64, Dordrecht: Springer.

Heckman, J.J. 1979. 'Sample bias as a specification error', *Econometrica* 47, 153–61.

Heckman, J.J. and J.R. Walker 1990. 'The third birth in Sweden', *Journal of Population Economics* 3 (4), 235–75.

Hotz, V.J., J.A. Klerman and R.J. Willis 1997. 'The economics of fertility in developed countries', in M.R. Rozenzweig and O. Stark (eds.), *Handbook of Population and Family Economics*, vol. IA., Amsterdam: Elsevier.

Kalwij, A.S. 2006. 'Household consumption, saving and employment around the time of births in the Netherlands', in S. Gustafsson and A. Kalwij (eds.), *Education and Postponement of Maternity: Economic Analysis of Industrialized Countries*, 207–24, Dordrecht: Springer.

Kantorová, V. 2006, 'Education and entry into motherhood in the Czech Republic during state socialism and the transition period (1970–1997)', in S. Gustafsson and A. Kalwij (eds.), *Education and Postponement of Maternity: Economic Analysis of Industrialized Countries*, 237–58, Dordrecht: Springer.

Kenjoh, E. 2004. 'Balancing work and family life in Japan and four European countries: econometric analyses on mothers' employment and timing of maternity', Amsterdam: Thela Thesis.

2005. 'New mothers' employment and public policy in the U.K., Germany, the Netherlands, Sweden and Japan', *Labour* 19: 5–49.

Klauw, W. van der 1996. 'Female labour supply and marital status decisions: a life-cycle model', *Review of Economic Studies* 63 (2), 199–235.

Kohler, H.P. 1999. 'The Swedish baby boom and bust of 1985–1996 revised: the role of tempo, quantum and variance effects', *MPIDR Working Paper* WP 1999-2007.

Kohler, H. P. and D. Philipov 2001. 'Tempo effects in the fertility decline in Eastern Europe: evidence from Bulgaria, the Czech Republic, Hungary, Poland and Russia', *European Journal of Population* 17: 37–60.

Kohler, H. P., F. C. Billari and J. A. Ortega 2002. 'The emergence of lowest-low fertility in Europe during the 1990s', *Population and Development Review* 28 (4), 641–80.

Kreyenfeld, M. 2006. 'Maternity in East and West Germany before and after unification', in S. Gustafsson and A. Kalwij (eds.), *Education and Postponement of Maternity: Economic Analysis of Industrialized Countries*, 225–36, Dordrecht: Springer.

Lam, D. 1988. 'Marriage markets and assortative mating with household public goods: theoretical results and empirical implications', *Journal of Human Resources* 23 (4), 462–87.

Lesthaege, R. and P. Willems 2002. 'Is low fertility a temporary phenomenon in the European Union?', *Population and Development Review* 25 (2), 211–28.

Mare, R. D. 1991, 'Five decades of educational assortative mating', *American Sociological Review* 56 (1), 15–32.

Matsuo, H. 2003. *The Transition to Motherhood in Japan: A Comparison with the Netherlands*, Doctoral dissertation, University of Groningen. Amsterdam: Rozenberg Publishers.

Mincer, J. 1962. 'Labor force participation of married women,' in NBER, *Aspects of Labor Economics*.

1963. 'Market prices, opportunity costs and income effects', in S. Christ *et al.* (eds.), *Measurement in Economics: Studies in Mathematical Economics in Honor of Yehuda Grunfeld*, Stanford, CA: Stanford University Press.

1974. *Schooling, Experience and Earnings*, New York: National Bureau of Economic Research.

Naz, G., Ø. Anti-Nilsen and S. Vagstad 2006. 'Education and completed fertility in Norway', in S. Gustafsson and A. Kalwij (eds.), *Education and Postponement of Maternity: Economic Analysis of Industrialized Countries*, 285–306, Dordrecht: Springer.

Ono, H. 2002. 'Women's economic standing, marriage timing and cross-national contexts of gender: the case of Japan, US and Sweden', Working Paper, University of Michigan, Ann Arbor.

Philopov D., and H. P. Kohler 2001. 'Tempo effects in the fertility decline in Eastern Europe: evidence from Bulgaria, the Czech Republic, Hungary, Poland, and Russia', *European Journal of Population* 17: 37–60.

Schultz, T. W. (ed.) 1974. *Economics of the Family: Marriage, Children, and Human Capital*, Chicago and London: University of Chicago Press.

Skirbekk, V., H.P. Kohler and A. Prskawetz 2006. 'The marginal effect of school leaving age on demographic events: a contribution to the discussion on causality', in S. Gustafsson and A. Kalwij (eds.), *Education and Postponement of Maternity: Economic Analysis of Industrialized Countries*, 65–85, Dordrecht: Springer.

Symeonidou, H. and G.P. Mitsopoulpos 2003. 'The timing of the first, second and third childbirths in Greece', Working Paper, National Centre for Social Research (EKKE), Athens.

UNESCO 2002. http://portal.unesco.org/

Wetzels, C. 2001. *Squeezing Birth into Working Life: Household Panel Data Analyses Comparing Germany, Great Britain, Sweden and The Netherlands*, Aldershot: Ashgate Publishing.

Willis, R. 1973. 'A new approach to the economic theory of fertility behavior', *Journal of Political Economy* 81: S14–S64.

Wolpin, K. 1984. 'An estimable dynamic stochastic model of fertility and child mortality', *Journal of Political Economy* 92: 852–74.

7   Motherhood and wages

Cécile Wetzels

7.1   Introduction

In many industrialised countries, women's educational levels and labour force participation have increased strikingly in recent decades and equal pay legislation was brought into force in the 1970s and 1980s. However, the stagnation in gender wage equalisation that has occurred after a sharp improvement has led to an increasing focus on the effects of family responsibilities on women's wages as one of the explanations of the apparent paradox of this stagnation. The original empirical model of wage determination was developed in Mincer (1974), based on a lifecycle earnings model, and contains only age as a measure of the individual work history and years of pre-labour-market schooling. This model is most appropriate for samples of men taken from the entire population who are working practically all their lives. In this chapter we are interested in motherhood and wages, and therefore we wish to focus not only on the effect of personal characteristics such as investments in education, but also on household characteristics, and the effect of the labour market and social policies (see Part I).

The Mincer type models, the question of what variables to include in the wage model and gender wage discrimination have already been reviewed extensively (Cain 1986; Blau and Ferber 1987; Gundarson 1989; Blau 1998; Kunze 2000). Here, we review studies focusing on four important aspects of the link between motherhood and wages: the wage effects of parental childcare; the wage effects of working part-time; the wage effect of spending non-employment hours in childcare or other housework rather than in leisure; and the potential endogeneity of children.

7.2   The facts

In order to compare gross hourly wages[1] across European countries, we make use of the latest wave of the European Community Household

---

[1] Since we work with gross wages, we refrain from the effects of taxation regimes as regards individualisation of taxes of household members. The hourly wage is constructed

Panel (ECHP) data set. We select women in their fertile years and who are less likely to be in school: women who are between 22 and 45 years old. Different public policies on the family may make women with the same human capital behave differently between countries. This different labour market behaviour is likely to have consequences for mothers' wages. These may depend purely on the quantity and quality of human capital (accumulation, depreciation and restoration during career breaks, training and promotion, working part-time) but, in addition, on the number of non-employment hours spent on childcare, and this may in turn depend on making use of non-parental childcare, and having a partner who shares childcare work.

Table 7.1 shows the outcome of women's participation rates according to motherhood and the number of children in some European countries included in the (ECHP) data set. The ranking of the countries reflects, in ascending order, the difference between women's (mothers') and men's (fathers') labour force participation rate. The ranking in Table 7.1 begins with countries, which have developed welfare states on an individual and equal role-sharing basis, e.g. the Nordic countries, and ends with countries that are characterised by welfare state regimes with a breadwinner orientation (see Sainsbury 1996;[2] Part I of this volume). And, as the columns with the heading R show, the order does not change much if we rank according to the difference in participation rates of mothers and fathers, and even if we rank the difference in participation rates of mothers and fathers according to the number of children in the household.[3]

The data in Table 7.1 are in line with the employment rates presented in Part II Chapter 5, (this volume): the differences in participation rates

---

from monthly gross earnings and divided by the number of hours in the main job including paid overtime multiplied by 4.3. We used purchasing power parity (PPP) specific coefficients provided by Eurostat in the ECHP data set to make earnings comparable across countries.

[2] Sainsbury (1996) makes a distinction in this typology between the breadwinner, the individual and equal role-sharing in social policy by applying the principles of maintenance or care. The breadwinner dimension is characterised by the following: family ideology with a strict division of labour (husband = earner; wife = carer); employment and wage policies that give priority to men; caring work being unpaid and a primarily private sphere of care; entitlements differentiated among spouses, the basis of entitlement belonging to the breadwinner; and joint taxation with deductions for dependants. The opposite dimension is the individual model which is characterised by a family ideology of shared roles (both parents earn and care); employment and wage policies aim at both sexes; caring work has a paid component with a strong state involvement in the sphere of care; entitlements are uniform; and there is separate taxation with equal tax relief.

[3] The ranking may also give us a first indication of the ranking of selection for employment that may bias wage estimations.

Table 7.1 *Women's labour force participation (lfp) rates and the differences between men's and women's lfp in households according to having children and number of children*

	Labour force participation (%)													
	All					1 child			2 children			>=3 children		
Country	Women	Diff. Men-Women	Mo	Diff. Fa-Mo	R	Mo	Diff. Fa-Mo	R	Mo	Diff. Fa-Mo	R	Mo	Diff. Fa-Mo	R
Sweden	.67	.047	.82	.089	(1)	.81	.057	(1)	.84	.089	(2)	.75	.146	(2)
Denmark	.72	.077	.85	.102	(2)	.81	.123	(3)	.89	.084	(1)	.84	.104	(1)
UK	.64	.101	.69	.170	(3)	.68	.122	(2)	.74	.184	(4)	.63	.245	(4)
Germany	.58	.131	.64	.221	(5)	.66	.140	(4)	.66	.240	(5)	.49	.415	(6)
Belgium	.55	.153	.71	.183	(4)	.63	.201	(6)	.79	.137	(3)	.67	.244	(3)
Netherlands	.56	.181	.66	.264	(6)	.66	.216	(7)	.70	.243	(6)	.57	.386	(5)
France	.49	.204	.58	.271	(7)	.57	.198	(5)	.65	.261	(7)	.47	.430	(7)
Italy	.36	.283	.39	.330	(8)	.39	.257	(8)	.41	.359	(8)	.33	.455	(9)
Greece	.34	.294	.41	.378	(9)	.36	.296	(9)	.44	.425	(9)	.42	.434	(8)
Spain	.31	.319	.32	.401	(10)	.30	.307	(10)	.36	.457	(10)	.29	.469	(10)
All*	.49	.21	.54	.283		.52	.219		.57	.301		.49	.376	

Notes: * = All countries included in ECHP;

Explanation of abbreviations: Diff: difference; Fa = fathers; Mo = mothers; R = ranking in ascending order; child(ren) living at home.

Source: Data from European Community Household Panel of 2000 (see Eurostat 2002, Locatelli *et al.* 2001).

Table 7.2 *Women's gross hourly wages in EU countries: means and (standard deviation) in € PPP*

Country	Women	Mothers	Mothers 1 child	Mothers 2 children	Mothers 3 or more child
Denmark	13.940 (4.08)	14.263 (4.08)	14.587 (4.09)	14.193 (4.14)	13.860 (3.89)
UK	9.943 (4.62)	9.739 (4.61)	10.334 (5.05)	9.472 (4.20)	9.001 (4.41)
Germany	10.266 (5.30)	10.151 (5.85)	10.156 (6.26)	10.133 (5.20)	10.208 (6.75)
Belgium	12.444 (4.59)	12.600 (4.52)	11.940 (4.19)	12.989 (4.75)	12.825 (4.46)
Netherlands	13.459 (4.97)	13.508 (5.14)	13.991 (4.79)	13.115 (5.24)	13.846 (5.38)
France	10.212 (4.84)	10.317 (4.87)	10.312 (4.88)	10.557 (4.75)	9.734 (5.09)
Italy	10.478 (4.58)	10.819 (4.79)	10.426 (4.47)	11.177 (5.00)	10.867 (5.02)
Greece	7.703 (4.40)	7.859 (4.37)	7.552 (4.30)	8.565 (4.67)	6.115 (2.60)
Spain	9.079 (5.90)	9.475 (6.27)	8.960 (5.68)	9.770 (6.79)	9.798 (5.93)
All countries[a]	10.169 (5.29)	10.189 (5.45)	9.907 (5.43)	10.393 (5.35)	10.297 (5.74)

[a] *Notes:* = all countries in the ECHP with wage information. The ECHP does not contain information on hourly wages in Sweden.
Explanation of abbreviations: PPP = purchasing power parities; child(ren): child(ren) living at home.
Source: Own calculations based on European Community Household Panel (ECHP) of 2000 (see Eurostat 2002, Locatelli *et al.* 2001).

among men and women with figures below 7.7% in the Nordic countries and as high as 32% in Spain are extraordinary. The difference between labour force participation rates of fathers and mothers increases from around 10% in Scandinavian countries to 40% in Spain. This difference in labour force participation rates becomes most prominent in households with two or more children in most Southern European countries but, in Spain, it also occurs in households with one child. These strong differences occur despite higher participation rates among mothers than among all women, which indicate the increase in women's participation in all countries.

Table 7.2 presents women's gross hourly wages according to motherhood and number of children. Gross hourly wages differ significantly

Table 7.3 *Difference in men's and women's mean gross hourly wages in* € *PPP according to parenthood in EU countries*

Country	Diff. men- women	R	Diff. Fa-Mo	R	Diff. Fa-Mo 1 child	R	Diff. Fa-Mo 2 children	R	Diff. Fa-Mo >=3 children	R
Denmark	3.02	7	2.92	6	2.96	7	2.91	6	2.82	4
UK	3.65	8	4.15	8	3.02	8	5.04	9	4.51	8
Germany	2.91	6	3.26	7	2.75	6	3.53	7	3.78	7
Belgium	2.35	4	2.33	4	2.14	5	2.12	4	3.02	5
Netherlands	3.97	9	4.58	9	4.09	9	4.69	8	5.10	9
France	2.37	5	2.63	5	1.79	4	2.92	5	3.71	6
Italy	0.97	1	0.82	1	0.72	1	0.89	1	0.64	1
Greece	1.33	2	1.34	3	1.39	3	0.95	2	2.46	3
Spain	1.37	3	1.29	2	0.74	2	1.43	3	1.72	2

Notes: Explanation of abbreviations: PPP = purchasing power parities; Fa = fathers; Mo = mothers; R = ranking in ascending order; child(ren): child(ren) living at home.
Source: Source: Own calculations based on data from the European Community Household Panel (ECHP) of 2000 (see Eurostat 2002, Locatelli *et al.* 2001).

between the countries in Table 7.2, with Greek women earning around one half in PPPs[4] compared with Danish women. Wage differentials within countries between women and mothers are very small. There is no clear pattern of countries in wage differentials and labour force participation rates. However, we observe lower wages for mothers with one child in the household than for all women in countries with more breadwinner welfare states (Germany, Italy, Greece and Spain).[5] Furthermore, as Table 7.3 shows, the gender market wage differentials are highest in the Netherlands, the UK and Denmark, whereas they are lowest in Southern European countries such as Italy, Greece and Spain, where the differences in labour force participation rates between men and women are highest. These patterns in wage differentials are not so marked for fathers and mothers.[6]

Appendix 7.A (pp. 256–63) presents a series of figures based on observed gross hourly wages in six European countries which represent

---

[4] PPPs = purchasing power parities.
[5] A similar pattern is found for net hourly wages (not shown here).
[6] In a comparison of net wage differentials according to gender and parenthood (not presented here) Germany showed the widest gap, although Germany ranked 6 out of 9 in Table 7.3 on differences in gross hourly wage between men and women. The Southern European countries still showed the lowest net wage differentials according to gender and parenthood.

different social policy environments (see Part I, Chapters 2, 3 and 4). The ECHP data does not provide any information on maternity leave. Appendix Figures 7.A.1–7.A.3 depict mothers' wage graphs concerning the use of paid childcare.[7] These graphs show by country in the left panel the wage rates of parents who do not make use of paid childcare, and in the right panel the wage rates of parents if they do use paid childcare.

In Denmark where paid childcare is heavily subsidised and available (see Part I, Chapter 3), we expect the mother's wages to be less associated with using paid care. In contrast, in countries, such as the UK and the Netherlands, where paid childcare is available but much less subsidised than in Denmark, we expect a stronger association between women's wages and use of paid care. We also expect mothers' wages and partners' wages to be more equal at the higher ranges of hourly wages in countries where childcare is available, affordable and of high quality. Appendix Figure 7.A.3 confirms these expectations as regards the use of paid care in Denmark and the UK. Furthermore, similar to the UK, in Italy and Spain the use of paid care is associated with higher and more equal wages between the spouses than those for couples who do not use paid childcare. The graph depicting the Netherlands shows different shapes of wage age profiles both for parents not using paid care and for parents who do. In the other countries, mothers are more likely to be with a partner who has an equal or higher wage, especially with respect to those parents using paid childcare. In the Dutch situation, women may have a higher hourly wage than their partner and not use paid care, but if both parents have a relatively high wage they may also not be using paid childcare. A possible reason is the peculiar Dutch situation in which there is paid childcare and informal childcare available (Wetzels 2005) in combination with the widespread availability of part-time jobs that are relatively better paid than in the UK. On the other hand, Dutch mothers who do not have a high wage, but one that is a bit higher than their partner's, may use paid childcare, and so do couples where the partner has a much higher hourly wage than the mother. Again this may also show that when Dutch women do not have a high wage, they remain in the labour market working part-time. However, when paid childcare is used, there is no clear association with either women's wages

---

[7] The questions on paid childcare are phrased as follows: 1. Are any of the children in the household looked after on a regular basis by someone other than their parent or guardian, whether at home or outside, such as at a crèche or kindergarten? (yes, no); 2. Does your household have to pay for any of the children looked after on a regular basis? (yes, no). If both answers are 'yes': we interpret this to mean that the household uses paid childcare.

or the difference in wage between the mother and her partner in the Netherlands.

Appendix Figure 7.A.2 shows parents' earnings according to whether the father cares for the children for 28 hours or more per week. This type of childcare shows a different picture than Appendix Figure 7.A.1 In France, households with this type of childcare are the households where the parents have the most equal wages. Also in Italy, Spain and the Netherlands, households where the father cares for the children at least 28 hours per week seem to be the households where the spouses have more equal hourly wages, but in Italy and Spain the hourly wage for such spouses is much lower than among couples who use paid care, whereas in the Netherlands it is higher. In Denmark, the households with this type of care have less equal hourly wages compared with households in which the father does not provide childcare for 28 hours per week or more. Appendix Figure 7.A.3 distinguishes between households which use both paid childcare and in which the partner cares for the children between 14 and 28 hours per week and households which do not have this childcare situation.

In Denmark, Italy and Spain, log hourly wages between mothers and their partner are more equal in households which are characterised by this childcare situation. The shape of the wage–age profile for households which use paid care and in which a father cares for his children is very similar to the shape of the wage–age profile in households who use only paid care (Appendix Figure 7.A.1).

In Appendix Figure 7.A.4 we present parents' wages according to whether the mother works full-time or part-time. In Denmark, mothers who work part-time earn slightly less per hour compared with full-time working mothers who have similar earning to their partner. In the UK the hourly wages of part-time working mothers are lower compared with full-time working mothers who have similar earnings to their partner. The Dutch situation shows that part-time working mothers earn much less per hour than full-time working mothers with a partner who has equal earnings, and the range of their partner's wages is very wide. This seems in line with part-time work being less restricted to a particular group (Gustafsson *et al.* 2003). However, the 'part-time penalty' is higher than expected (Gustafson *et al.* 2003). In Southern European countries part-time working mothers' wage–age profile is higher than that of full-time working mothers if their partner earns a log hourly wage of 2.5 or more.

Appendix Figures 7.A.5 and 7.A.6 depict women's log hourly wage according to age categories of giving birth to the first child. We distinguish between three age categories of giving birth for the first time: 23 and younger; between 23 and 27; and older than 27, and between three education levels (tertiary education, secondary education and lower education). We expect, according to the reasoning and findings reported in Gustafsson and Wetzels (2000), Wetzels (2001), and Part II, Chapter 6, that women's hourly wages are the highest and mostly increase with age for women who postponed the birth of their first child (in Appendix Figure 7.A.5 graph (3,1)) in each country. However, in countries in which social policies aim at combining paid work and children (such as Denmark), we expect that employed mothers' wage curves are less affected by taking time out of the labour market due to childcare duties and taking part-time jobs, since these countries are full-time economies (Gustafsson, Kenjoh and Wetzels 2003). The descriptive graphs confirm that in all countries highly educated mothers who postpone having their first child till they are 27 or older have a higher wage–age profile. Some of the countries in Appendix Figure 7.A.5 show a U-shape association between wage and age[8] which may point to the effect of having a career break or the change to part-time work when having children. The overall impression from Appendix Figure 7.A.5 is that most of the mothers' wage–age curves are flat, except for highly educated Danish mothers who had their first child when they were aged 23 or younger, and Italian women. Furthermore, it seems that Spanish women have an increase in their wages from age 30.

Appendix Figure 7.A.6 depicts the mother's log wage and her partner's log wage. The picture describes whether giving birth at a younger age (and, associated with this, specialising in home care (the mother) and in market work (the partner) at a younger age), is associated with more unequal wage rates between the mother and her partner (the flatter curves in Appendix Figure 7.A.6) compared with those couples who have children at a later age. For Italy, we may say that the graphs do indicate this. But, in the other countries, we only observe flatter curves of mothers' and partners' wages for a particular age at first birth and a particular type of education. In France we only observe a flatter curve in the category for the earliest age at first birth for mothers with medium and low education, and similarly, in Denmark only for those with the lowest education. In the UK this flatter curve is observed for youngest mothers with a low level of education and for mothers with a medium level of education who have postponed having their children until age 27

---

[8] These are the wage–age profiles for: medium-educated women and low-educated 'late' mothers in Denmark, medium-educated 'early' mothers in the UK; highly educated 'early' mothers in the Netherlands, France and Italy; and low-educated 'late' mothers in Italy; and medium- educated and 'late' mothers in Spain.

or older compared with having their first child between age 23 and 27. In contrast, in Spain we only find some 'specialisation of work and care in the household' effects in the highest education group who postpone their first child.

Appendix Figures 7.A.7 and 7.A.8 show women's log hourly wages by motherhood and education level (Appendix Figure 7.A.7), and by log hourly wages of their partner (Appendix Figure 7.A.8). The upper panel in each country in Appendix Figure 7.A.7 shows childless women's wages, the lower panel mother's wages. In general we find the expected positive effect of education level on women's wages and more so for childless women in all countries. Appendix Figure 7.A.8 shows very different patterns of the association between women's and partners' log hourly wages in the different countries, and even more so when childless couples and parents are compared. In Chapter 8 (this volume) we will analyse women's wages as regards motherhood in these six countries.

7.3   Issues

The conceptual framework for the analysis of an individual's acquisition of earning power and the distribution among groups of individuals originates in Becker's theory of human capital (1964). Investment in people is time consuming. Each additional year of schooling or on-the-job training postpones the time of the individual's receipt of earnings or reduces the span of his/her working life if he/she retires at a fixed age. The deferral of earnings and the possible reduction of earning life are costly. These time-cost plus money outlays make up the total cost of investment. Because of these costs, investment is not undertaken unless it raises the level of the deferred income stream. Hence, at the time it is undertaken, the present value of real earnings streams, with and without investment, are equal only at a positive discount rate. This rate is the internal rate of return on the investment. Since earnings are a return on cumulated net investments, they also rise at a diminishing rate over the working life, and decline when net investment becomes negative, as in old age. The typical logarithmic working life earnings profile is therefore concave from below. Its rate of growth is a positive function of the amount invested and of the rate of return. Its degree of concavity depends on how rapidly investments decline over time. See Appendix 7.A for a simple model of wage determination that nests most specifications that have been estimated in the empirical literature on women's wages.

Here, we review studies focusing on four important aspects of the link between motherhood and wages: the wage effects of maternal child-care; the wage effect of working part-time; the wage effect of spending non-employment hours in childcare or other housework rather than in leisure; and the potential endogeneity of children. Appendix Table 7.A.1 summarises some of the literature based in Europe, which we will discuss by country, data and results.

7.3.1   Taking time out of the labour market for childcare, and wages

A woman's transition out of the labour market may be a result of her decision to care for their own child while on leave or by reducing work hours, and this decision to exit the labour market is determined by social policies that differ across European countries (see Part II, and Part II, Chapter 5, Gustafsson et al. 1996; Wetzels, 2001, Del Boca and Pasqua 2005). In order to take into account the more interrupted work histories of women, extensions to the wage model that included variables for actual work experience as well as home-time were first specified in Mincer and Polachek (1974). This study found that beyond the human capital accumulation and tenure that is lost as a result of having a career break, human capital also depreciates during the time of unemployment. Mincer and Ofek (1982) accounted for the 'restoration' or 'repair' of depreciated human capital. The intermittent worker's decision whether and when to invest in human capital will depend jointly on the relative sizes of the depreciation and restoration effects and the probability of returning to work. Corcoran et al. (1983) suggest that the restoration is not explained by the higher efficiency of reconstructing occupational skills rather than building new skills, as Mincer and Ofek suggest, but by the matching process on the labour market. Both employers, and employees who seek jobs after a career break, find a match in which the initial wage is low but improves considerably when the match appears successful. Another explanation for the wage effects of career breaks is found in signalling, as different types of non-labour-market participation of equal duration have different effects on wages (Albrecht et al. 1999).

A wide variety of studies employing extensive data sets have indeed found that wages fall during periods of non-employment. The estimated decline in the USA ranges from 0.6% to over 5% annually, but averages around 2%. The findings reported by Stratton (1995) attest to the robust nature of earlier work on the rate of wage depreciation during interruptions in work experience but, more importantly, demonstrate a major shortcoming of this work. The estimated depreciation rates remain in the order of 2% even as a new data set is employed, part-time and full-time jobs are better distinguished, more accurate and shorter measures of non-employment are introduced, and a new sampling technique which focuses more directly upon withdrawals and which makes greater use of the available data is tested. Even a specification which permits the level of full-time and part-time wages to vary does not significantly change estimates of the depreciation rate. These stable estimates lend considerable credence to the earlier results. Unfortunately, this specification appears to be sensitive to sample selection bias of a sort not previously noted. While researchers have introduced controls for very gross sample selection criteria, such as the existence of two reported wage values, they have not typically considered the decisions which might lead to an interruption in, and subsequent re-entry to, employment. However, theory clearly tells us there is a link between wages and labour force behaviour. There is likely to be a positive correlation between re-entry spell length and the apparent depreciation rate. A test of this hypothesis by Stratton (1995) reveals that women who remained employed for three or more years following re-entry did not experience any significant wage 'depreciation' during their interruption; women who re-exited employment more rapidly did. Estimates of a depreciation rate are, therefore, very sensitive to the manner in which the labour supply decision is handled. A much more complex model which incorporates a period-by-period or continuous-time labour supply decision is needed to truly measure the effect that interruptions in work experience have on subsequent earnings. Future research will have to fill this gap.

7.3.1.1 Labour market experience: measurement and wage effects Studies based in European countries have replicated and extended the US-based studies by including the effects of the reason for interruption (Albrecht *et al.* 1999), taking account of the extent to which social policies aim at combining paid work and family care. However, most studies of European women's wages are based in one country and a number of studies based in Europe do not contain the actual work experience of women (for an excellent review of empirical studies on the gender wage gap, see Kunze 2000) and, hence, proxies such as age or potential experience are used instead.[9] Appendix Table 7.A.2 compares

[9] To circumvent using age or potential work experience, alternative approaches have been applied in the literature. For example, studies use imputed experience instead of potential work experience as a proxy for actual work experience for females or estimate wage regressions for samples of single females, rather than single and married females pooled. Both of these approaches are, however, problematic. The former, which implies the estimation of imputed work experience, depends on the estimation of a participation equation for women. In this case, the identification of its parameters again depends on the exclusion restrictions made: for example, that the variable 'number of children' is exogenous, which is debatable. The latter approach, to estimate wage regressions only for single females, may suffer from non-random selection problems since it may be

the measure of actual experience which is crucial to examine the effect of labour market experience and the years of interruption(s) due to childcare on mothers' wages. Most UK, US and Nordic studies include actual experience, whereas most Dutch studies do not account for actual experience, except for more recent studies (Wetzels 2002a,b; Wetzels and Zorlu 2003; Albrecht *et al.* 2004).[10] There are very few studies on women's wages in Southern European countries.[11] Furthermore, few studies take a cross-country comparative perspective on the family wage gap.

It is also relevant to ask: Do studies account for part-time work (experience) and how? In the study on Sweden by Albrecht *et al.* (1999), detailed information on monthly activities has been used to calculate experience in full-time equivalents. However, they have information only on work experience of more than 15 hours per week. In the Netherlands this selection would lead to the exclusion of a substantial proportion of female workers.[12] Measuring experience in full-time equivalents seems an inappropriate measurement of improvements in productivity by on-the-job training in the Dutch part-time economy (Visser 2002; Wetzels 2002b). In the Dutch setting ten years part-time work is not equal to five years' full-time work experience, as the former has experienced ten years of organisational and work changes. However,

---

argued that single women older than, say, forty may be extremely dedicated to their careers or extremely averse to marriage and, hence, their characteristics may differ from the average female population.

[10] The latter study uses actual experience but excludes some observations if no actual experience is reported and for a number of non-workers actual experience is set to zero.

[11] For example, there is only one study known to us on Greek women's wages (Kanellopoulos and Mavromaras 2002). The study analyses male–female labour market participation and wage differentials in Greece finding that adverse treatment of female labour market participation is the largest identifiable reason why there is a gender wage gap in Greece and why it increased. There is no analysis that investigates the child gap in Greek women's wages. In addition, studies in Italy do not have a focus on the family gap in pay. In Italy, the ratio between the average female wage and the average male wage is higher than in the European Union (80.9% against 76.8%). This depends mainly on the institutional characteristics of the Italian labour market, where most of the wage bargaining occurs at national level, leaving little room for bargaining at firm level. In addition to workers' protection, the other major objective of Italian unions in the 1970s and the beginning of the 1980s was to equalise wages. The unions' actions had positive implications for women's earnings (Del Boca and Pasqua 1999). In Belgium, the data used to analyse the gender wage gap do not permit the analysis of the child gap in pay.

[12] For example, in the Netherlands 17.7% of women's jobs have fewer than 12 working hours per week, 16.9% between 12 and 20 hours per week, 31.1 between 20 and 35 hours per week, and 33.2% of the jobs are full-time jobs. For jobs held by men, the percentages for the respective categories are 6.0, 3.1, 8.7 and 82.3 (Statistics Netherlands 2000).

the experience built up during part-time work will also not equate to experience built up during full-time work. The question: 'Which recalculation is the best?' requires further research. Studies concerning women's wages in the UK, the USA and Canada explicitly use the information on full-time and part-time experience to test for the effect of working part-time. Studies on Denmark and Germany (Datta Gupta and Smith 2002; Ejrnaes and Kunze 2004; Beblo and Wolf 2002) have not included part-time work in their analyses of women's wages.[13]

Albrecht et al. (1999) analyse career interruptions and subsequent earnings in Sweden. If human capital depreciates during time at home, then the effect of time out for different types of unpaid household work should be similar. In the cross section the effects of time out vary both by type of time out and by gender. In panel estimates with control for individual fixed effects, most of the difference in effects across different types of time out is eliminated, but the difference across genders on the effects of time out remains. Therefore, Albrecht et al. (1999) conclude that the human capital depreciation interpretation of the negative coefficient on total time out in earnings functions estimates does not explain the entire effect of time out on wages: employers may use leave-taking behaviour as a signal of future career commitment. However, according to Datta Gupta and Smith (2002), analysing the family gap in Denmark, the main effect of children seems to be loss of human capital accumulation during childbirth periods, and the wage effect will diminish over time. In contrast, Skyt Nielsen, Simonsson and Verner (2004) analyse the segregation of the labour market into a family-friendly and a non-family-friendly sector and its implication that women self-select into sectors depending on institutional constraints, preferences for family-friendly working conditions and expected wage differences. They take this sector dimension into account and find a severe penalty after birth-related leave in the non-family-friendly sector, so that women who would be affected by this penalty self-select into the family-friendly sector. The penalty is a combination of a large human-capital depreciation effect, a child penalty and no recovery.

For Canada, a country with a similar generous leave arrangement and high female labour force participation rates as in the Scandinavian countries, Phipps et al. (2001) show that full-time female workers experience no income penalty associated with time out without job

---

[13] This is motivated in Datta Gupta and Smith (2002) by a study by Naur et al. (1994) showing that part-timers tend to have the same wage functions as full-timers in Denmark, and by earlier studies based on Danish longitudinal data showing that there are measurement errors for part-time workers. In Germany, the data used do not provide the information.

change. There is, however, a significant penalty associated with time out followed by a job change. Even for women who have always worked full-time after their interruptions, switching jobs following a child-related interruption has significant negative consequences for current income.

However, findings by Waldfogel (1998) show that women in the UK who had leave coverage and returned to work after childbirth received a wage premium that offset the negative wage effects of children. On the other hand, Joshi *et al.* (1999) find that in the UK, among full-time employees, women who left employment at childbirth were subsequently paid less than childless women. In contrast, mothers who maintained employment continuity were as well paid as childless women.

Countries that have changed from being a strong breadwinner state in the 1960s to a more individualised welfare state (e.g. the Netherlands in the 1990s[14]), are characterised by a female labour supply, a considerable proportion[15] of whom has experienced a long career interruption, e.g. of eleven years in the Netherlands (Allaart and de Voogd 1994; Wetzels and Tijdens 2002). Wetzels and Tijdens (2002) find a strong significant effect of time out on Dutch women's wages after controlling for actual human capital. Beblo and Wolf (2002) analyse German social security data matched with administrative data and find that, whereas men's wages seem to be only somewhat affected by recent non-labour-market participation experience, periods of absence from the labour force lead to substantial wage cuts for women even if they occurred several years ago, whereas formal parental leave periods show no effects on the current wage rate. In the latter study, training generates only positive wage effects, especially for men. But allowing for unobserved individual heterogeneity and endogeneity of the work history results in lower estimated returns for experience, particularly for women. Using panel data and first difference estimation, Ejrnæst and Kunze (2004) analyse the similar German data set on the effect of career interruption for full-time

---

[14] Only in 1973 did Dutch women gain the same protection that Swedish women secured in 1939: namely, legislation making it unlawful for employers to dismiss a woman because of pregnancy, childbirth or marriage. In Swedish political rhetoric, no one questions that a job is an essential right, and Swedish active labour market policies since 1968 also officially include women. Therborn cites a debate between the Catholic premier Van Agt and the Labour leader Den Uyl in the Netherlands in 1980, where Van Agt did not agree with the social democratic idea that you can only completely, humanely and socially function in society when you have a paid job (Wetzels 2001).

[15] In the period from 1995 to 1999, a period characterised by a tight labour market in the Netherlands, women re-entering the market made up 34% of all individuals who entered the labour market (Wetzels and Tijdens 2002). The latter study provides a review of studies on re-entrants in the Dutch labour market.

working German women having a first birth. Their study provides evidence of a large drop of 11% for each year of interruption after the first birth for the unskilled, 16% for the skilled and only 4% for graduates.

7.3.2 Part-time work and wages

After having the first child or having a career break due to having children, mothers return to jobs which can be combined with their time-consuming childcare responsibilities (e.g., jobs which offer reduced working time, shorter commuting time, etc.) (Gustafsson *et al.* 1996; Gustafsson *et al.* 2001; Wetzels 2002a; Del Boca and Pasqua 2005), that is, if such jobs are available. Choosing jobs with working conditions that are more compatible with parenthood offers employers the possibility of filling jobs for lower wages if they offer non-pecuniary amenities that some workers, e.g. mothers, will trade off against wages. The reduced mobility and the increased costs of any potential search associated with family responsibilities may reduce the elasticity of supply and make workers more vulnerable to monopsonistic behaviour of the employer. Such mechanisms that lower the relative pay of mothers would be additional to those operating through the effect of motherhood on experience and might work through the division between full-time and part-time work.[16] From Del Boca and Locatelli, Part II, Chapter 5 of this volume and Table 5.1, it follows that part-time employment is most prevalent in the Netherlands and the UK. In addition, the growth in part-time employment was the highest in the UK. Secondly, part-time employment is more gender biased in Germany and the UK than in the Netherlands and Sweden. Mothers seem, in all four countries presented in Table 7.4, more likely to be employed in non-standard jobs than childless women.[17]

British empirical literature identifies differences in the payment of full-time workers and part-time workers (Ermisch and Wright 1993; Manning and Robinson 2004). Joshi *et al.* (1999) disentangles three elements of the pay gap between mothers and childless women in the UK: (1) a 'within full-timers' component; (2) a 'within part-timers'

---

[16] A study on the USA by Budig and England (2001) includes variables measuring a high number of job characteristics, e.g. working hours, effort, cognitive skill, authority and time spent commuting, and shows that working part-time is the only 'mother friendly' characteristic of the job that explains some of the child penalty.

[17] In a study of the Netherlands, Wetzels and Tijdens (2002) show that 67% of women re-entering the workforce in 2000 worked in a different sector than that which they had earlier exited. It is likely that they return to a job where they are able to make use of their generic qualifications (for reference to other countries, see also Part II, Chapter 5, this volume.)

Table 7.4 *Comparison of employment in some European countries: women and mothers*

	Germany	Netherlands	Sweden	UK
Part-time employment as %, of total, 1990–97	13.2–15.0	27.3–29.1	14.5–14.2	20.8–23.1
Women's share in part-time employment 1990–97	91.7–87.6	69.4–78.9	81.1–76.3	87.6–82.8
% employed in non-profit business sector:[a]				
women	49.5	56.5	51.8	44.3
mothers	49.0	66.9	50.4	46.2
% employed in standard work in non-profit business sector:				
women	22.5	12.9	21.4	21.5
mothers	6.9	5.4	28.7	14.8

[a] Earlier draft of Gustafsson *et al.* 2003, using household panel data of 1998. Standard work = full-time permanent contract.

component; and (3) a composition effect. This last effect measures the extent to which the relatively low pay of mothers can be explained by their concentration in part-time jobs. Comparing two cohorts of British women of age 33, born in 1946 and in 1958, they conclude that the crude pay gap between mothers and childless women was similar for both cohorts, but low pay in part-time work became more important in explaining this gap and human capital less so.

The studies in the Netherlands are less conclusive on the effect of working part-time on wages. Gustafsson *et al.* (2003) and Zorlu (2002) do not find a significant effect of working part-time for the Netherlands. Maassen van den Brink (1994: 91) concludes that the wage effect of working part-time compared with full-time is even found to be positive in the Netherlands: 'An average female part-time worker earns 49% [per hour] more then she would have earned if she had a full-time job. A woman working full-time, however, earns almost 57% [per hour] less then she would have received if she had a part-time job. This suggests that women trade a lower wage rate for more hours of work. Females pay for working full-time.'[18] Albrecht *et al.* (2004) find a gender wage

[18] Russo and Hassink (2005) analyse the part-time wage penalty in the Netherlands, focusing on the probability of job promotion and its wage effect by using data on firms and employees and find a reduced probability of promotion for part-time workers. However, there is no clear distinction between employees who are parents or not, because that was not the object of their analysis.

gap in the Netherlands using quantile regression decomposition, in which they include the effects of working part-time by correcting their wage estimation for being selected for full-time work. Most of the gender gap is accounted for by differences in how men and women are rewarded.

7.3.3   Non-employment hours spent in childcare and wages

Mothers spend more of their non-employment hours in childcare or other household work instead of in leisure than men and probably childless women do, and leisure takes less energy thus leaving more energy for paid work, and hence mothers' leisure deficiency may lead to lower wages for them (Becker 1985). There is evidence that women do more housework than men. Hersch and Stratton (1994) argue that, in part, women do so because they earn less on average than their husbands (see also Appendix Figure 7.A.2). Further, the greater amount of time spent by women on housework exacerbates this earning differential.

Hersch (1991) provides evidence that in the USA, household responsibilities affect the wages of women not only by reducing human capital investments but perhaps also by reducing the amount of effort available for market work. She finds no such effect on men's wages, for which she offers two possible explanations: (1) the negative effects of housework on wages may begin at a point beyond the number of hours typically spent by men on housework; (2) the timing of housework done by men and women may be different. Any reduction of effort available for labour market work caused by housework should be more pronounced if housework is timed closely with market work. Stratton (2001) demonstrates that neither reduced work effort nor compensating wage differentials associated with more flexible jobs can explain the housework penalty, again in the USA and without reference to mothers. There is no study that investigates the differences between mothers and childless women in how housework affects women's labour-market work.

A US-based study by Anderson et al. (2003) found that younger children impose a higher penalty than older children, a pattern that is consistent with a work effort explanation. However, the largest differences in the penalty arise among educational groups in Anderson et al. (2003). Medium-skilled mothers (high-school graduates) suffered more prolonged and severe wage losses than either low or highly skilled mothers, which is not to be explained by work effort. Instead, Anderson et al. (2003) reason that high-school graduates are likely to hold jobs requiring their presence during regular office hours, and are unlikely to be able to gain flexibility by finding work at other hours or by taking work home in the evening.

In Europe, different social policies on the combination of work and family (see Part I, this volume) may have an effect on mothers' energy for work, not only by providing affordable non-parental childcare, but also by increasing fathers' childcare hours. In the Netherlands, since the 1990s, a more equal distribution of 'the second shift' (Hochschild 1989) between mothers and fathers in households has been at the heart of the debate on policies to combine work and children.[19] However, there is no research yet that examines the effect of a more equal distribution of hours on paid work and care work on household members' wages in the Netherlands. Wetzels (2001: ch. 5) reveals that some German fathers adjust their incomes downwards after the arrival of a second child. Swedish fathers, on the other hand, increase their earnings by about 10% on average after the first and second child, which would be the normal expectation for a three-year period for a young male without adjusting work hours.[20]

7.3.4   *Potential endogeneity of children in wages*

There are an increasing number of studies that analyse the child gap in women's pay: whether mothers still have a relatively low wage rate compared with childless women after correcting for the period of time for childcare and after controlling for unobserved heterogeneity?[21] To estimate this effect, studies report on the wage effect of one or more dichotomous variables that take up the independent wage effect of

---

[19] The legal right to reduce and expand working hours is viewed as a way to facilitate this equal sharing of both paid work and care work. As a result, some fathers with children in the age group 0–2 have adjusted their working hours. However, part-time jobs, while more prevalent among Dutch men than among men in other countries, are found mostly among students and retired men (Gustafsson *et al.* 2003).

[20] The motives given for wishing to return to paid work show clearly that re-entrants in the Netherlands are secondary earners (Wetzels and Tijdens 2002). The motive for re-entry 'because the income is needed' is only cited by a quarter of the women. The most frequently cited motives are 'my children are growing up/ becoming more independent', 'because of the social contacts', and 'I want to develop myself.' A comparison of the current and previous jobs of the re-entrants shows that 26% apparently earn more in their current job than in their previous job; 28% do not indicate a difference in the two salaries; and 26% report that the current job pays less well than the previous job. The remainder of the respondents did not provide this information.

[21] If OLS estimations find an effect of children on women's wage in addition to actual experience, then panel estimations that correct for unobserved heterogeneity can sort out whether the child penalty falls to zero, becomes larger or is not affected. Three possible effects can occur: (a) if women with lower unobserved earning power are more likely to have children, the child penalty will fall close to zero; (b) if women who have children and are observed working are those with higher unobserved earning power, the child penalty is larger; and (c) if having children is uncorrelated with unobserved earning ability, the child penalty might be unaffected by controlling for fixed effects.

children.[22] Estimates of the child gap in women's wages in European countries are presented in Appendix Table 7.A.3 showing that the effects differ in magnitude according to the method used and the measurement of human capital. Studies in the UK and USA find a negative effect of children, e.g. after controlling for actual human capital (Waldfogel 1995, 1998) and for unobserved heterogeneity (Korenman and Neumark 1992; Neumark and Korenman 1994; Waldfogel 1998). Similar results are found in the USA by Avellar and Smock (2003), and they also find that the association between motherhood and lower wages has not weakened across cohorts in the USA. This is in contrast with the results of studies performed in Scandinavian countries and with the results found for the Netherlands in Wetzels (2002b).

Wetzels and Zorlu (2003) show a significant child gap of 8.7% in a wage regression using only human capital covariates measured by calendar years and a child dummy in the Netherlands. If age is used instead of experience, this gap is even 9.3% in the latter study. When this last model is extended, the child gap may be 6.7% at the 10% significance level. On the other hand, the extended model with experience in calendar years generates insignificant and smaller coefficients for the child gap. Finally, the inclusion of full-time equivalent of experience in the regressions makes the child gap disappear convincingly both in a short model and an extended version. These results suggest that there would be no child gap in the Netherlands if we corrected women's wage function for differences in the human capital of childless women and mothers.[23] The results for the Netherlands in Wetzels and Zorlu (2003) also suggest that the number of hours worked are more important in raising human capital accumulation than the continuity of employment in the form of fewer hours distributed over time. On the other hand, the connection with the labour market in part-time jobs with low hours may increase employment probability, a supposition which is not verified in their paper.

Endogeneity may bias wage models if children, experience or time out are not exogenous. Browning (1992) and Joshi et al. (1999) found the

---

[22] It is not always clear whether this refers to children living at home or whether it also includes children not living at home. Phipps et al. (2001) explicitly looked at the different effects of including a 'child ever dummy' instead of a 'child now dummy', but they did not find a different result.

[23] There is no other study analysing data from the Netherlands on women's wages and motherhood that uses actual experience in the labour market, except for Wetzels (2002b), which uses an Internet survey of workers. In line with Wetzels and Zorlu 2003, the latter study did not find a child gap between mothers and childless women's wages when controlling for actual human capital.

number and age of children to be endogenous to the model. However, Korenman and Neumark (1992) show that the exogeneity of children in the wage equation is not rejected.[24] Similarly, Waldfogel (1995) reports on a Hausman test, using a working partner and partner's pay as instruments. This test did not reject exogeneity of experience in the wage equation.

7.3.5   Bias in wage estimation from sample selectivity

In addition, women's wage estimations may be biased because wages are known only for workers, who may be more productive than non-workers. The standard method to correct wage estimation models for selection for employment is laid out in Heckman (1979). In the studies reviewed, some employed the standard Heckman method (Waldfogel 1995; Datta Gupta and Smith 2003; Harkness and Waldfogel 2003), while others did not (Albrecht *et al.* 1999; Budig and England 2001). Datta Gupta and Smith (2003) found a selection effect. Harkness and Waldfogel (2003) found the selection correction term to be significant and positive in the USA, and not in the other six countries in their analyses. Selection bias from employment was not found by Waldfogel (1995). Wetzels and Zorlu (2003) correct the estimations of wage differentials between mothers and childless women for the selectivity bias resulting from two double selection processes: first, the motherhood decision and the employment decision: and, secondly, the motherhood decision and the decision to be employed in a less demanding job. They use a representative sample of the Dutch population and construct an indicator for less demanding jobs. Their estimations indicate that the motherhood decision is strongly correlated with both employment and having a less demanding job. This suggests that ignoring these correlations will lead to inconsistent parameter estimations of wage equations. The selectivity-corrected estimation of women's wage differentials indicates that a large part of the wage differential is composed of discrimination compared with estimations without correction for selectivity.

---

[24] The problem of endogeneity bias can be handled by instrumenting the child variables, or by estimating separate wage functions and controlling for the selection into the group of mothers and non-mothers (Joshi *et al.* 1999). It is not possible to use valid instruments (variables that affect the choice of having children but not the human capital and earning capacity of women) for the data used by Datta Gupta and Smith (2003).

7.4   Conclusion

Human capital theory implies that children affect wages because they demand time-inputs which cannot be invested in education or on-the-job training. Which time-inputs (the amount, the quality, and the timing) lead to which wage effects is a research question still awaiting careful analysis. In particular, the timing of time-inputs has received insufficient attention.[25] Most studies analysing women's wages have focused on the human capital accumulation, and depreciation during career interruption and restoration after career interruption. In this chapter these studies are reviewed from a social policy on combining paid work and family care perspective.

The ranking of European countries according to the gross hourly wage differentials in purchasing power parities by gender and parenthood does not coincide with the ranking of countries according to the gaps in labour force participation rates between mothers and fathers. This may be due to selection into employment of women with favourable labour market characteristics in countries where their labour force participation is low. Descriptive graphs of gross hourly wages in six European countries according to childcare arrangements and partner's gross hourly wages show cross-country differences and give a preliminary indication that postponement and choice of childcare arrangement (paid care/father) does show associations with the country's social policies to combine paid work and children (childcare policies and possibilities to work part-time) and 'equality' of mothers' and fathers' wage rates.

The findings of the studies reviewed indicate that care-related leave-taking behaviour may not only have consequences for human capital accumulation, but also have signalling effects. Even in a single country, Denmark, one study finds that the effects of taking leave for care are only temporary (Datta Gupta and Smith 2002); but another study does not find that these effects diminish over time (Skyt et al. 2004). So there is still a puzzle to be solved. The effect of working part-time has not been researched in the Scandinavian countries but has gained a lot of

---

[25] The demographic developments, such as postponement of the first child in a woman's life, and a higher proportion of childless women (see also Wetzels 2001; Part II, Chapter 6 of this volume) affect the composition of women and mothers in the labour force, and, depending on whether and how labour market productivity is affected by motherhood, women's wage structure may be affected accordingly. The number of studies that analyse the impact of these demographic aspects on women's wages is quite limited. An example is Amuedo-Dorantes and Kimmel (2006) who find that it pays for American college-educated women to postpone the first child until after turning 30.

attention in studies from the UK. It is a well-known finding that part-time jobs are paid less per hour in the UK. No such clear effect is found in the Dutch part-time economy.

Another peculiar aspect of women's wages in the UK is the 'exogenous' child effect in women's wages. After controlling for actual human capital, unobserved heterogeneity, past part-time experience, and controlling for holding a part-time job, there is still an effect of children revealed by dummy variables in the wage equation, at least for fairly young women, not older than age 33. No such significant effect is found in the Netherlands or in Scandinavian countries.

In most of the Central and Southern European countries, there are still very few studies analysing the effect of leave and maternal and non-maternal childcare on mother's wages. Research on the effects of time out on wages has also not yet accounted for the number of transitions in and out of the labour market around the time of childbirth. More-over, the component of labour market training, which is found to be so important in market wage determination, has not been analysed according to parenthood.

Appendix 7.A

Wage model specification and the OLS estimator   A simple model of wage determination that nests most specifications that have been estimated in the empirical literature on women's wages is:

$$\ln W_{it} = X_{it}\,\beta + \varepsilon_{it} \tag{1}$$

where i indexes individuals and t indexes time periods. The dependent variable is the logarithmic wage, $\ln W_{it}$. The vector of explanatory variables X_{it} includes measures for observed individual human capital characteristics which can be time varying or time invariant, so that X_{it} can be partitioned such as $X_{it} = [X(1)_{it}, X(2)_i]$. More specifically, the vector of variables, X_{it}, usually includes measures for investment in human capital, such as years of schooling and work experience, and non-investment, such as time out of work due to childbearing and rearing – summarised by the variable home time for females. The parameter estimates are then interpreted as the effect of changes in these variables on wages. A constant is included in the vector X_{it}. The error term, ε_{it}, defined as:

$$\varepsilon_{it} = \nu_i + u_{it} \tag{2}$$

contains an individual specific component, v_i, which is constant over time, and an idiosyncratic error term, u_{it}, with mean zero and constant variance σ_u^2. The unobserved individual specific component, v_i, captures unobserved individual specific skills. Such characteristics may incorporate motivation and ability which may be sustained all through life. The common error term component, u_{it}, picks up macro-shocks or luck.

The traditional estimator applied to the general model specified in equations (1) and (2) is the ordinary least squares estimator (OLS). Consistent estimation of the parameters of interest requires that the following orthogonality condition holds:

$$E[v_i + u_{it}|X_{it}, d_{it}^\star > 0] = 0 \qquad (3)$$

where the latent index variable $d_{it}^\star$ is positive if an individual i participates in the labour market and non-positive otherwise. Obviously, the validity of the orthogonality condition in equation (3) demands the implementation of restrictive assumptions since it may be violated by endogeneity of the explanatory variables of the model, including non-random sample selection. Endogeneity means that explanatory variables in a regression model are correlated with the error term

$$E[\varepsilon_{it}|X_{it}] \neq 0, \text{ or } E[v_i + u_{it}|X_{it}] \neq 0.^{26}$$

In the final section of this chapter, we discuss the bias in wage estimations from non-random sample selection. Below we will first explain and discuss the bias in women's wage estimations caused by measurement error of employment experience and, second, we explain the bias in women's wage estimation from unobserved heterogeneity and the methods that have been applied to reduce this possible bias.

Measurement error in explanatory variables

Measurement error in explanatory variables causes consistency problems with the OLS estimates of the corresponding slope coefficients of the

---

[26] In most cases, it is economically reliable to assume that the time varying variables contained in the vector X_{it} are not strictly exogenous, but are predetermined and, thus, $E[u_{is}|X_{it}] = 0$ if $s \geq t$. The intuition behind predeterminedness is that while shocks in the present are likely to have an impact on future decisions, shocks in the present and future do not affect present decisions. Although predeterminedness does not imply violation of the orthogonality assumption, equation (3), correlation of the unobserved individual-specific error term component, i, with the explanatory variables and measurement error problems in the variables used for the estimation of the model may do.

model. In general, for any variable x_{it}, $x_{it} \in X_{it}$, that is measured with error, we can write:

$$X_{it} = X_{it} + m_{it} \qquad (4)$$

The observed variable x_{it}^* measures x_{it}, the true value of the characteristic, with a random error m_{it} that may vary across individuals and time. As a result, a downward bias of the corresponding estimated coefficient by OLS is induced. It can be shown that the bias of the estimated coefficient of x_{it} is proportional to $\frac{\sigma_m^2}{\sigma_m^2 + \sigma_x^2}$ where σ_m^2 is the variance of the measurement error m and σ_x^2 of x correspondingly.

Two cases may be captured by the specification in equation (4). One case is that the observed variable is only an estimate of its counterpart in economic theory. Thus, the reason for the occurrence of measurement error problems may be due to reporting or computing errors and random non-response errors. The second case is that the variable of interest has no observed counterpart at all and, hence, some indicator or proxy is used. Examples for the latter are the use of age and potential work experience to proxy actual work experience in cases when the data source does not contain information on actual work experience.

Use of instrumental variables/fixed effects estimation

Despite the availability of precise measures for the variables actual work experience and home-time, the application of OLS to the model specified in equations (1) and (2) may still result in biased estimates of the parameters of interest due to the correlation of the unobserved individual specific effect and the regressors of the model, $E[\nu_i | X_{it}] \neq 0$, where $x_{it} \in X_{it}$, which causes OLS applied to the coefficient of the variable x_{it} to be inconsistent.[27]

Therefore, either instrumental variables estimation procedures[28] or fixed effects estimators (FE) are more appropriate in order to identify the parameters of interest. However, the consistency of FE can only be achieved under restrictive assumptions. The FE procedure implies that, in the first step, all individual varying, but time-invariant, observed and

---

[27] The direction of the bias depends on the sign of the correlation of ν_i and x_{it}. Hence, if $E[\nu_i | x_{it}] > 0$, the corresponding component of β is estimated by OLS with an upward bias, and if $E[\nu_i | x_{it}] < 0$ with a downward bias.

[28] Given valid instruments, standard instrumental variable estimation (IV) is consistent but not efficient under most general assumptions. Generalised method of moments estimator – hereafter GMM – leads to more efficient estimates. In the following, we refer to all of these estimators as IV.

unobserved components of the model are removed. This can be achieved either by correction of all variables by individual means, the within-groups estimator, or by taking first differences, the first difference estimator (FD). As a result, also, the major source of endogeneity is removed from the model. In the second step, OLS is applied to the transformed equation. Implied in the use of FE, is that individuals are followed over at least two periods. We will refer to FE in our review of studies below.[29]

Identification of the parameters of interest by application of IV depends on the following factors. First, identification requires that the instruments do not determine wages (the exclusion restriction). In general, if there are k endogenous variables in the regression model, there should be at least k instruments, or k exclusion restrictions. This is the order condition. The instruments, then, have to be correlated with, or determine the endogenous variables. This is the rank condition. Since finding of instruments is often difficult and controversial, it is important to test the exclusion restrictions, the order and the rank conditions.[30]

---

[29] FD results that have been reported in wage growth studies would be consistent estimates of the parameters of interest under the assumption that the time varying regressors in the wage level model are strictly exogenous and that the sample selection process is time constant. However, although the latter assumption may be economically reliable, it is not reasonable to assume strict exogeneity for the variables work experience and time out of work. In fact, it is difficult to justify why economic shocks in the present should not have an impact on choices regarding work experience and home time, or time out of work, in the future.

Further identification problems may be introduced by FD due to the possible multicollinearity of the change in actual work experience variable and the change in home-time, or time out of work.

[30] Tests for endogeneity of the regressors in the wage equation and of the order condition can also be formulated in the expanded regression framework. To investigate the validity of the instruments in terms of explaining variation in xk, F-tests can be applied, where H0: $\pi l = 0$. Examples of variables assumed to be exogenous in empirical studies are: parental education, number of children, variables for region, gender, race, age and occupation. While correlation with home-time and work experience for all of them can be expected, the assumption that they are orthogonal to the error term components in equation (2) is debatable.

Table 7.A.1 *Summary of European based studies published after 1990 that explain women's pay*

Authors	Country	Data	Results[a]
Joshi et al. 1999	US and UK	MRC 1978 and NCDS 1991	Study disentangles three elements of the family pay gap in the UK: (a) a 'within full-timers' component; (b) a 'within part-timers' component; and (c) a composition effect. This last effect measures the extent to which the relatively low pay of mothers can be explained by their concentration in part-time jobs. Comparing two cohorts of British women age 33, born in 1946 and in 1958, they conclude that the crude pay gap between mothers and childless women was similar, but low pay in part-time work became more important in explaining this gap, human capital less so.
Waldfogel 1998	US and UK	NCDS 1991; NLSY in 1991	Regression results indicate a negative effect of children on women's wages even after controlling for observable characteristics such as education; controlling for unobserved heterogeneity did not significantly reduce the estimated child penalties; controlling for actual experience was important in reducing the child gap. However, the majority remained. Women who had leave coverage and returned to work after childbirth received a wage premium that offset the negative wage effects of children.
Albrecht et al. 1999	Sweden	Family and Work 1992 1993, matched with wage data Statistics Sweden	In the CS the effects of time out vary both by type of time out (formal parental leave has no effect on women's subsequent wages, whereas other types of time out have negative effects), and by gender (the effects are stronger for men than for women). PE with controls for individual FE eliminates most of the difference in effects across different types of time out, but the difference across genders in the effects of time out remains. HC depreciation interpretation of the negative coefficient on total time out in earnings functions estimates does not explain the entire effect of time out on wages.

Authors	Country	Data	Results[a]
Datta Gupta and Smith 2002	Denmark	Administrative data	For the cohorts born after 1960: the accumulated experience could be split into experience obtained before the first birth, during the childbirth period and after the birth of the last child. When controlling for time constant unobserved heterogeneity the negative effect of children on mothers' wages disappears. There is no indication that children have long-term effects on the earnings potential of their mothers, holding experience constant.
Skyt Nielsen et al. 2004	Denmark	Administrative data	Taking long birth-related leave has a negative effect on wages both in the public and private sector in Denmark, with no evidence of reduction of the negative effect over time.
Wetzels and Zorlu 2003	Netherlands	Work and IT survey 2001	Mothers in demanding jobs earn 4.5% more than childless women in demanding jobs; mothers in less-demanding jobs earn 6.5% less than childless women. When selectivity is accounted for, the wage premium for mothers in demanding jobs is 20.5% and the wage loss to mothers in less demanding jobs is 37.1%.
Ejrnaes and Kunze 2004	Germany	IABS +administrative data 1975–95	Study of full-time working mothers having the first child. Simple descriptives show a drop in wage after the parental leave period of 15–20% (a higher drop than for other types of interruptions such as unemployment). In the wage regression framework with a rich set of instruments, the consistent parameters suggest that the loss is larger than 11% for each year of interruption for the unskilled; 16% for skilled, and only 4% for graduates.
Gustafsson et al. 2003	Netherlands, Germany, Britain, Sweden	OSA 1998; GSOEP 1998 BHPS 1998; HUS 1998	Part-time work is not restricted to a particular group of workers in the Netherlands. Women and mothers are more likely to work in non-standard work arrangements (not only part-time but also in temporary work).

Table 7.A.1 (*cont.*)

Authors	Country	Data	Results[a]
Harkness and Waldfogel 1999	Australia, Canada, UK, USA, Germany, Finland, Sweden	LIS and LNU for S: most 1994; UK 1995; FI and SE 1991.	OLS with controls for age, age squared, education, race or ethnicity, region and urban residence, and marriage and dummies for having 1, 2, 3 and more children; also corrected for sample selection bias, only significant for USA. Child gap in pay in UK and G; This child gap is largest in the UK.
			1. Higher propensity of UK mothers to work in low-paid part-time jobs; 2. Among full-time working women mothers are relatively lower paid in UK than are mothers in other countries. 2. The variation in the child gap in pay across countries is not primarily due to differential selection into employment or to differences in the wage structure.

Note: [a] We only present here the results relevant for our review on women's wages.

Table 7.A.2 *Studies on women's wages:* * *Data sources and measurement of employment experience*

	Country	Data	Measure of Experience
Harkness and Waldfogel (2003)	Aus, Can, UK, US, GE, FI, SE	LIS and LNU for SE: most 1994, UK 1995; FI and SE 1991.	Not included
Gustafsson *et al.* (2003)	NL, G, UK, SE	OSA 1998; GSOEP 1998 BHPS 1998; HUS 1998	Not included
Albrecht *et al.* (1999)[a]	SE	Family and Work 1992–93, matched with wage data Statistics Sweden	Actual (from age 17) in ft-equivalents, excludes activities of $\leq$ 3 months; only persons working $\geq$ 15 hours pw.
Datta Gupta and Smith (2002)[b]	DK	1980–95 Only individuals with an annual employment of $>$ 1,000 hours.	Actual: accumulated. For cohorts born after 1960 split into: before 1st birth, during the childbirth period and after last childbirth
Ejrnaes and Kunze (2004)	GE	IABS +administrative data 1975–95	Select: only ft workers

Wetzels and Zorlu (2003)	NL	Work and IT survey 2001	Actual
Joshi, *et al.* (1999)	UK, US	MRC 1978 and NCDS 1991	Actual
Waldfogel (1998)[c]	UK, US	NCDS 1991; NLSY in 1991	Actual NCDS: pre-1981 from 1981 survey 1981–91 from the 1991 survey; LSY: sum of actual exp. from 1978 as recorded, plus potential exp. for pre-1978 period for those who left school before 1978

Notes:

[a] Wage data are adjusted to a full-time basis. Wages from Statistics Sweden are based on employers' reports of individual wages once per year;

[b] Annual wage income divided by number of working hours, which is calculated from the register on supplementary pension payment (ATP);

[c] Waldfogel: 'NCDS wage from current job at the age of 33 interview in 1991, if available, for the late wage; if not, I work backward to find the most recent wage. For this reason not all women are age 33 at the time of the late wage. For the early wage, I use the current job at the age 23 interview in 1983, if available; if not I work backward to the most recent job, or if none is available in 1983, I use an intermediate wage from the period between 1983 and 1991. Thus not all women are age 23 at the time of the early wage.'

Explanation of abbreviations: pw = per week; ft = full-time work; exp. = experience.

Countries: Aus = Australia; Can = Canada; DK = Denmark; FI = Finland; GE = Germany; NL = Netherlands; SE = Sweden; UK = United Kingdom; US = United States;

Data sets:

LIS: Luxembourg Income Study.

OSA: Organisatie voor Strategisch Arbeidsmarkt-onderzoek; GSOEP German SocioEconomic Panel; BHPS British Household Panel Survey; HUS HUShallen ekonomiska levnadsforhallenden.

IABS: Institut fur Arbeitsmarkt and Berufsforschung Sample.

MRC: Medical Research Council's National survey of Health and Development provides data on a cohort born in a week in March 1946;

NCDS: National Child Development Study of every child born in the UK during the first week of March 1958, with surveys conducted at birth age 7, age 11, age 16, age 23 and age 33 in 1991;

NLSY: National Longitudinal Survey of Youth is a national probability sample of individuals age 14–21 in 1979 followed annually, Blacks and Latinos over sampled;

Source: Wetzels 2002b.

Table 7.A.3 *Review of estimates of the 'exogenous effect of children in women's wages' in Europe*

Research	Country[a]	Age distribution of women	Empirical estimation: type of data and method	Wage effect by children	Wage gap by children after control for actual experience
Datta Gupta and Smith (2002)	DK	18–40 (1980) 18–55 (1955)	Panel data; random/fixed effects and Heckman		Disappears after controlling for time-constant unobserved heterogeneity
Gustafsson, Kenjoh and Wetzels (2003)	GE NL SE UK	16–64	CS; OLS	n.s. in GE, NL, SE and UK	Not available
Harkness and Waldfogel (2003)	GE FI SE UK	25–44	CS; OLS	First child: GE: n.s.; FI: 42%. SE: n.s. UK: 8.2% Corrected for sample selectivity: GE: n.s. FI: 4.4% SE: n.s.; UK: 9.3%;	Not available
Wetzels (2002a)[b]	NL	18–64	CS; OLS	−8.2%	Disappears

Study	Country	Age	Method		
Wetzels (2002b)[b]	NL	21–30 31–40 41–50	CS; OLS		1 child: 9% 2 children: 9% 1 child: 4% 2 children n.s. 1 child: n.s. 2 children: −3%
Wetzels and Zorlu (2003)[b]	NL	18–64	CS; OLS	8.7%	Disappears
Albrecht et al. (1999)	SE	24–44	CS and Panel, OLS and fixed effects	n.a.	n.s.
Waldfogel (1995)	UK	23 and 33	CS, first differences, fixed effects	1 child: −10%; >=2 children: −20%.	Lowered but remained
Waldfogel (1998)	UK	33	Panel; fixed effects/first differences	−20%	Lowered, but majority remained

Notes: [a] some studies include comparisons with the US or other countries.

[b]These results come from OLS estimations without correction for selection.

Explanation of abbreviations: DK = Denmark; FI = Finland; GE = Germany; NL = Netherlands; SE = Sweden; UK = United Kingdom; CS: cross-section data; Panel: Panel data; OLS = ordinary least squares estimation; GLS = Generalised Least Squares estimations; n.s. = not significant

Denmark   UK   Netherlands

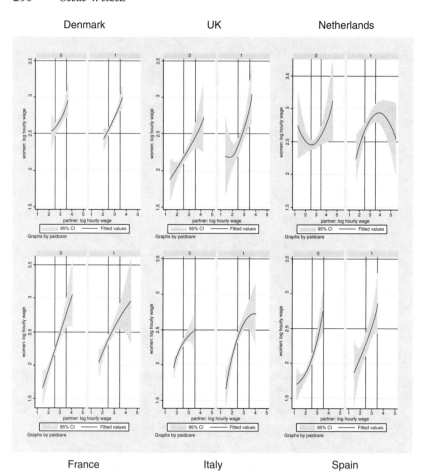

France   Italy   Spain

Figure 7.A.1 Mothers' log hourly wages in € PPP and partner's log hourly wages in € PPP by use of paid care (0 = no paid childcare; 1 = use paid childcare) in European countries, women's age 22–45. Own calculations using data from the European Community Household Panel (ECHP) 2000.

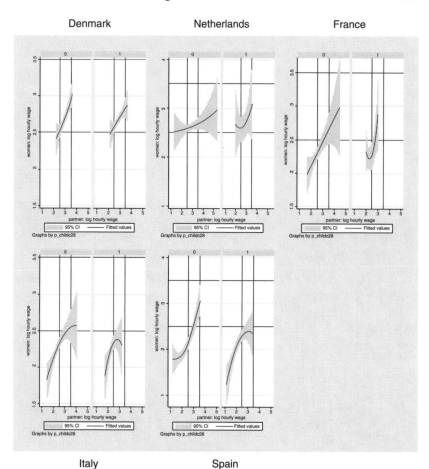

Figure 7.A.2 Mothers' log hourly wages in € PPP and partner's log hourly wages in € PPP by partner cares for children at least 28 hours per week (0 = partner does not care for children 28 hours or more per week; 1 = yes, partner does care for children at least 28 hours per week) in European countries, women's age 22–45. Own calculations using data from the European Community Household Panel (ECHP) 2000.

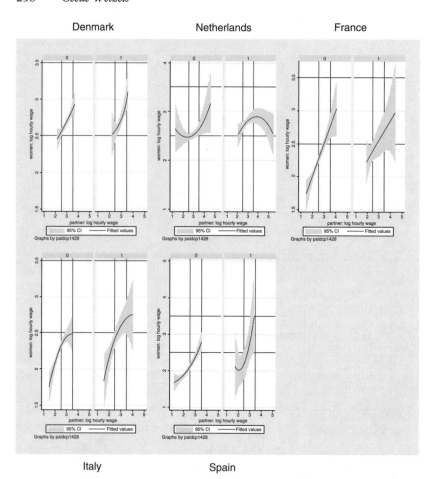

Figure 7.A.3 Mothers' log hourly wages in € PPP and partner's log hourly wages in € PPP by using paid care and partner takes care of children 14–28 hours per week (0 = no; 1 = yes) in European countries: women aged 22–45. Own calculations using data from the European Community Household Panel (ECHP) 2000.

Denmark   UK   Netherlands

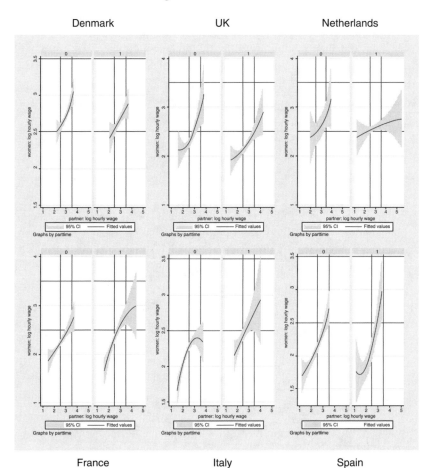

France   Italy   Spain

Figure 7.A.4 Mothers' log hourly wages in € PPP and partner's log hourly wages in € PPP by mother working part-time (0 = working full-time; 1 = working <35 hrs per week) in European countries, women aged 22–45. Own calculations using data from the European Community Household Panel (ECHP) 2000.

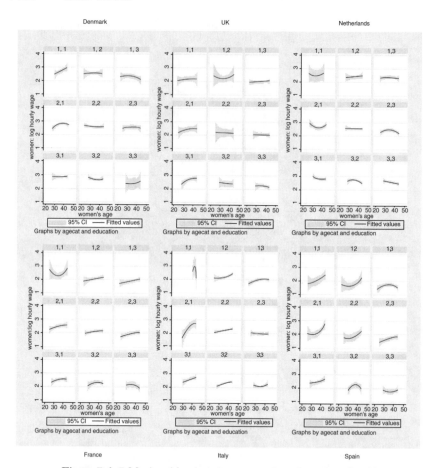

Figure 7.A.5 Mothers' log hourly wage and age by age at first birth (1 = 23 and younger, 2 = between 23 and 27; 3 = older than 27), education (1 = highest, 2 = medium, 3 = lowest level of education) in European countries: women aged 22–45. Own calculations using data from the European Community Household Panel (ECHP) 2000.

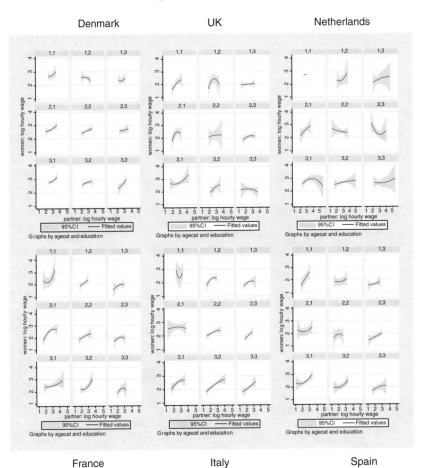

Figure 7.A.6 Mothers' log hourly wages in € PPP and partner's log hourly wages in € PPP by mothers' age at first birth (1 = 23 and younger, 2 = between 23 and 27; 3 = older than 27), mothers' education (1 = highest, 2 = medium, 3 = lowest level of education) in European countries: women's age 22–45. Own calculations using data from the European Community Household Panel (ECHP) 2000.

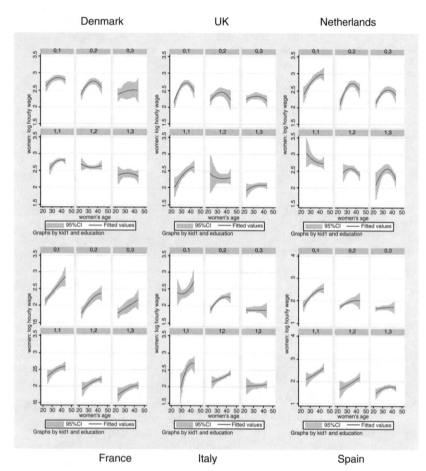

Figure 7.A.7 Women's log hourly wages in € PPP and age by having children and education level (children: 0 = no children; 1 having children, education level: 1 = highest level, 2 = medium level, 3 = lowest level) in European countries, women aged 22–45. Own calculations using data from the European Community Household Panel (ECHP) 2000.

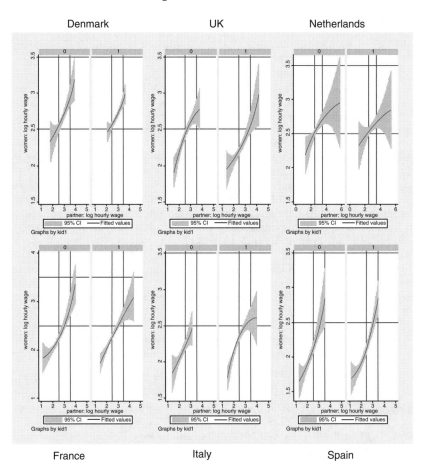

Figure 7.A.8 Women's log hourly wages in € PPP and partner's log hourly wages in € PPP by having children (0 = no children; 1 = having children) in European countries, women aged 22–45. Own calculations using data from the European Community Household Panel (ECHP) 2000.

References

Albrecht, J. W., A. van Vuuren and S. B. Vroman 2004. 'Decomposing the gender wage gap in the Netherlands with sample selection adjustments', IZA Discussion Paper No. 1400, November.

Albrecht, J. W., P. A. Edin, M. Sundström and S. B. Vroman 1999. 'Career interruptions and subsequent earnings: a re-examination using Swedish data', *Journal of Human Resources* 34 (2), 295–311.

Allaart, P. and M. de Voogd 1994. 'Herintredende vrouwen', *OSA Research Memorandum 9402*, The Hague.

Amuedo-Dorantes, C. and J. Kimmel 2006. 'USA: Can the family earnings gap be reduced by postponing maternity?', in S. Gustafsson and A. Kalwij (eds.), *Education and Postponement of Maternity: Economic Analysis for Industrial Countries*, 175–206. Dordrecht: Springer.

Anderson, D. J., M. Binder and K. Krause 2003. 'The motherhood wage penalty revisited: experience, heterogeneity, work effort and work schedule flexibility', *Industrial and Labor Relations Review* 56 (2), 73–94.

Avellar, S. and P. Smock 2003. 'Has the price of motherhood declined over time? A cross-cohort comparison of the motherhood wage penalty', *Journal of Marriage and the Family* 65 (3): 597–607.

Beblo, M. and E. Wolf 2002. 'The wage penalties of heterogeneous employment biographies: an empirical analysis for Germany', Working Paper No 02–45, Centre for European Economic Research (ZEW), Mannheim.

Becker, G. S. 1964. *Human Capital: A Theoretical and Empirical Analysis with Special Reference to Education*, Chicago: University of Chicago Press, 1993, 3rd edn.

    1985. 'Human capital, effort, and the sexual division of labor', *Journal of Labor Economics* 106 (4), 979–1014.

Blau, F. D. 1998. 'Trends in the well-being of American women, 1970–1995', *Journal of Economic Literature* 36 (1), 112–65.

Blau, F. D. and M. A. Ferber 1987. 'Discrimination: empirical evidence from the United States', *American Economic Review* 77 (2), 316–20.

Browning, M. 1992. 'Children and household economic behaviour', *Journal of Economic Literature* 30 (3), 1434–75.

Budig, M. J. and P. England 2001. 'The effects of motherhood on wages in recent cohorts', *American Sociological Review* 66 (2), 204–25.

Cain, G. G. 1986. 'The economic analysis of labor market discrimination: a survey', in Orley, Ashenfelter and Richard Layard (eds.), *Handbook of Labor Economics*, vol. I, 693–785, Amsterdam: Elsevier.

Corcoran, M., G. Duncan and M. Ponza 1983. 'A longitudinal analysis of white women's wages', *Journal of Human Resources* 18 (4), 497–521.

Datta Gupta, N. and N. Smith 2002. 'Children and career interruptions: the family gap in Denmark', *Economica* 69 (276), 609–29.

Dekker, R., R. Muffels and E. Stancanelli 2000. 'A longitudinal analysis of part-time work by women and men in the Netherlands', in Siv Gustafsson and Danièle Meulders (eds.), *Gender and the Labor Market: Econometric Evidence of Obstacles to Achieving Gender Equality*, 260–87. London/Basingstoke: Macmillan.

Del Boca, D. and S. Pasqua 1999. 'Trade union policies and women's work', Dipartimento di Economia Cognetti de Martiis, Università degli Studi di Torino.

2005. 'Labor supply and fertility in Europe and the U.S.', in T. Boeri, Daniela Del Boca and C. Pissarides (eds.), *Women at Work: An Economic Perspective*, 126–53. Oxford: Oxford University Press.

Ejrnæst, M. and A. Kunze 2004. 'Wage dips and drops around first birth', IZA Discussion Paper No. 1011.

Ermisch, J. and R. Wright 1993. 'Wage offers and full-time and part-time employment by British women', *Journal of Human Resources* 28 (1), 111–33.

Eurostat 2002. ECHP UDB Description of variables, Data Dictionary, Codebook, and Differences between countries and waves, Doc Pan 166/2002–12.

Gustafsson, S. and C. Wetzels 2000. 'Optimal age for first birth: Germany, Great Britain, the Netherlands and Sweden', in S. Gustafsson and D. Meulders (eds.), *Gender and the Labour Market: Econometric Evidence of Obstacles to Achieving Gender Equality*, 188–209. London: Macmillan.

Gustafsson, S. S., E. Kenjoh and C. M. M. P. Wetzels 2001. 'Does part-time and intermittent work during early motherhood lead to regular work later? A comparison of labor market behaviour of mothers with young children in Germany, U.K., Netherlands and Sweden', *Vierteljahrshefte* 1: 15–23.

2002. 'First time mothers' labor force transitions in Britain, Germany, the Netherlands and Sweden', in Hugh Mosley, Jacqueline O'Reilly and Klaus Schömann (eds.), *Labor Markets, Gender and Institutional Change: Essays in Honour of Günther Schmid*: 185–211, UK: Edward Elgar Cheltenham.

2003. 'Employment choices and pay differences between non-standard and standard work in Britain, Germany, Netherlands and Sweden', in S. Houseman and M. Osawa (eds.), *Non-standard Work Arrangements in Japan, Europe, and the United States*, 215–66, Upjohn Institute for Employment Research.

Gustafsson, S. S., C. M. M. P. Wetzels, J. D. Vlasblom and S. Dex 1996. 'Labor force transitions in connection with childbirth: A panel data comparison Between Germany, Great Britain, and Sweden', *Journal of Population Economics* 9: 223–46.

Harkness, S. and J. Waldfogel 2003. 'The family gap in pay: evidence from seven industrialized countries', *Research in Labor Economics* 22: 369–414.

Heckman, J. 1979. 'Sample selection bias as a specification error', *Econometrica* 47: 153–61.

Hersch, J. 1991. 'Male–female differences in hourly wages: the role of human capital, working conditions, and housework', *Industrial and Labor Relations Review* 44 (4), 746–59.

Hersch, J. and L. S. Stratton 1994. 'Housework, wages, and the division of housework time for employed spouses', *American Economic Review* 84 (2), 120–5.

Hochschild, A. 1989. *The Second Shift: Working Parents and the Revolution at Home*, New York: Viking Press.

Joshi, H., P. Paci and J. Waldfogel 1999. 'The wages of motherhood: better or worse?', *Cambridge Journal of Economics* 23: 543–64.

Kanellopoulos, C. N. and K. G. Mavromaras 2002. 'Male–female labour market participation and wage differentials in Greece', *Labour* 16: 771–801.

Korenman, S. and D. Neumark 1992. 'Marriage, motherhood and wages', *Journal of Human Resources* 27: 222–55.

Kunze, A. 2000. 'The determination of wages and the gender wage gap: a survey', IZA Discussion Paper 193, Bonn.

Locatelli, M., V. Moscato and S. Pasqua 2001. 'The European Community Household Panel (ECHP): elements for users with special focus on labour and household economics', Child Working Paper 24.

Maassen van den Brink, H. 1994. 'Female labor supply, marital conflict and childcare', Doctoral dissertation. Amsterdam: Amsterdam University Press.

Manning, A. and H. Robinson 2004. 'Something in the way she moves: a fresh look at an old gap', *Oxford Economic Papers*, 168–88.

Mincer, J. 1974. *Schooling, Experience and Earnings*. New York: Columbia University Press.

Mincer, J. and H. Ofek 1982. 'Interrupted work careers', *Journal of Human Resources* 17: 3–24.

Mincer, J. and S. Polacheck 1974. 'Family investments in human capital: earnings of women', *Journal of Political Economy* 82 (2), 76–108.

Naur, M., M. Rosholm and N. Smith 1994. 'Wage differentials between men and women in the 1980s', *Nationalokonomisk Tidsskrift* 132: 260–85.

Neumark, D. and S. Korenman 1994. 'Sources of bias in women's wage equations: results using sibling data', *Journal of Human Resources* 29: 379–405.

Phipps, S., P. Burton and L. Lethbridge 2001. 'In and out of the labor market: long term-income consequences of child related interruptions to women's paid work', *Canadian Journal of Economics* 34 (2): 411–29.

Russo, G. and W. Hassink 2005. 'The part-time wage penalty: a career perspective', IZA Discussion Paper 1468.

Sainsbury, D. 1996. *Gender, Equality and Welfare States*. Cambridge: Cambridge University Press.

Skyt Nielsen, H., M. Simonsen and M. Verner 2004. 'Does the gap in family-friendly policies drive the family gap?', *Scandinavian Journal of Economics* 106 (4), 721–44.

Statistics Netherlands 2000, 2002. *Statline*.

Stratton, L. S. 1995. 'The effect interruptions in work experience have on wages', *Southern Economic Journal* 61 (4), 955–70.

2001. 'Why does more housework lower women's wages? Testing hypotheses involving job effort and hours flexibility', *Social Science Quarterly* 82 (1), 67–76.

Visser, J. 2002. 'The first part-time economy in the world: a model to be followed?', *Journal of European Social Policy* 12 (1), 23–42.

Waldfogel, J. 1995. 'The price of motherhood: family status and women's pay in a young British cohort', *Oxford Economic Papers* 47: 584–640.

1998. 'The family gap for young women in the United States and U.K.: can maternity leave make a difference?', *Journal of Labor Economics* 16 (3), 505–45.

Wetzels, C. M. M. P. 2001. *Squeezing Birth into Working Life: Household Panel Data Analysis Comparing Great Britain, Germany, the Netherlands and Sweden*, Aldershot, Hampshire: Ashgate Publishing.

2002a. 'Dutch women's productivity in the labor market: is there a double selection into motherhood and less demanding jobs?', Working Paper presented at IZA Bonn workshop: The Future of Family and Work: Evaluation of Family Friendly Policies, 10–11 May.

2002b. 'Does motherhood really make women less productive? The case of the Netherlands', Working paper presented to EALE 2002 Conference, Paris.

2005. 'Supply and price of childcare and female labour force participation in the Netherlands', *Labour* 19: 171–210.

Wetzels, C. M. M. P. and K. G. Tijdens 2002. 'Dutch women's return to work and the re-entry effect on wage', *Cahiers Economiques Bruxelles* 45 (20), 169–89.

Wetzels, C. M. M. P. and A. Zorlu 2003. 'Wage effects of motherhood: a double selection approach', Working Paper presented to the joint workshop of research networks on family and labor market dynamics on quantitative methods', European Commission, Bruxelles, 18–19 February.

Zorlu, A. 2002. 'Absorption of immigrants in European labor markets, the Netherlands, U.K. and Norway.', *Doctoral dissertation*, 177–206, Tinbergen Institute Research Series no 279.

Part III

8 An empirical analysis of the effects of social policies on fertility, labour market participation and hourly wages of European women

Daniela Del Boca, Silvia Pasqua, Chiara Pronzato and Cécile Wetzels

8.1 Introduction

In this chapter, we explore the impact of social policies on the joint decisions of women's labour market participation and fertility and on wages. We use the European Community Household Panel (ECHP), a longitudinal survey coordinated and supported by Eurostat. The survey involves a representative sample of households and individuals interviewed for eight years (1994–2001) in each of the fifteen European Union (EU) Member States existing at that time.[1] The standardised methodology and procedure in data collection yield comparable information across countries, making the ECHP a unique source of information for cross-country analyses at the European level. The aim of the survey, in fact, is to provide comparable information on the EU population, representative at both the longitudinal and the crosswise level. The data collected cover a wide range of topics on living conditions (income, employment, poverty and social exclusion, housing, health, migration and other social indicators). Therefore, the ECHP survey allows us to make analyses of how individuals and households experience change in their socio-economic environment and how they respond to such changes, and analyses of how conditions, life events, behaviour and values are linked to each other dynamically over time.

This empirical chapter is organised as follows: section 8.2 contains an empirical analysis of the simultaneous women's choice of working and

---

[1] Austria (from 1995), Belgium, Denmark, Finland (from 1996), France, Germany, Greece, Italy, Ireland, Luxembourg, the Netherlands, Portugal, Spain, Sweden (from 1997) and the UK.

271

having children in which the results of different specifications are presented and compared. In section 8.3 an empirical analysis of women's wages determinants is presented. Section 8.4 concludes.

8.2   Women's choices of labour market participation and fertility

As discussed in Del Boca and Locatelli's survey Part II, Chapter 5, the labour market participation decision, and fertility are considered as joint decisions, being the outcome of the maximisation of household expected utility under budget and time constraints (Cigno 1991; Rosenzweig and Wolpin 1980; Hotz and Miller 1988; Francesconi 2002; Del Boca 2002). The relationship between participation and fertility depends not only on prices, incomes and household characteristics, but also on variables related to the characteristics of the social environment in which the household is embedded. In this empirical analysis we attempt to determine the extent to which different combinations of currently existing social and labour market policies (e.g. part-time employment opportunities, subsidised childcare provision, parental leave and welfare support for women with children) affect the decision to participate in the labour market and to have children. As discussed above, countries differ markedly in the ways governments support women's choices in their labour market and fertility decisions. In fact, while in the Nordic European countries, the fertility decline in the 1970s raised important concerns and stimulated governments to design social policies supporting working women to have the desired number of children, in the Southern European countries governments have intervened in a less significant way.

In this empirical application we explore the effect on participation and fertility of not only personal and household characteristics but also of important social policies such as childcare and parental leave. We use the rankings proposed in Part I, Chapters 2 and 3.

8.2.1   *The econometric specification*

In order to estimate the effects of individual characteristics, household characteristics, and childcare provision generosity on the joint decision to work and to have a child, we use a bivariate probit model that allows us to estimate the joint probability of working and having a child in the period considered.

The econometric specification of the fertility and labour supply decision rules are assumed to be quasi-reduced form representations of the demand functions representing the solutions to the optimisation problem. A latent variable structure is assumed for both decisions. To illustrate this, we consider a two-equation system. Let the net value of being employed in period t be given by:

$$P_{1,t}^* = H_{i,t}\beta_1 + Y_{i,t}\beta_2 + E_{i,t}\beta_3 + u_{i,t},$$

where $H_{i,t}$ is the row vector containing the observed variables measuring the human capital of the woman in household i at time t; $Y_{i,t}$ is the vector of the household's income at time t, and includes the husband's earnings; and $E_{i,t}$ represents the environment she faces in terms of social policies. The term $u_{i,t}$ is a disturbance term.

The latent variable representing the net returns of an additional child in period t is given by:

$$B_{1,t}^* = H_{i,t}\delta_1 + Y_{i,t}\delta_2 + E_{i,t}\delta_3 + v_{i,t},$$

where the disturbance term $v_{i,t}$ is not assumed to be distributed independently of $u_{i,t}$. Let the variable $d_{i,t}^p = 1$ if woman in the household i participates in the labour market in period t, and $d_{i,t}^p = 0$ if she does not. Treat the birth outcome in a similar way, that is, let $d_{i,t}^f = 1$ if there is a birth in household i during period t, and 0 if this is not the case. Then we have that:

$$d_{i,t}^p = 1 \Leftrightarrow p_{i,t}^* > 0 \text{ and } d_{i,t}^f = 1 \Leftrightarrow B_{i,t}^* > 0,$$

Assume that $d_{i,t}^{p^*}$ and $d_{i,t}^{f^*}$ are normally distributed with unit variance. Therefore, we have that:

$$P(d_{i,t}^P = 1) = \Phi(H_{i,t}\beta_1 + Y_{i,t}\beta_2 + E_{i,t}\beta_3)$$

and

$$P(d_{i,t}^f = 1) = \Phi(H_{i,t}\delta_1 + Y_{i,t}\delta_2 + E_{i,t}\delta_3)$$

The joint probability of working and having children is given by:

$$P(d_{i,t}^P = 1, d_{i,t}^f = 1) = F_P(H_{i,t}\beta_1 + Y_{i,t}\beta_2 + E_{i,t}\beta_3, H_{i,t}\delta_1 + Y_{i,t}\delta_2 + E_{i,t}\delta_3),$$

where F_p is the bivariate normal distribution function with zero means, unit variance and correlation ρ.

8.2.2   Data and variables

As already mentioned, for our empirical analysis we use the European Community Household Panel (ECHP). The unit of analysis of the ECHP is the family, and, within the households, all individuals older than 16 years, although it is also possible to have information (mainly demographic information) on children under 16 years. In almost every country the concept of 'family' is based on the two criteria: sharing a house and the common daily matters. A *household* is therefore defined as 'one person living alone or a group of persons (not necessarily related) living at the same address with common housekeeping – i.e. sharing a meal on most days or sharing a living or sitting room' (Eurostat 1999; p. 25).

The ECHP has many advantages: it covers the whole population, including non-working persons; as a household data set, it includes a lot of useful and harmonised information (for example, number and age of children, marital status). Moreover, it is possible to link household-level information to individual data so that it allows us to study, for example, the labour supply decisions of the female partner in a couple, accounting not only for her own personal characteristics but also for those of her male partner.

We use the panel for the period 1994–2000, and we introduce dummies for countries grouped according to the generosity of their childcare provision and their parental leave policy, respectively (see Part I, Chapters 2 and 3). Since our main aim is to study participation and fertility for our analysis in all specifications, we selected all households in which women are in the age range 21–45, married or cohabiting, in order to exclude those women who might still be enrolled in school or may be already retired. For the analysis of fertility, the age restriction helps to ensure that women included in the final sample will have a high probability of being fertile.

The variables used in our estimates can be grouped in the following three categories:

(i)   *Personal characteristics*

- wife's age (and squared age)
- wife's education: we use three dummy variables (third level of education; second level of education; and less than second level of education; the last is the excluded one).

(ii) *Household's characteristics*

- presence of children (4 different age groups: 0–2, 3–5, 6–14, older than 14); the excluded dummy is 'no children'

- presence of grandparents (i.e., presence in the household of either the wife's or the husband's parents)
- wife's non-labour income, which includes all household sources of income except the wife's labour income and social transfers (in euros and divided by 1,000)
- social transfers to the household, which represents income from public transfers (in euros and divided by 1,000)

(iii) *Social policies*

In the first specification:

- dummies for the generosity of childcare provision: four dummy variables that group the countries according to the availability and generosity of childcare services for children 0–3 years old. Group 1 includes only Denmark, where childcare supply is very generous; Group 2 includes France and Finland, with quite generous childcare policies; Group 3 includes Ireland, Austria, Portugal, the UK, Italy, Luxembourg, Germany and the Netherlands with less generous childcare policies; and Group 4 (excluded) includes Spain and Greece where the public provision of childcare is scarce.

In the second specification:

- dummies for the generosity of the parental leave policy: four dummy variables that group the countries according to the generosity of their parental leave policy, which depends on its attractiveness (in terms of duration, protection and replacement wage) and on incentives for the fathers to take advantage of it (higher, if the right to the leave is individual and the replacement wage is also good for men). Group 1 includes Luxembourg, Italy and Portugal, where parental leave is not long (6–12 months which can be split between the parents), but good in terms of protection, wage replacement and seniority rights and where months cannot be transferred from the father to the mother. In Group 2 we find Finland and Denmark, which score less than the Group 1 countries from a gender-equality point of view, as the whole period can be transferred from the father to the mother. Group 3 includes a heterogeneous bunch of countries (the UK, Greece, Ireland, France, Germany and the Netherlands). The UK, Ireland, the Netherlands and Greece appear weak from a protective point of view (no paid period, no seniority rights, not even job protection in the Netherlands) while France and Germany offer very long leave

(36 months) but it is badly paid and transferable, implying an unbalanced division of work between the couple. Finally, the two countries in Group 4, Austria and Spain, show the worst performance: both of them have long parental leave (36 months) (very badly protected in Spain), are supportive of the traditional distribution of tasks between the parents, are not flexible in terms of minimum time allowed, and restrictive in terms of the age of the child by which the leave must be taken.

The information concerning income has been made comparable using purchasing power parity (PPP)-specific coefficients provided by Eurostat in the ECHP data set. In our empirical analysis we consider the effect of all the above-mentioned variables on the probability for a woman to work and to have a child. Table 8.1 reports the descriptive statistics for the sample we use.

The data show a picture quite consistent with the empirical evidence discussed in the previous chapters in this book. The percentage of women working is higher in Denmark, Finland, the UK and Portugal, while it is much lower in Spain, Luxembourg, Greece and Italy (Figure 8.1).

Important differences concern childcare availability for children 0–3 years which is extremely low in the Southern European countries (and in the UK), and very high in Denmark. The family structure shows different features across countries: the percentage of households where we observe coresidence between married children and their parents is relevant only in Southern European countries, where the lack of public services makes the role of the extended family important. Finally, public transfers to the household are much higher in the Northern and Central West European countries than in the Southern European ones. Table 8.2 shows the sample size for all countries considered.

8.2.3   *The empirical results*

Tables 8.3 and 8.4 show the results of the empirical analysis of the probability of working and having a child and uses the ranking proposed in Part I, Chapters 2 and 3, for childcare and for parental leave. The results show that age has a positive (but decreasing) effect on both the probability of working and the probability of having a child. Education has the expected positive effect on the probability of working, but also it has a positive effect on fertility. This can be interpreted as the prevalence

Table 8.1 Descriptive statistics, ECHP (1994–2000)

	GE	DK	NL	LU	FR	UK	IE	IT	EL	ES	PT	AT	FI
% of working women	63.7	78.2	57.1	46.6	62.6	68	49.6	48.8	47.7	40.5	68	65.2	74.5
% of women who had a child in the year	5.7	9.4	6.8	7.9	8.8	8.1	9.3	7.6	6.7	6.9	6.9	6.3	8.8
Women's age	34.2	33.8	34.9	34	34.3	33.8	35.8	35.4	34.8	35	34.5	34.8	34.9
% of women with tertiary education	18.1	36.5	18	15.1	30.1	35.4	15.4	8.1	23.7	21.2	8.6	8.9	43.9
% of women with secondary education	61.1	44.7	54.7	34.5	41.3	16.2	47.8	42.2	30.6	20.3	13.3	66.4	42.9
Presence of grandparents in the household (%)	2.1	0.5	0.1	6	0.9	2.1	4.2	6.4	14.6	9.5	16.4	13.7	1.5
Woman's non-labour income (€, PPP)	17,832	16,046	18,556	30,088	17,734	18,188	18,575	15,194	13,805	14,065	9,877	18,110	20,315
Social transfers to the household (€, PPP)	2,925	4,775	2,229	5,699	3,415	2,317	3,092	1,241	1,032	1,753	1,463	5,252	5,520
N. obs.	16,418	6,220	13,312	5,267	14,715	11,379	6,850	16,963	11,515	14,742	11,325	6,268	6,406

Table 8.2 Sample selection and attrition

	1994		1995		1996		1997		1998		1999		2000	
	Women 16+	Final sample Women 21–45	Women 16+	Final sample Women 21–45	Women 16+	Final sample Women 21–45	Women 16+	Final sample Women 21–45	Women 16+	Final sample Women 21–45	Women 16+	Final sample Women 21–45	Women 16+	Final sample Women 21–45
Germany	6,347	2,460	6,497	2,603	6,379	2,502	6,240	2,414	5,987	2,226	5,847	2,159	5,689	2,054
Denmark	3,053	1,067	2,824	1,028	2,542	930	2,373	877	2,153	801	2,042	775	1,965	743
Netherlands	4,953	2,040	4,853	2,008	4,905	1,954	4,792	1,963	4,671	1,853	4,745	1,796	4,714	1,698
Luxembourg	1,057	–	3,483	947	2,877	798	2,963	921	2,788	868	2,710	906	2,521	839
France	7,493	2,509	6,933	2,331	6,808	2,264	6,320	2,061	5,851	1,964	5,562	1,825	5,383	1,761
UK	4,860	1,663	4,780	1,620	4,826	1,615	4,789	1,615	4,799	1,646	4,726	1,629	4,685	1,591
Ireland	4,982	1,426	4,268	1,224	3,736	1,062	3,440	984	3,195	876	2,748	721	2,320	557
Italy	9,070	2,593	9,077	2,603	9,037	2,553	8,469	2,399	8,158	2,400	7,897	2,286	7,487	2,129
Greece	6,590	2,020	6,393	1,916	6,059	1,756	5,740	1,615	5,228	1,461	4,997	1,411	4,917	1,336
Spain	9,276	2,590	8,435	2,325	8,116	2,222	7,642	2,094	7,139	1,929	6,811	1,844	6,396	1,738
Portugal	6,064	1,626	6,167	1,624	6,128	1,651	6,089	1,637	5,987	1,608	5,911	1,596	5,824	1,584
Austria	–	–	3,872	1,204	3,788	1,142	3,629	1,061	3,408	1,030	3,240	968	2,994	863
Finland	–	–	–	–	4,126	1,518	4,073	1,413	3,722	1,272	3,587	1,231	2,853	972

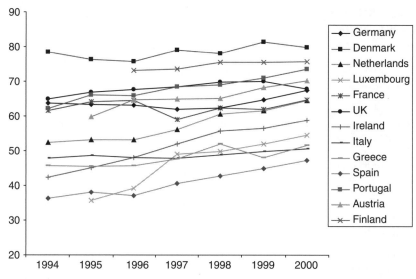

Figure 8.1 Percentage of women aged 21–45 working (ECHP 1994–2000)

of the income effect over the substitution effect on the demand for children (assumed as normal goods). Women's non-labour income (both from other household sources and from public transfers) has the expected negative sign on the probability of being employed, while it is not significant in the fertility equation.

The presence of children in the household decreases the probability of working and having another child, but the effect is different according to the age of the children. In fact, younger children have a stronger negative impact on the probability of being employed, while the presence of older children negatively affects the probability of having an additional child. The presence of grandparents in the household has a positive coefficient in the working equation. This can be interpreted in two ways. On the one hand, grandparents when coresiding may be able to facilitate women going out to work, by helping in the household with various chores and compensating for the rigidities of childcare schedules. On the other hand, the presence of these elderly people in the household could be an additional economic burden that requires women to provide additional income, by working in the labour market.

As far as ranking based on childcare is concerned, we choose to focus our analysis on the provision of childcare for the 0–3 age group, since

Table 8.3 *Bivariate probit estimates (std. errors in parentheses), ECHP (1994–2000)*

	Problem of working	Problem of having a child
Women's age	.164** (0.010)	.309** (0.012)
Women's age squared	−.002** (0.000)	−.005** (0.000)
Tertiary education	.860** (0.020)	.035* (0.016)
Secondary education	.354** (.016)	−.046** (0.013)
Woman's non-labour income	−.007** (0.001)	.003** (0.000)
Social transfers to the household	−.051** (0.002)	.008** (0.001)
Presence of grandparents in the household	.459** (0.030)	.026 (025)
Children 0−2	−.346** (0.013)	−.543** (0.017)
Children 3−5	−.363** (0.012)	.015 (0.013)
Children 6−14	.324** (0.013)	−.493** (0.014)
Children >14	−.052** (0.018)	−.538** (0.029)
Group 1	1.121** (0.0351)	.076** (0.029)
Group 2	.719** (0.025)	.109** (0.020)
Group 3	.505** (019)	−.006 (0.015)
1995	.023** (0.008)	−.052* (0.021)
1996	.050** (0.010)	−.018 (0.020)
1997	.074** (0.011)	.008 (0.020)
1998	.128** (0.011)	−.003 (0.020)
1999	.153** (0.012)	.013 (0.021)
2000	.213** (0.013)	−.151** (0.022)
Cons	−2.924** (0.173)	−5.134** (0.194)
N. obs.	136,092	
Log likelihood	−112,845.03	
Rho	−.051** (0.007)	

(**) = significant at the 99% level.
(*) = Significant at the 95% level.

there is more variability of childcare for this age across countries and within countries, and the provision of such childcare has been shown to be more crucial for supporting women's choices (Del Boca 2002; Del Boca and Pasqua 2005; D'Addio and Mira d'Ercole 2005).[2] The effect of the country ranking is very much in line with our discussions

---

[2] We also used other ranking indicators in our analysis, and in particular the generosity of childcare for children aged 3–6 years. However, the results are less straightforward than those presented here.

Table 8.4 *Bivariate probit estimates (std. errors in parentheses) – ECHP (1994–2000)*

	Prob. of working	Prob. of having a child
Women's age	.157** (0.010)	.305** (0.012)
Women's age squared	−.002** (0.000)	−.005** (0.000)
Tertiary education	.831** (0.020)	.568*(0.016)
Secondary education	.385** (0.016)	−.038** (0.013)
Woman's non-labour income	−.006** (0.000)	.003** (0.000)
Social transfers to the household	−.043** (0.002)	.009** (0.001)
Presence of grandparents in the household	.347** (0.030)	.009 (025)
Children 0−2	−.353** (0.013)	−.542** (0.017)
Children 3−5	−.366** (0.012)	.016 (0.013)
Children 6−14	.329** (0.013)	−.488** (0.014)
Children >14	−.076** (0.018)	−.533** (0.029)
Group 1	239** (0.023)	.055** (0.018)
Group 2	.399** (0.028)	.120** (0.024)
Group 3	.250** (020)	−.026 (0.017)
1995	.041** (0.008)	−.055*(0.021)
1996	.049** (0.009)	−.020 (0.020)
1997	.073** (0.010)	.005 (0.020)
1998	.129** (0.011)	−.007 (0.021)
1999	.152** (0.012)	.009 (0.021)
2000	.212** (0.012)	−.155** (0.022)
Cons	−2.632** (0.173)	−5.086** (0.022)
N. obs.	136,092	
Log likelihood	−114,012.33	
Rho	−.0466** (0.007)	

(**) = significant at the 99% level.
(*) = Significant at the 95% level.

above, especially with respect to the coefficients of the employment equation. Being in countries where there is more availability of childcare increases the probability of working and having a child (i.e. only when the provision is very generous, as in the first two country groups (e.g. Denmark in Group 1, Finland and France in Group 2).

Table 8.4 presents the results of our estimates when we use the dummies for the generosity of the parental leave schemes offered by each country (Group 1 includes the most generous countries; Group 4 – the excluded category– the least generous). When we look at the coefficients related to the parental leave arrangements, we see that the probability of working and having children is higher in the three groups displayed than in the excluded group. All countries included in the analysis have a better work performance than Austria and Spain: the coefficients for Groups 1 and 3 are very close to each other in size, and the coefficient for Group 2 (Denmark and Finland) is the largest one. To explain the large coefficient relating to Group 2, it is important to consider that the social policies may be correlated: residing in Denmark or Finland increases the probability of working and having children, given also the greater availability of childcare when the leave expires.

The empirical results presented here illustrate the importance of analysing labour market and fertility choices in a framework which allows us to consider not only the impact of personal and household characteristics but also the characteristics of the environments where these choices are made. In fact, the variables related to the country rankings have a relevant influence on women's employment and fertility and they are as important (and in some cases even more important) than individual and household characteristics. Our empirical specification illustrates the use of country rankings as 'parsimonious indicators' of the generosity of social policies in the analysis of women's employment and fertility decisions.

8.3   Women's wage analysis

In the second part of the empirical analysis we analyse the determinants of women's wages considering not only personal and household characteristics but also the impact of the social policies that characterise the different countries of the ECHP sample.

The ECHP cross-country comparison information allows analyses of women's wages across Europe to be carried out. We present a cross-sectional analysis of wages for women of 21–45 years of age in 2000. Although the panel aspect of this data set may be used to correct the potential bias from unobserved heterogeneity in wages as explained in Part II, Chapter 7 the attrition of wage information is high. Furthermore, as Table 7.2 in that chapter shows, hourly wages in PPP are still quite different across countries. Pooling wage data across countries and using dummy variables to capture country effects would lead to a mixed effect of country difference in wages and social policies affecting wages.

We start by showing simple OLS wage regressions for four countries for which we have the most relevant information in the ECHP. We include Denmark as a representative of a country second in ranking according to generosity of parental leave policies, and with the highest ranking according to availability and generosity of childcare services for children aged 0–3; Belgium with ranking 2 on parental leave generosity, and ranking 3 on childcare generosity; Italy which is first in ranking according to generosity of parental leave policies, and ranks 3rd according to availability and generosity of childcare services for children aged 0–3; and Spain as a representative country which is last in both rankings. Since the countries differ less in childcare provision for children aged 3–6 we do not expect large differences across countries, and therefore this information is left out.

In Appendix Table 8.A.1, we define all the variables used in our analysis. The dependent variable, women's hourly wage, appears in its logarithmic form. Women's hourly wage was constructed from monthly gross earnings and divided by the number of hours in the main job including paid overtime per week multiplied by 4.3 weeks. We used PPP-specific coefficients provided by Eurostat in the ECHP data set to make earnings comparable across countries. The independent variables we use to explain women's wages can be divided into three main groups.

The first group includes indicators for investment in human capital. In Part II, Chapter 7 in this volume it was explained that actual employment experience is essential in estimating the effect of having children on women's wages. The only information related to years of employment experience that ECHP provides is: the calendar year when leaving full-time education; year of finishing the highest completed level of education; year when starting working life; the time period between the previous job and the current job; tenure in current job, and whether the current job is the first paid job. It is not specified whether first jobs are student jobs or involve helping in the parents' business. We include the time between leaving full-time education and finding a paid job, since entering the labour market is difficult and unemployment rates are high, especially in the Southern European countries (De Luca and Bruni 1993). We take the period between the previous job and the current job as an indication of time out of the labour market. However, we do not know whether this time out was taken to care for children.[3] We control the analyses for the effect of the highest education level obtained. We expect differences between the four countries. First, we expect human capital to have less effect on women's wages in the social democratic welfare regime in Denmark because of the narrower wage distribution there, than in other countries. As regards leave schemes, we expect the countries which are generous, such as Italy and Denmark, to show that years of employment while having children is less productive in the labour market. On the other hand, full-time, affordable high-quality

---

[3] However, we do not have information on whether the woman had other career breaks, on when she started her first 'real paid job' and on how many years she was in part-time employment.

childcare, as in Denmark, may make these years in employment more productive. The time that passes between leaving the previous job and the current job is also expected to have a negative effect, since a career break leads to less human capital accumulation, especially in countries where it is more difficult to re-enter after a career break. In a relatively highly regulated labour market with few part-time jobs, and relatively fewer permanent jobs, such as in the Southern European countries (Bologna and Fumagalli 1997), we expect more difficulties in re-entering than in other countries.

The second group of exogenous variables in the wage equation aims to estimate the effects of labour market and job characteristics such as working part-time. Working part-time does not lead to a wage penalty in Italy (Cebrian *et al.* 2001; Garrone and Villosio 2001; Del Boca *et al.* 2005), whereas in Belgium, Denmark and Spain the literature reports a few results which do not give a clear idea of the effect of working part-time on wages. We also include variables that have not been specifically analysed in connection with mothers' wages, but which are important in wage determination. These variables are our control variables and include whether the current job is a paid apprenticeship or provides special training, which would relate to a negative wage effect, as the employer is likely to trade off wages against investments in the human capital of the employee. Furthermore, we include the type of contract. Working in temporary contracts increased from 1988 to 1998 in all countries that we analyse, especially in Spain (Carré 2003). We also include a variable that indicates working in a supervisory job as well as working in the private sector. Finally, we include whether the reasons for leaving the previous job were related to the type of contract or the employer's choice to end the contract, or another reason. We do not know whether this is due to having children.

The third group of exogenous variables relates to the energy of paid work, measured by the energy that is taken away by activities other than leisure or sleep and other personal care activities, in line with Becker's theory on labour market productivity (1985). Our data only permits us to include indirect indicators for this energy, e.g. high satisfaction with the distance from home to workplace (we interpret this as a shorter commuting time), high satisfaction with working hours (if working hours fit, this may have a positive effect on an employee's energy to work), and being overqualified (the job is not too difficult, but may also be unsatisfying and tiring in that respect). Unfortunately, there is no information on time spent on household care tasks. Instead, we include duration of marriage and duration of divorce or separation which may indicate the number of years when the woman was putting less effort into the labour market due to specialisation in household tasks after marriage. Alternatively, being married compared with living in a consensual union may also indicate a more promising future for the relationship, and therefore lead to relying more on the breadwinner or the primary earner in the household. We expect to find this in those countries which are low in the ranking on generosity of parental leave and on generosity of childcare. We also expect that in such countries household services will be less available or more expensive than in countries where formal childcare serves the needs of working mothers. Furthermore, husbands in Southern Europe spend less time on household work compared with other husbands, even though their wives work longer hours than women in other countries.

Table 8.5 presents OLS wage regressions for women in Denmark, Belgium, Italy and Spain.

As expected, we find that education has stronger wage effects in Italy, Spain and Belgium than in Denmark. Contrary to our expectations, we find a very similar negative effect from years between leaving education and entering paid work in all countries at the 1% significance level. In line with our expectations, the wage effect of tenure is only strong and significant at the 1% level in the Southern European countries; in Italy, the effects of tenure on wage decrease with tenure. This seems to indicate that Italian women remain working in their job after their wage increase starts to decline. This points to reaching peaks in wages early in their job or a less mobile pattern of Italian women in the labour market.

As expected, we only find negative effects of the time passed between previous and current jobs in Italy and Spain at the 5% significance level.

Giving birth to the first child at a later age (or having no child yet) affects hourly wages positively. We interpret this as a reward for longer years of pre-maternity employment experience. If a Danish woman gives birth to a child before starting working life, this has a positive effect on hourly wages but we do not find any effect in the other countries. This is not in line with the idea of increasing your earnings before taking maternity leave in Denmark because the financial benefits are a percentage of your pre-maternity earnings. Nevertheless, it fits the idea that women's labour market participation is less of a choice in the Nordic countries because the social democratic regime goes hand-in-hand with full employment. In other countries, women may see having children early in life as the end of their career possibilities, whereas in the full employment economy of Denmark women are expected to work.

Doing short part-time jobs has a highly significant positive wage effect in the Southern European countries. In Belgium, only working long part-time jobs is paid at a better hourly rate than working full-time. In the Danish full-time economy, no wage effects of working part-time are found.

Table 8.5 *OLS women's log hourly wage in PPP in four European countries (age 21–45, in partnership)*

	Denmark	Belgium	Italy	Spain
Less than secondary education	−0.105 (0.030)***	−0.091 (0.046)**	−0.113 (0.026)***	−0.075 (0.039)*
Tertiary education	0.145 (0.023)***	0.234 (0.029)***	0.182 (0.036)***	0.215 (0.037)***
Time period between leaving education and starting working life	−0.009 (0.002)***	−0.008 (0.004)**	−0.008 (0.002)***	−0.008 (0.003)***
Time period between previous job and current job	0.000 (0.006)	−0.004 (0.007)	−0.013 (0.006)**	−0.012 (0.005)**
Tenure	0.009 (0.006)	0.002 (0.009)	0.022 (0.006)***	0.026 (0.009)***
Tenure squared	−0.000 (0.000)	0.000 (0.000)	−0.001 (0.000)**	−0.001 (0.000)
Started working life after having children	0.103 (0.061)*	0.052 (0.070)	0.014 (0.039)	0.046 (0.069)
Current job is paid apprenticeship	−0.394 (0.062)***	−1.507 (0.291)***	−1.393 (0.274)***	0.972 (0.353)***
Current job special training	−0.226 (0.088)**	0.066 (0.295)	−0.546 (0.110)***	0.102 (0.250)
Part-time job less than 20 hours	0.030 (0.023)	0.016 (0.030)	0.192 (0.027)***	0.198 (0.040)***
Part-time job 20−34 hours	0.011 (0.051)	0.082 (0.040)**	0.355 (0.035)***	0.120 (0.054)**
Permanent contract	0.108 (0.035)***	−0.005 (0.043)	−0.018 (0.041)	0.138 (0.039)***
Contract less than 6 months	0.076 (0.078)	0.006 (0.115)	−0.162 (0.067)**	0.020 (0.063)
Supervisory job	0.089 (0.037)**	0.153 (0.056)***	0.128 (0.042)***	0.122 (0.063)*
Overqualified for current job	−0.025 (0.019)	−0.071 (0.056)	−0.027 (0.021)	−0.051 (0.028)*
Previous job ended because of contract	−0.026 (0.027)	−0.049 (0.039)	0.003 (0.035)	0.009 (0.033)
Previous job ended because employer obliged me to leave	−0.045 (0.032)	−0.068 (0.045)	0.060 (0.038)	−0.016 (0.057)
Employer provides training	0.103 (0.031)***	0.083 (0.028)***	0.124 (0.028)***	0.207 (0.033)***
Private sector	0.105 (0.020)***	0.012 (0.057)	−0.199 (0.024)***	−0.168 (0.035)***
Satisfaction with distance is high	−0.051 (0.019)***	−0.064 (0.028)**	−0.037 (0.027)	−0.110 (0.039)***

Table 8.5 (cont.)

	Denmark	Belgium	Italy	Spain
Satisfaction with	0.026	0.049	0.018	0.131
working time is high	(0.020)	(0.031)	(0.031)	(0.042)***
Women's age	0.010	0.006	0.008	0.010
(at 1st birth)	(0.002)***	(0.003)*	(0.002)***	(0.003)***
Years married	−0.001	−0.001	0.003	0.006
	(0.002)	(0.002)	(0.002)*	(0.002)**
Years separated	−0.008	0.019	0.043	−0.005
	(0.009)	(0.011)*	(0.023)*	(0.022)
Always lived in the	−0.060	−0.085	−0.032	0.034
same region	(0.047)	(0.045)*	(0.042)	(0.069)
Migrated to this region	−0.021	0.046	−0.031	0.131
	(0.047)	(0.064)	(0.051)	(0.074)*
Constant	2.085	2.118	1.927	1.424
	(0.088)***	(0.107)***	(0.089)***	(0.131)***
N. obs.	511	492	705	646
R squared	0.50	0.39	0.52	0.54

* significant at the 10% level;
** significant at the 5% level;
*** significant at the 1% level; Secondary education is base; full-time job is base.
Source: Own estimations using ECHP 2000. See Table 8.A.1 for definitions.
Standard errors in parentheses.

Being overqualified for the current job has only a highly significant and negative wage effect in Spain. On the other hand, being satisfied with the distance to work has negative effects on wages. The latter effect seems to be an indication that women pay a price for saving energy by working closer to their home (if high satisfaction with the distance to work means working closer to the home).

The number of years married has a small positive, but very significant, effect in the Southern European countries, which may point to stability in the home situation that is rewarded in wages, or learning-by-doing in the balancing act of combining household work and paid work. In line with the analysis on the hourly child gap in women's wages (Waldfogel 1995), we include in an alternative specification (not presented here), a dichotomous variable that measures the effect of children on top of all other variables. We only found a significant positive effect in Belgium at the 10% level.[4]

---

[4] In line with Waldfogel (1995), we estimated women's wage regressions in seven countries including fewer variables (since some were not available in all countries), and a dummy for having a child or not. From these regressions the child effects that may indicate the estimated negative effect of children in addition to human capital differences and differences in job characteristics were only found in the UK (at the 10% level).

Furthermore, in most countries, women's wages are strongly positively affected by a supervisory position, and working with an employer who provides training. The latter effect is stronger in the Southern European countries than in the Nordic countries and the UK.[5]

8.4   Mothers' and childless women's wages

8.4.1   Descriptive statistics of separate samples of mothers and childless women

Appendix Table 8.A.2 summarises the means of the crucial explanatory variables in women's wage analysis for separate samples of mothers and childless women. The descriptive statistics on the separate samples show constructed years of actual experience from current age, minus age at the beginning of working life, minus the period between beginning the current job minus the year of leaving the previous job. This is a crude measure of actual experience.[6] However, in cross-country comparison it is revealed that mothers of a similar mean age have proportionately[7] the highest employment experience in countries with extensive social policies to keep mothers in the labour market, as in Denmark (ranked 2 in parental leave generosity and ranked 1 in childcare generosity in Part I, Chapters 2 and 3). This proportion is similarly high among mothers in the liberal welfare state of the UK which is ranked 3 in both

---

[5] A contract that lasts less than 6 months has only a significantly negative effect on Italian women's wages compared with a permanent contract and a contract which is temporary but lasts longer. Also, Davia and Hernanz (2002) found that working while covered by a temporary contract did not have a negative effect on wages in Spain once job and employee's characteristics were controlled for. However, our results for Spain show a positive effect for working in a permanent contract and no effect for working in a temporary contract that lasts less than 6 months. Working in the private sector pays worse than working in the public sector, except for women in Denmark who are better paid in the private sector, all else being equal. Although the proportion of women in paid apprenticeships or in jobs that involve special training is low in all four countries, being in these programmes has a highly significant negative effect on wages in all countries, except in Spain, where the effect is positive. This result for Spain is a bit puzzling. In Italy and Spain, paid apprentices and trainees show the highest poverty indicators, especially in Spain (Cebrián *et al.* 2003). A possible explanation that we considered was that other explanatory variables would correlate with the paid apprenticeship, for example training by the employer (as was found in Istat 2000 and Isfol 1998). However, this is not the case.

[6] We do not correct here for composition of the education levels nor for length of education. Also, we do not have information on other career breaks.

[7] The proportion we use is the mean of years of employment experience as a proportion of the mean years of age.

parental leave and childcare generosity in Part I, Chapters 2 and 3. All other countries show lower proportions.

As expected, more mothers are working part-time, but especially in the UK, the Netherlands, Belgium and Italy, mothers are much more likely than childless women to work in short part-time jobs (less than 20 hours per week). The proportion of women working part-time in Southern European countries is higher than figures provided by statistical offices on women of all ages (15.8% for women of all ages in Italy and 17.8% of women of all ages in Spain (Cebrian *et al.* 2003)). But we also selected women who are between 25 and 45 years of age and are most likely to be in these jobs.

Next, we show the statistics related to mothers having a more vulnerable position on the labour market independent of working part-time. Leaving the previous job because the employer obliged them them to, is higher for mothers than for childless women in France (13% for mothers), the UK (9%) and Spain (7%). The percentage of women whose reason for leaving the previous job was the end of a fixed-term contract is only low in the UK. All other countries show a proportion between 9% and 16% with Spain showing figures as high as 27% for mothers, but even 49% for childless women. Moreover, in countries with less generous social policies to combine paid work and family care, fewer mothers compared with childless women have a supervisory position (the Netherlands, the UK and Italy) which may be for reasons related to the lack of energy to work outside the home as a result of care work without public support.

However, the proportion of women employed on a permanent contract is much higher for mothers than for childless women in Denmark and France, and in the Southern European countries (where the proportion of both mothers and childless women who have a permanent contract is much lower than in the other countries).[8]

8.4.2.   *Correction for sample selection bias*

Section 8.2 and Part II Chapter 5, showed that fertility and labour market participation are jointly determined decisions. Therefore, OLS wage regressions should be corrected for sample selection bias caused by these simultaneous decisions.[9] In this subsection we will provide an

---

[8] The statistics for the Southern European countries are in line with figures for all women all ages presented in Cebrian *et al.* (2003) using the European Labour Force survey in 1999.

[9] For more details on method and double selection in women's wages, see Wetzels (2002). Here, we present an example. However, the results should be interpreted with caution since ECHP has very limited information that may be used to identify the equations for double sample selection bias estimations of having a child, as opposed to not having a child.

estimation of these effects, although there may be problems related to identification. For the selection terms in our wage equations, we use a similar bivariate probit model as described in section 8.2. The specification of our equations is different since we wish to correct for selectivity into motherhood as opposed to being childless and not for selectivity of having a child in the next year (section 8.2).

Appendix Table 8.A.3 summarises the results for the selection models in the seven countries considered. We include different sets of variables in the two equations to identify the model (as recommended by Abowd and Farber 1982).[10] As expected, the correlation between the probability of women's employment and the probability of motherhood in the simultaneous bivariate probit models is in all countries significantly negative. Only in Denmark and Belgium is the correlation less significant, whereas in the other countries the correlation is strong. See Appendix Table 8.A.3 for a detailed description.

We wish to correct the OLS wage regressions for sample selection bias caused by the simultaneously determined fertility and labour market participation decisions (as presented in Appendix Table 8.A.3). We are interested in the selections for the probability of employed motherhood. As pointed out earlier, wage estimation models may be biased since the wage of a worker is observed only if he/she is employed. Thus, for the ith worker: $w_i = z_i\delta + \epsilon_{wi}$ if $EMP_i = 0$; and $= 0$, otherwise (1) where EMP_i denotes the employment status of the ith worker and z_i denotes the vector of characteristics that affect her wages. Let DES_i denote the ith worker's labour force participation status. Define DES_i as the woman's decision to have a child. Thus:

$$EMP_i = 1 \ \textit{if} \ DES_i = 1 \cap \times (SEL_i | DES_i = 1) = 1 \qquad (2)$$

$$= 0 \ \text{otherwise}$$

$$DES_i = 1 \ \textit{if} \ Y_{1i} > 0 \qquad (3)$$

[10] Strictly speaking, our model is basically identified by functional form because the bivariate probit model is non-linear. However, we decided to adopt an additional strategy in order to avoid multicollinearity problems and to ensure identification of the model. The key element of this strategy is to find at least one instrument variable that affect women's participation decision, but not the decision to have a child. The difficulty here is that we expect very similar factors to influence both the probability of having a job and having a child. Since a formal econometric test that could indicate the correct specification is not available, any argument as to why specific variables are expected to influence one equation and not the other has to be of a substantive theoretical nature.

$$= 0 \text{ otherwise}$$

$$(SEL_i|DES_i = 1) = 1 \text{ if } Y_{2i} > 0 \qquad (4)$$

$$= 0 \text{ otherwise}$$

where y_{1i} denotes the difference between a worker's expected market wage rate and the reservation wage rate.

The y_{2i}, on the other hand, denotes the i_{th} woman's preference function for a child which is measured by the difference between the woman's expected benefit from motherhood and the opportunity costs of motherhood. In their reduced forms, they may be expressed as follows:

$$Y_{1i} = x_{1i}\beta_1 + \epsilon_{1i} \qquad (5)$$

$$Y_{2i} = x_{2i}\beta_2 + \epsilon_{2i} \qquad (6)$$

When defined for the whole population, the error terms in Equations 1, 5 and 6 are assumed to follow a multivariate normal distribution with zero means, and variances and covariances defined at follows:

$$V(\epsilon_{wi}) = \sigma_w^2, \ Cov(\epsilon_{wi}, \epsilon_{1i}) = \sigma_{1w},$$

$$Cov(\epsilon_{wi}, \epsilon_{2i}) = \sigma_{2w}, V(\epsilon_{1i}) = 1 = V(\epsilon_{2i}), \ Cov(\epsilon_{1i}, \epsilon_{2i}) = \rho^2$$

Unfortunately, wages are observed only for employed workers, and consequently:

$$E(\epsilon_{wi}|EMP_i = 1) = \sigma_{1w}\lambda_{1i} + \sigma_{2w}\lambda_{2i}, \qquad (7)$$

where $\lambda_{1i} = \phi(a_i)\Phi(A_i)/F(a_i, b_i; \rho)$ and $\lambda_{2i} = \phi(b_i)\Phi(B_i)/F(a_i, b_i; \rho)$ are selectivity variables, $a_i = x_{1i}\beta_1, b_i = x_{2i}\beta_2, A_i = (b_i - \rho a_i)/\sqrt{(1 - \rho^2)},$ $B_i = (a_i - \rho b_i)/\sqrt{(1 - \rho^2)}, \phi$ is the univariate standard normal density function, Φ is the univariate standard normal distribution function, and F is the bivariate standard normal distribution function.

From Equation 7, it follows that:

$$E(In \ w_i|EMP_i = 1) = z_i\delta + \sigma_{1w}\lambda_{1i} + \sigma_{2w}\lambda_{2i} \qquad (8)$$

The selectivity variables in Equation 8 are estimated from the bivariate probit models in Appendix Table 8.A.3. Tunali (1986) provides an extensive discussion on the correction of selectivity bias under different variants of bivariate selection rules.

The estimated effects of the selection terms on mothers' wages are presented in Table 8.6. The selection terms for motherhood are significant in the Northern (Denmark) and the Southern European countries (France and Italy). Employed mothers have higher hourly wages compared with all employed women in the labour market in these countries. Only in Denmark do we also find a selection effect for the employment decision, but not a very significant one. This effect is positive, which suggests, surprisingly, that if non-employed women's characteristics were taken account of, the employed mothers would have lower wages than the sample of all women in Denmark, including women who are not participating in paid work. However, since the correlation in the selection model is not highly significant, we should be careful in interpreting these effects in Denmark. A possible explanation might be that only mothers with extremely high-earning husbands and high earnings potential (but not working women) can still make a living in Denmark, whereas couples with low earning potential have to participate in the market since a one partner earning household is not an option for them.

8.5   Discussion and conclusion on wages

In section 8.3 of this chapter we analysed the effect of social policies and labour market characteristics on women's wage structure in countries that differ in their historical and actual social policies and labour market structures. Two potential effects were discussed: (1) the 'direct' effects of social policies and labour market characteristics on women's wages, and in particular on mothers' wages; and (2) the effect of the selection of employed mothers on hourly wages.

We find that human capital is far less important as a determinant of mothers' wages in Denmark than in the other countries, which we regard as a reflection of the total package of social policies in combination with a more narrow wage distribution. Moreover, the Northern European countries are also characterised as full-time economies, with decreasing part-time participation rates, and working part-time being considered as part-time unemployment, with the exception of the reduced working hours for parents. In fact, we did not find an effect of part-time workers being paid better or worse than full-time workers in the Northern European countries. We did not find a significant effect of variables that related to women's energy to work in Denmark except for the negative highly significant effect of job satisfaction and a highly positive effect of an employer providing training, and of having a

Table 8.6 *OLS hourly log wage in PPP (mothers, aged 21–45, in partnership)*

	Denmark	UK	Netherlands	Belgium	France	Italy	Spain
Less than sec. educ	−0.232	−0.079	−0.023	−0.186	−0.121	−0.167	−0.161
	(0.052)***	(0.061)	(0.035)	(0.063)***	(0.048)**	(0.033)***	(0.051)***
Tertiary education	0.173	0.204	0.181	0.272	0.248	0.272	0.274
	(0.028)***	(0.054)***	(0.039)***	(0.058)***	(0.053)***	(0.054)***	(0.053)***
Experience	0.008	0.040	0.034	0.008	−0.001	0.021	0.009
	(0.011)	(0.013)***	(0.007)***	(0.013)	(0.009)	(0.007)***	(0.011)
Experience sq.	−0.000	−0.001	−0.001	−0.000	−0.000	−0.001	−0.000
	(0.000)	(0.000)***	(0.000)***	(0.000)	(0.000)	(0.000)***	(0.000)
Job 20–34 hours	0.017	−0.028	0.023	0.033	0.042	0.201	0.165
	(0.024)	(0.041)	(0.042)	(0.035)	(0.040)	(0.032)***	(0.049)***
Job < 20 hours	−0.013	−0.106	−0.010	0.023	0.023	0.278	0.038
	(0.061)	(0.045)**	(0.043)	(0.043)	(0.065)	(0.036)***	(0.066)
Permanent contr.	0.220	0.018	0.230	0.066	0.206	0.252	0.331
	(0.033)***	(0.076)	(0.042)***	(0.047)	(0.055)***	(0.041)***	(0.045)***
Private sector	0.112	−0.161	−0.093	−0.033	−0.142	−0.185	−0.277
	(0.023)***	(0.037)***	(0.027)***	(0.060)	(0.038)***	(0.027)***	(0.043)***
Supervisory pos.	0.117	0.305	0.321	0.175	0.210	0.243	0.178
	(0.041)***	(0.047)***	(0.059)***	(0.067)***	(0.077)***	(0.052)***	(0.080)**
Previous job ended because of contract	−0.035	0.119	−0.076	−0.074	−0.079	−0.020	−0.009
	(0.030)	(0.077)	(0.046)*	(0.045)*	(0.044)*	(0.041)	(0.043)
Previous job ended employer obliged	−0.029	−0.021	−0.110	−0.084	−0.082	−0.018	−0.081
	(0.035)	(0.061)	(0.061)*	(0.054)	(0.048)*	(0.045)	(0.070)
Married	−0.085	0.025	−0.038	−0.072	−0.142	−0.079	−0.206
	(0.056)	(0.093)	(0.047)	(0.071)	(0.060)**	(0.117)	(0.160)

Table 8.6 (cont.)

	Denmark	UK	Netherlands	Belgium	France	Italy	Spain
Separated/divorced	-0.004	0.109	-0.121	0.062	-0.192	0.085	-0.009
	(0.066)	(0.109)	(0.082)	(0.085)	(0.112)*	(0.153)	(0.209)
Always lived same region	-0.024	0.026	-0.082	-0.088	0.040	0.023	-0.035
	(0.023)	(0.047)	(0.040)**	(0.041)**	(0.038)	(0.035)	(0.043)
λ_{11}	0.360	-0.072	-0.100	0.069	-0.193	0.050	0.044
	(0.201)*	(0.311)	(0.076)	(0.192)	(0.235)	(0.139)	(0.118)
λ_{12}	-0.516	0.231	0.099	-0.126	-0.413	-0.165	-0.117
	(0.193)***	(0.222)	(0.110)	(0.216)	(0.163)**	(0.062)***	(0.085)
Constant	2.430	1.798	2.258	2.272	2.398	1.947	2.069
	(0.195)***	(0.307)***	(0.119)***	(0.227)***	(0.197)***	(0.174)***	(0.247)***
N.obs.	421	603	571	438	552	612	436
R-squared	0.40	0.26	0.28	0.27	0.27	0.45	0.49

Notes: λ_{11}: Measures the possible selection bias from employment for employed mothers based on bivariate probit models in Appendix Table 8.A.3; λ_{12}: Measures the possible selection bias from the motherhood decision for employed mothers based on bivariate probit models in Appendix Table 8.A.3; Standard errors in parentheses.
* significant at the 10 % level; ** significant at the 5 % level; *** significant at the 1 % level.
Source: Own calculations based on European Community Household Panel (ECHP) of 2000. See Appendix Table 8.A.1 for definitions.

supervisory job. However, similar effects were found for satisfaction with distance to work in Belgium, and for training and supervisory jobs in all countries.

Central West European countries which have policies focused on childcare (France and Belgium, see Part I), make human capital accumulation possible for parents, but similar to the Northern European countries, these policies seem to indicate that the human capital that is built up has insignificant effects on mothers' wages compared with childless women's wages. Part-time work with 20–34 working hours had a positive effect on Belgian women's wages. Years of marital separation showed a positive effect on Belgian women's wages.

Human capital (education, tenure, actual employment experience) is an important determinant of mothers' wages in the Southern European countries. It seems unlikely that this is the result of social policies for very small children: while Italy scores highest on parental leave and second on childcare, at the other end of the spectrum Spain scores worst on both. Furthermore, although very limited in supply, employment in part-time jobs, even in short part-time jobs, affects hourly wages positively compared with full-time jobs. The most striking feature of the Southern European labour markets is the lack of labour mobility and the relatively highly regulated labour markets. Moreover, in the Southern European countries mothers who are employed in a permanent job show a more positive wage effect from having this contract than the effect of working in a supervisory job (especially in Spain), whereas in other countries the opposite holds. Since all mothers in our cross-country analysis have a similar mean age, future research should analyse whether mothers' career progress, measured by job status, in Southern Europe is restricted by institutional factors (since there are proportionately fewer mothers in supervisory jobs, the wage effect of being in these jobs is weaker than in other countries, and we find, for example, that the positive years of tenure only increase at a decreasing rate in Italy). Interestingly, we also found that in countries where mother's wages are strongly affected by being in a supervisory job, the effect of a higher age at the time of the first birth leads to more positive wage effects than in countries where mothers gain less from being employed in a supervisory job. We only found a significant effect of being overqualified on Spanish women's wages which may be due to the local labour market characteristics, but it may also indicate that women, and more likely mothers, end up in jobs that are below their level and with low pay.

Table 8.A.1 *Definitions of variables used in wage analyses based on ECHP (2000)*

Dependent variable	
Ln hourly wage	Log of women's gross hourly wage in PPP 2000
Independent variables	
Human capital	
Less than secondary education	ISCED 0–2; less than second stage of secondary education; 0 otherwise
Tertiary education	ISCED 5–7; recognised third level of education; 0 otherwise
Medium-level education = base	ISCED 3; second stage of secondary education; 0 otherwise
Time period full-time education and start working	Time between stopping of full-time education and starting working life in years (n.a. for NL, FR and UK)
Time between current and previous job	Time between starting current job and ending previous job in years; 0 if current job is first job
Tenure (squared)	2000 minus year of start of current job (squared)
Labour Market Characteristics	
Current job is paid apprenticeship	1 if working with an employer in paid apprenticeship; 0 otherwise
Current job is special training	1 if working with an employer in training; 0 otherwise
Part-time job 20–34 hours	Number of hours incl. paid overtime in main job is between 20–34
Part-time job less than 20 hours	Number of hours incl. paid overtime in main job is less than 20
Full-time job=base	Number of hours including paid overtime in main job 35 or more
Permanent contract	1 if type of employment contract is permanent; 0 otherwise
Supervisory job	1 if job status is supervisory, 0 if intermediate, non-supervisory
Previous job ended: contract	1 if reason is ending previous job: end of contract or temporary job, 0 otherwise
Previous job ended: employer	1 if reason is ending previous job: obliged to stop by employer, 0 otherwise
Employer's characteristics	
Employer provides training[11]	1 if education or training provided by employer (free or subsidised), 0 otherwise
Private sector	1 if private sector, including non-profit private organisations, 0 otherwise
Energy to work	
Overqualified for current job	1 if person has skills or qualifications to do a more demanding job; 0 otherwise
High satisfaction, distance to work	1 if fully satisfied with distance to job, 0 for other 5 lower categories of satisfaction

High satisfaction, working time	1 if fully satisfied with working times, 0 for other 5 lower categories of satisfaction
Married	1 if present marital status is married, 0 otherwise
Separated or divorced	1 if present marital status is separated or divorced, 0 otherwise
Years married	Duration of present marriage in years, 0 if not married, (f.o. in France)
Years separated or divorced	Duration of present separation or divorce, 0 if not separated/ divorced (f.o. in France)
Women's age (at birth of 1st child)	Women's age at first birth for mothers; women's current age for childless women
First birth occurs before starting working life	1 if age at first birth is younger than age at starting working life, 0 if no child or age at starting working life is earlier than age at maternity
Always this region	1 if person born in the country of present residence, and has lived in the same region since birth, 0 if otherwise

Source: See also Eurostat (2002). n.a. = not available; f.o. = few observations

[11]The ECHP provides information on whether the employee has received training since January in the year of the survey, the type of course, the number of hours spent on the course, and whether the employer has paid for (part) of this training. However, there are very few observations, and some countries do not include this information.

Table 8.A.2 *Descriptive statistics according to motherhood status in seven countries: women aged 21–45 in partnerships, wages observed, ECHP (2000) (means)*

	Denmark		UK		Netherlands		Belgium		France		Italy		Spain	
	mothers	childless	mothers	childless	mothers	childless	mothers	childless	mothers	childless	mothers	childless	mothers	childless
Less than secondary education	0.138	0.142	0.452	0.229	0.377	0.523	0.113	0.064	0.205	0.167	0.284	0.269	0.383	0.306
Tertiary education	0.394	0.268	0.377	0.569	0.188	0.150	0.513	0.407	0.318	0.323	0.140	0.099	0.400	0.419
Experience (1)	16.854	10.126	17.254	9.960	15.377	10.822	15.429	8.436	15.266	6.294	14.561	8.740	16.434	9.492
Part-time job 20–34 hours	0.298	0.126	0.306	0.057	0.449	0.361	0.311	0.221	0.279	0.162	0.197	0.149	0.170	0.101
Part-time job less than 20 hours	0.033	0.055	0.246	0.020	0.416	0.124	0.178	0.064	0.088	0.066	0.162	0.079	0.087	0.093
Previous job ended because of contract	0.157	0.110	0.052	0.057	0.088	0.112	0.153	0.121	0.170	0.258	0.112	0.120	0.268	0.411
Left previous job because employer obliged me	0.117	0.102	0.090	0.031	0.051	0.050	0.100	0.114	0.133	0.045	0.086	0.103	0.076	0.058
Permanent contract	0.864	0.756	0.945	0.955	0.880	0.816	0.851	0.814	0.900	0.798	0.877	0.806	0.705	0.601

Private sector	0.425	0.575	0.642	0.680	0.635	0.675	0.078	0.250	0.621	0.657	0.504	0.682	0.662	0.795
Supervisory position	0.080	0.047	0.177	0.249	0.057	0.064	0.056	0.057	0.059	0.051	0.063	0.074	0.054	0.043
Married	0.791	0.370	0.845	0.533	0.86	0.433	0.860	0.500	0.794	0.409	0.971	0.810	0.964	0.783
Separated/divorced	0.033	0.031	0.065	0.059	0.037	0.020	0.056	0.021	0.029	0.020	0.017	0.017	0.018	0.012
Womens' age (2)	36.068	29.921	36.502	30.759	37.103	31.226	36.598	29.893	36.163	28.653	37.068	31.045	36.563	29.740
Women's age (at first birth)	26.646		26.192		27.586		26.293		25.724		27.002		26.559	
Always lived in the same region	0.392	0.528	0.759	0.578	0.196	0.281	0.793	0.821	0.572	0.616	0.831	0.789	0.765	0.767
N. obs.	426	127	631	353	631	353	450	140	713	198	649	242	447	258
(1)/(2)	0.47	0.34	0.47	0.32	0.41	0.35	0.42	0.28	0.42	0.22	0.39	0.28	0.44	0.32

Source: *Source*: Own calculations based on European Community Household Panel (ECHP) of 2000. See Appendix Table 8.A.1 for definitions.

Table 8.A.3 Determinants of employment and having a child, estimations from a simultaneous bivariate probit model

	Denmark		UK		Netherlands		Belgium		France		Italy		Spain	
	Mean	Robust st. error	Mean	Robust st. error	Mean	Robust st. error	Mean	Robust st. error	Mean	Robust st. error	Mean	Robust st. error	Mean	Robust st. error
Prob. of Employment (1 = yes)														
Experience (in years)	0.034	0.010	0.023	0.005	0.037	0.004	0.015	0.007	0.026	0.004	0.050	0.003	0.017	0.004
Tertiary education (1 = yes)	0.163	0.152	0.136	0.104	0.396	0.115	0.653	0.129	0.449	0.085	0.725	0.124	0.503	0.094
Less than secondary education (1 = yes)	−0.643	0.151	−0.248	0.102	−0.076	0.086	−0.647	0.136	−0.345	0.080	−0.655	0.064	−0.456	0.082
Partner: tertiary education (1 = yes)	−0.017	0.151	−0.149	0.084	−0.130	0.108	−0.193	0.129	−0.077	0.095	0.010	0.115	−0.036	0.092
Partner: less than secondary education (1 = yes)	0.138	0.189	−0.042	0.091	0.190	0.089	−0.271	0.142	−0.291	0.079	−0.153	0.065	−0.190	0.076
Married (1 = yes)	0.194	0.134	−0.045	0.096	−0.690	0.097	−0.267	0.151	−0.204	0.077	−0.710	0.157	−0.450	0.144
Separated or divorced (1 = yes)	−0.224	0.302	0.120	0.158	−0.470	0.234	−0.257	0.272	−0.134	0.214	0.070	0.289	−0.007	0.295
Constant	0.513	0.134	0.498	0.119	0.835	0.108	0.867	0.147	0.314	0.077	0.501	0.158	0.394	0.150
Prob. of Child in the Household (1 = yes)														
Age (in years)	0.078	0.012	0.043	0.006	0.066	0.006	0.094	0.011	0.081	0.008	0.076	0.006	0.109	0.008
Tertiary education (1 = yes)	0.032	0.140	−0.142	0.100	−0.232	0.106	0.129	0.124	−0.060	0.094	−0.050	0.127	−0.239	0.103

	(1)		(2)		(3)		(4)		(5)		(6)		(7)	
Less than secondary education (1 = yes)	0.115	0.164	0.311	0.104	−0.057	0.089	0.239	0.207	0.140	0.114	0.274	0.075	0.224	0.098
Partner: tertiary education (1 = yes)	−0.071	0.140	0.191	0.084	0.661	0.123	−0.054	0.130	0.045	0.107	0.237	0.133	0.114	0.104
Partner: less than secondary education (1 = yes)	−0.007	0.205	0.443	0.100	0.358	0.088	0.083	0.197	0.112	0.108	0.448	0.079	0.505	0.089
Years married	0.762	0.117	0.573	0.082	1.062	0.080	0.871	0.122	0.722	0.082	0.838	0.135	0.784	0.139
Constant	−2.341	0.342	−1.469	0.213	−2.809	0.221	−3.043	0.339	−2.283	0.238	−2.776	0.241	−3.877	0.273
N. obs.	746		1566		1806		877		1719		2204		1752	
Log pseudo-likelihood	−624.903		−1603.93		−71.74		−817.35		−1674.25		−2167.73		−1799.62	
Rho	−0.278	0.089	−0.445	0.049	−0.258	0.050	−0.171	0.088	−0.238	0.052	−0.318	0.043	−0.340	0.045

Notes: Equation 1 (women's probability of paid job): other specifications include presence of grandmother in the household, and exclude women's experience in the labour market; Equation 2 (probability of child in household): other specifications include partner's employment status (1 = employed; 2, 3, 4 and 5 = non-employment) and presence of grandmother in the household.

Source: Own estimations based on European Community Household Panel (ECHP) of 2000. See Appendix Table 8.A.1 for definitions.

References

Abowd, J. M. and H. S Farber 1982. 'Job queues and the union status of workers', *Industrial and Labour Relations Review* 43: 354–67.

Becker, G. S. 1985. 'Human capital, effort, and the sexual division of labour', *Journal of Labour Economics* 106 (4), 979–1014.

Bologna, S., and A. Fumagalli 1997. *Il lavoro autonomo di seconda generazione*. Milan: Feltrinelli.

Carré, F. 2003. 'Nonstandard work arrangements in France and the United States: institutional contexts, labour market conditions, and patterns of use', in S. Houseman and M. Osawa (eds.), *Nonstandard Work in Developed Economies: Causes and Consequence*: 131–74, Kalamazoo, MI: W. E. Upjohn Institute for Employment Research.

Cebrían, I., G. Moreno and L. Toharia 2001. 'Trabaja a tiempo parcial y duración de la jornada en la Unión Europea: Características, salarios, pobreza', in L. Garrido and L. Tohario (eds.), *Análisis del Panel de Hogares de la Unión Europea*, Madrid: Instituto Nacional de Estadística.

Cebrían, I., G. Moreno, M. Samek, R. Semenza and L. Toharia 2003. 'Nonstandard work in Italy and Spain: the quest for flexibility at the margin in two supposedly rigid labour markets', in S. Houseman and M. Osawa (eds.), *Nonstandard Work in Developed Economies: Causes and Consequence*: 89–130, Kalamazoo, MI: W. E. Upjohn Institute for Employment Research.

D'Addio, A. C. and M. Mira d'Ercole 2005. 'Trends and determinants of fertility rates: the role of policies', OECD Social Employment and Migration Working Papers 27, OECD Directorate for Employment, Labour and Social Affairs.

Davia, M. A. and V. Hernanz 2002. 'Temporary employment and segmentation in the Spanish labour market: an empirical analysis through the study of wage differentials', *Documento de Trabajo 2002–26*, Madrid: FEDEA.

De Luca, L. and M. Bruni 1993. *Unemployment and Labour Market Flexibility: Italy*, Geneva: International Labour Organization.

Del Boca, D. and S. Pasqua 2005. 'Labour supply and fertility in Europe and the U.S.', in T. Boeri, D. Del Boca and C. Pissarides (eds.), *Women at Work: An Economic Perspective*, Oxford: Oxford University Press.

Del Boca, D., S. Pasqua and C. Pronzato 2005. 'Employment and fertility decisions in Italy, France and the U.K.', *Labour* 19 (special issue), 51–77.

Eurostat 1999. *Demographic Statistics*. Luxembourg: Office for official Publications of the European Communities.

   2002. ECHP UDB Description of variables, Data Dictionary, Codebook, and Differences between countries and waves, doc Pan 166/2002–12.

Garrone, G. and C. Villosio 2001. 'Un'analisi longitudinale dei percorsi lavorativi e dei differenziali retributivi degli occupati part-time', in M. Samek Ludovici and R. Semenza (eds.), *Le Forme del Lavoro*: 181–204, Milan: Franco Angeli.

Heckman, J. 1979. 'Sample selection bias as a specification error', *Econometrica* 47: 153–61.

Hotz, V. J. and R. A. Miller 1988. 'An empirical analysis of lifecycle fertility and female labor supply', *Econometrica* 56 (1), 91–118.

Isfol 1998. 'Il lavoro in Italia: profili, percorsi, politiche', Unpublished manuscript.

Istat 2000. *Rapporto Annuale: La situazione del paese nel 1999* Rome: Istat.

Rosenzweig, M. and K. I. Wolpin 1980. 'Life-cycle labor supply and fertility: casual inferences from household models', *Journal of Political Economy* 88 (2), 328–48.

Tunali, Insan 1986. 'A general structure for models of double selection and an application to a joint migration/earnings process with remigration', *Research in Labour Economics* 8 (part B), 235–82.

Waldfogel, J. 1995. 'The price of motherhood: family status and women's pay in a young British cohort', *Oxford Economic Papers* 47: 584–640.

Wetzels, C. 2002. 'Dutch women's productivity in the labour market: is there a double selection into motherhood and less demanding jobs?', Working paper, presented at IZA Bonn workshop: The Future of Family and Work: Evaluation of Family Friendly Policies, 10–11 May.

Index .